*f*P

THE REHNQUIST CHOICE

THE UNTOLD STORY OF THE

NIXON APPOINTMENT

THAT REDEFINED THE

SUPREME COURT

———

JOHN W. DEAN

The Free Press

New York   London   Toronto   Sydney   Singapore

THE FREE PRESS
A Division of Simon & Schuster, Inc.
1230 Avenue of the Americas
New York, NY 10020

THE FREE PRESS and colophon are trademarks
of Simon & Schuster, Inc.

Designed by Leslie Phillips
Manufactured in the United States of America

1   3   5   7   9   10   8   6   4   2

Library of Congress Cataloging-in-Publication Data
Dean, John W. (John Wesley)
The Rehnquist choice : the untold story of the Nixon appointment that
redefined the Supreme Court / John W. Dean.
p.   cm.
Includes bibliographical references and index.
1. Rehnquist, William H., 1924–   2. Nixon, Richard M. (Richard Milhous), 1913–
3. Judges—Selection and appointment—United States.   4. United States.
Supreme Court.   5. Political questions and judicial power—United States.
6. Civil rights—United States.   I. Title.
KF8745.R44 D43 2001
347.73'2634—dc21   2001040675
ISBN 0-7432-2607-0

For information regarding special discounts for bulk purchases,
please contact Simon & Schuster Special Sales:
1-800-456-6798 or business@simonandschuster.com

For Mo and Professor Stanley I. Kutler

For Mo and Professor Stanley P. Fisher

Acknowledgments

This book is dedicated to my wife and to University of Wisconsin professor of history Stanley Kutler, but I owe them both a special note of thanks.
Mo, for her loving support and for encouraging me to tell this story. She
also read it in draft form and made countless helpful suggestions. Professor Kutler for his earlier lawsuit (handled by the able lawyers at Public
Citizen) that forced the Nixon tapes out of their indefinite hibernation,
so the history of the Nixon presidency could be fully reported using this
unique record. Stanley Kutler also had a suggestion when I told him I was
thinking about doing this story as a book. He encouraged me to do it with
his editor at Free Press, Bruce Nichols, who had published his *Abuse Of
Power: The New Nixon Tapes*. This proved itself a terrific idea.

Bruce is not only a masterful editor and delightful person, he was familiar with the Nixon tapes. When he recommended that this not be a book of
transcripts, I realized we were on the same wavelength. This is a three act
drama that is best told through dialogue. Bruce's good ear for the printed
word was indispensable assisting me edit the transcripts into dialogue, and
refining the material to tell the story. His helping hand is on every page.

In addition to Bruce, I must thank his Free Press/Simon & Schuster
colleagues Jennifer Weidman for her legal professionalism in vetting the
work, and Carol de Onís for copy editing. While I appreciate the skills and
efforts of all the people at Free Press, needless to say the responsibly for
any and all errors or mistakes is mine.

To gather the material for this book I spent several months at the National Archives and Records Administration in College Park (NARA).
Over many years I have come to know many of the archivists involved
with the Nixon White House tapes and papers. They are professionals,
not to mention enjoyable people to lunch with at their cafeteria. When I
told Karl Weissenbach at the Nixon Project my plans, he gathered key

staff in his office for me so we could discuss it. Their assistance was invaluable. John Powers was familiar with many of the tapes I sought, and made suggestions of others I should consider. Patty Anderson assembled literally thousands upon thousands of documents for me that I wanted to review. David Mengel proved indispensable at finding tapes, or listening equipment, when problems popped up.

Outside the Nixon Project, many others gave me assistance at NARA on this project. In particular David Paynter (who has been assisting me to locate Nixon administration documents for years in the files of the Watergate Special Prosecutor) once again came to the rescue when I found I needed material I had failed to gather when in College Park. In addition, there is a long list of people in the reading and listening rooms whose friendly assistance made several months of work less tedious. While I cannot recall all their names, I do owe special thanks to Vernon Early, Bill Deutscher, and Kevin Bradley.

NARA archivist, and friend (we share an undergraduate alma mater), Walter Hill helped me locate a research assistant. That was Sarah Shoenfeld who (as I mentioned in the Note on Sources) has a masters degree in history from Northeastern University. She assisted me at NARA on transcribing tapes, or locating documents, for five months. Sarah was joined by third year law student, Jennifer Gruda, from another alma mater, Georgetown Law Center. This was difficult and tedious work for these overqualified young women, but they remained undaunted. Jennifer had to leave for final exams, and bar exam preparation, but her contribution is much appreciated. Sarah went the distance, and now is working at NARA. Both young women were a pleasure to work with and became invaluable to the project.

Finally, Jim Warren, who has recently returned to Chicago from his post as the Washington Bureau chief of the *Chicago Tribune*. As one of the few journalists who periodically ventures out to NARA to sample the Nixon tapes, Jim was kind enough to share his transcripts, and thoughts, relating to several of the conversations in this story. Jim's information was helpful.

John W. Dean
Beverly Hills, CA
August, 2001

Contents

Cast of Characters

[positions at time of the story]

THE WHITE HOUSE:

Richard Nixon—President of the United States

H. R. "Bob" Haldeman—Assistant to the President (chief of staff)

John D. Ehrlichman—Assistant to the President (top domestic affairs adviser)

John W. Dean—Counsel to the President (reported to Haldeman and Ehrlichman)

Richard A. Moore—Special Counsel to the President (political and media adviser)

Egil "Bud" Krogh—Deputy Assistant to the President (Ehrlichman deputy)

David Young—Special Assistant to the National Security Council (Ehrlichman deputy)

THE JUSTICE DEPARTMENT:

John N. Mitchell—Attorney General

Richard Kleindienst—Deputy Attorney General

William H. Rehnquist—Assistant Attorney General (Office of Legal Counsel)

John W. Dean—Associate Deputy Attorney General (Legislation)

CANDIDATES CONSIDERED FOR THE SUPREME COURT
(LISTED ALPHABETICALLY):

Spiro Agnew (U. S. Vice President)

Sylvia Bacon (Judge, Superior Court, District of Columbia)

Howard Baker (U.S. Senator from Tennessee)

Alexander M. Bickel (law professor, Yale University Law School)

Robert Braucher (Justice, Supreme Judicial Court of Massachusetts)

Charles Breitel (Judge, U. S. Court of Appeals, 2nd Circuit)

William H. "Bob" Brown (Chairman of Equal Employment Opportunity Commission)

Robert Byrd (U.S. Senator from West Virginia)

Charles Clark (Judge, U.S. Court of Appeals, 5th Circuit)

Constance E. Cook (Member of the New York State Assembly)

David W. Dyer (Judge, U.S. Court of Appeals, 11th Circuit)

Herschel Friday (attorney, Little Rock, Arkansas)

Edward Thaxter Gignoux (Judge, U.S. District Court, Maine)

Harry D. Goldman (Judge, Appellate Division's Fourth Department, New York)

Martha W. Griffiths, (Member of Congress from Michigan)

Margaret M. Heckler (Member of Congress from Massachusetts)

Shirley M. Hufstedler (Judge, U.S. Court of Appeals, 9th Circuit)

Cornelia G. Kennedy (Judge, U. S. District Court, Eastern District of Michigan)

Jewel Lafontant (attorney, Chicago, Illinois)

Mildred L. Lillie (Justice, Court of Appeals, Second Appellate District of California)

Walter Mansfield (Judge, U.S. Court of Appeals, 2nd Circuit)

Soia Mentschikoff (law professor, University of Chicago Law School)

William H. Mulligan (Judge, U.S. Court of Appeals, 2nd Circuit)

Dorothy W. Nelson (Dean, University of Southern California Law School)

Ellen Peters (law professor, Yale University Law School)

Richard H. Poff (Member of Congress from Virginia)

Lewis Powell (attorney, Richmond, Virginia)

William "Bill" Pullman (attorney, location unknown)

Paul Reardon (Justice, Supreme Court in Massachusetts)

Charles S. "Chuck" Rhyne (attorney, District of Columbia)

Paul H. Rooney (Judge, U.S. Court of Appeals, 5th Circuit)

Susie Marshall Sharp (Associate Justice, Supreme Court of North Carolina)

William French Smith (attorney, Los Angeles, California)

Arlen Specter (U.S. Senator from Pennsylvania)

Harold Tyler (Judge, U.S. Court of Appeals, 2nd Circuit)

Caspar Weinberger (Director, Bureau of the Budget)

A Note to the Reader

From 1969 through 1971, the period of the events in this story, I served in the Nixon administration, first as associate deputy attorney general at the Justice Department, and then as counsel to the president at the White House. While I did so, Richard Nixon appointed four Supreme Court justices in two pairs, the first in 1969 and 1970, the second in 1971. I was involved in varying degrees in the process, especially the president's last selections: Lewis Powell and William Rehnquist.

The story of William Rehnquist's appointment has never been told. Indeed, hardly any Supreme Court appointments have ever been opened to public scrutiny. It is only thanks to Richard Nixon's taping system, the fruits of which are finally now being released to the public, that the full story of the Rehnquist selection can be revealed. Rehnquist's was a surprise appointment; at the time, he was a relatively young assistant attorney general, from the electorally modest state of Arizona.

I have some regrets about my role in this story. I have decided that the least I can do is tell it.

THE
REHNQUIST
CHOICE

1

INTRODUCTION: THE BACKSTORY

THE HEART OF THE STORY of William Rehnquist's appointment to the Supreme Court begins on September 17, 1971, and ends with an announcement on October 21, 1971. That story begins in the next chapter. First, it is important to understand the backstory.

It is well known that Richard Nixon made extraordinary use and abuse of his presidential powers. It is not widely known that those uses and abuses also related to the Supreme Court. More than any president since Franklin D. Roosevelt, he worked hard to mold the Court to his political liking. That meant not only making conservative appointments; it also meant *creating* appointments. William Rehnquist, who would be Nixon's most important appointment, was actively involved in the efforts to create vacancies on the Court while serving as an assistant attorney general. It is not an overstatement to say that Rehnquist, working with Nixon's attorney general, John Mitchell, and others, misused the resources and powers of the Department of Justice, and other executive branch agencies, to literally unpack the Court by removing life-tenured justices they found philosophically or politically unacceptable. It was all part of a strategy that commenced even before Nixon assumed office.

Resignation of Chief Justice Earl Warren

The scheme began during the 1968 presidential campaign. The vacancy on the Supreme Court awaiting Richard Nixon when he became president was not an accident. Nixon had made certain that that vacancy would be his to fill. During the 1968 presidential campaign, by a letter of June 13, 1968, Chief Justice Earl Warren informed President Lyndon Johnson that he wished to resign "not because of reasons of health or on account of any personal or associational problems, but solely because of age." Employing the easy candor that characterized all his decisions, Warren explained it was time "to give way to someone who will have more years ahead of him to cope with the problems which will come before the Court."[1]

Candidate Richard Nixon, and his campaign manager and law partner John N. Mitchell, knew exactly why Earl Warren had resigned when he did, five months before the November election decision.[2] The politically savvy Warren, a former governor of California, believed that Nixon would win. And Nixon's "law and order" presidential campaign often targeted Warren's Court. As Nixon biographer Stephen Ambrose observed, "By 1968, Nixon had become almost as critical of the Warren court as he was of the Johnson Administration. He was promising, as president, to appoint judges who would reverse some of the basic decisions of the past fifteen years. When Warren resigned, reports spread quickly that he had chosen this moment to do so because he feared that Nixon would win in November and eventually have the opportunity to appoint Warren's successor."[3] Nixon did not attack Earl Warren personally—as many conservatives did. But he made sure that, as president, he would select the next chief justice.

Less than two weeks after receiving word that Warren wished to retire, President Johnson called the press into the Oval Office to announce: "I have the nomination for the chief justice. The nomination will go to the Senate shortly. It is Justice Abe Fortas, of the State of Tennessee," whom Johnson had placed on the Court in 1965.[4] To fill the Fortas seat as associate justice, Johnson added, "I am nominating Judge [Homer] Thornberry, presently on the Fifth Circuit."[5] The Democratic president had nominated two of his closest cronies, men he knew would continue the judicial activism of the Warren Court and the liberalism that Lyndon Johnson had embraced throughout his political career. It would prove a mistake for all.

While no one could read the U.S. Senate better than Lyndon Johnson, given his many years as its majority leader, in this instance he misread his strength as a lame-duck president. With Johnson not seeking reelection, and his vice president Hubert Humphrey fading in the race with Nixon, Senate Republicans, joined by southern Democrats who were less than enamored with Justice Fortas's position on civil rights, decided to fight the Fortas nomination.

Publicly, Nixon remained above the fray. Privately, he encouraged Senator Robert Griffin (R-MI), to attack Fortas's elevation to chief justice.[6] The effort to block the nomination took several tacks. At the outset, Senator Griffin tried to make a point of Fortas's close relationship with President Johnson, but his Republican colleague on the Judiciary Committee, Senate minority leader Everett Dirksen, dismissed that avenue. Dirksen observed that presidents regularly appointed "cronies" to the Supreme Court, citing Abraham Lincoln selecting his campaign manager David Davis, President Harry Truman appointing his private adviser Fred Vinson, and more recently President Kennedy sending his lieutenant Byron White to the Court.

As his biographer Laura Kalman notes, Fortas's opponents then found an endless arsenal among his own opinions as a member of the Warren Court that could be used against him. For example, Republican senator Strom Thurmond of South Carolina spent several hours berating him about the Warren Court's criminal law holdings, even holding Fortas responsible for a ruling made before he arrived.[7] The Senate Judiciary Committee called a witness from the Citizens for Decent Literature, who had examined fifty-two of the Court's rulings and determined that Fortas's vote had prevented the Court from finding obscenity in forty-nine of the cases. In addition, the witness had a slide show (later reviewed by the senators, and press, in a closed session) to display the types of pornographic materials he found offensive but that Justice Fortas had tolerated.[8]

Most damaging, however, Senator Griffin received an anonymous tip from an American University employee, where Fortas was teaching a seminar at the law school, that the school had raised "an exorbitant sum from businessmen to pay Fortas's salary."[9] At that time it was not unusual for a justice to earn outside income by teaching; but in this case the amount was relatively large—and possibly tainted. This was reason to re-open the hearings, which revealed that Fortas's former law partner, Paul Porter, had gone to friends and clients to raise $30,000, with half going to the American University law school and the other half going to Fortas. Porter said that Fortas had not been told of this arrangement, but the Senate made much of the appearance of impropriety of Fortas's $15,000 fee, which amounted to 40 percent of a Supreme Court justice's salary at that time.

When the Fortas nomination came to the Senate floor, the Republicans mounted a historic filibuster—the first against a Supreme Court nomination. The Johnson White House lacked the political muscle to prevent this unless, it was said, Richard Nixon urged a halt. But Nixon refused to comment publicly, and through backchannels he sent advice and praise to the Republicans' effort.[10] On October 1, 1968, when the Senate failed to vote for cloture (thus ending the filibuster), Justice Fortas, realizing that his nomination was doomed, requested that Johnson withdraw it.[11] With the Fortas nomination defeated, the Thornberry nomination became moot. Given the limited time available, Johnson could name no successor to Chief Justice Earl Warren. The vacancy for chief justice awaited Nixon.

Ousting Abe Fortas

The story of how Richard Nixon created a second opening on the Court has never been fully told. After winning in November, Nixon arranged for retiring Chief Justice Earl Warren to remain on the Court until the end of the Court term in June 1969. This gave the new president six months to select his chief justice. Ostensibly to show Earl Warren his appreciation for remaining, but in truth because Nixon wanted to size up the remaining eight still on the Court for himself, he decided to have a White House dinner to honor the retiring chief justice.[12] Of particular interest to Nixon were five justices—William O. Douglas, Hugo Black, Thurgood Marshall, Abe Fortas, and William Brennan—who with Earl Warren formed the core of the Court's controlling liberal voting bloc.

The "Earl Warren Dinner" on April 23, 1969, was a lavish, black-tie affair, with the members of the Supreme Court and wives, Earl Warren's family, Nixon's cabinet and wives, and his former law partners and their wives heading the guest list.[13] Richard Nixon treated his old enemy Warren like a visiting head of state, starting with a private meeting with wives in the Yellow Oval Room in the family quarters, then a walk down the Grand Staircase with the Marine Band playing, where about 110 well-wishers including the chief's family and friends awaited and watched, and finally with "Ruffles and Flourishes" to usher everyone into the East Room for a formal dinner, which ended with a convivial, and witty, toast to the chief justice by the president. Astute observers could have noticed that the new president's guest list included three men he was actively considering for the Supreme Court: Thomas E. Dewey, Herbert Brownell, and Warren Burger.

Only a few Nixon aides knew of the president's thinking, and even fewer knew of his hidden agenda. Nixon wanted to create additional vacancies, and the Earl Warren Dinner was typical of the public misdirection that concealed his true plans. White House aide John Ehrlichman, then counsel to the president, reported in his memoir that "the Justice Department was hearing rumors [at this time] of Justice Abe Fortas' dealings with [convicted] financier Louis Wolfson. By May 1969, *Life* magazine had written an exposé of Fortas' agreement with Wolfson, and Nixon cleared his desk of other work to focus on getting Fortas off the Court."[14] Ehrlichman didn't say that it was the Department of Justice that was spreading rumors and leaking this information to *Life* reporter William Lambert.[15] Ehrlichman had been given advance proofs of the *Life* story several days prior to its publication, scheduled for Sunday afternoon, May 4. The Justice Department had passed along the fact that, while sitting on the Supreme Court, Fortas had accepted a $20,000 retainer from Louis Wolfson, who was under investigation by the Securities and Exchange Commission (SEC).[16] (He would later be indicted and convicted of fraud.) At the time of the investigation, Wolfson bragged that his friend Abe Fortas was going to help him.[17]

On May 1, three days before publication by *Life,* Assistant Attorney General William Rehnquist sent Attorney General Mitchell a memorandum providing a precedent for the Department of Justice to investigate the Fortas-Wolfson relationship. To date, this memo has not surfaced at the National Archives with other Department of Justice papers of the period.[18] Nonetheless, the contents of the memo and the reason it was written by Rehnquist have been reported. Veteran Washington journalist and author Robert Shogan interviewed John Mitchell in 1971 while he was still attorney general, and Mitchell in turn (after waiving any attorney-client privilege with his constitutional lawyer) opened the door for an interview with Rehnquist. Although additional information has surfaced in the years since Shogan published *A Question of Judgment: The Fortas Case and the Struggle for the Supreme Court* (1972), this book recorded Rehnquist's crucial role.

Mitchell told Shogan, "We were struggling to find answers to what we should or shouldn't do."[19] With good reason. For the Department of Justice, as an arm of the Executive Branch, to investigate or prosecute any federal judge, not to mention a Supreme Court justice, certainly raised fundamental legal issues, and the investigation of Fortas was uncharted. Article III of the Constitution provides: "The judicial power of the United States shall be vested in one Supreme Court and in such inferior courts as the Congress may from time to time ordain and establish. The judges, both of the Supreme and inferior Courts, shall hold their offices during good behavior." There is no express provision in the Constitution respecting removals, except for Article II, which provides for removal from office of "all civil officers of the United States" (including judges and justices) by impeachment. Alexander Hamilton wrote in *The Federalist No. 79*: "The standard of good behavior for the continuance in office of the judicial magistracy, is certainly one of the most valuable of the modern improvements in the practice of government." He added, "Nothing can contribute so much to firmness and independence [of the judicial branch] as permanency in office." Of impeachment, Hamilton further noted: "This is the only provision on the point which is consistent with the necessary independence of the judicial character, and is the only one which we find in our own Constitution in respect to our own judges."

Mitchell did not need a constitutional lawyer to understand the limits on his investigative powers relating to Abe Fortas. According to Shogan, he learned (I suspect from Henry Petersen, who had the necessary institutional memory) that the Justice Department had always "been hesitant to seem to threaten the independence of the judiciary."[20] Investigating a Supreme Court justice could place the Justice Department on thin ice, because the power of impeachment belonged exclusively to the Congress. It was for this reason that Mitchell turned to the "intellectual adroitness" of Rehnquist, a former Supreme Court law clerk, for help.[21] Shogan reported the following:

(1) Rehnquist "took no part in the direct investigation" of Fortas, which was handled by Will Wilson and Henry Petersen of the criminal division. Rather, Rehnquist was asked, as he himself put it, "to assume the most damaging set of inferences about the case were true" and to "determine what action the Justice Department could take."[22]

This was a remarkable assignment. The Justice Department was deciding how to deal with one of the nine highest judicial officials of the nation; whether and how to cross the constitutional divide of a judicial independence. Presumably Rehnquist was to make certain the Department of Justice acted in a constitutional manner. Yet he was told to ignore the facts and assume the worst and most damaging inferences. Common sense—and careful legal analysis—would demand facts, not inferences. The only thing more surprising is that he took the assignment. This is Alice in Wonderland, not legal analysis.

(2) The worst inference Rehnquist could draw was that Fortas, while sitting on the Supreme Court, had somehow intervened in the government's prosecution of Wolfson's stock market activities. (In fact he had not.) Based on this (false) inference, Rehnquist searched the federal criminal code, and found one provision that "seemed to cover the Fortas-Wolfson relationship, as Rehnquist understood it." It was a statute that made it a crime for "officers of the judicial branch" to be rewarded "for services rendered on behalf of another person before a Government department or agency in relation to any particular matter in which the United States is a party."[23] Shogan notes, "Just what services Fortas had been expected to render in return remained to be established, but this was not Rehnquist's responsibility."

(3) Having found a possibly relevant federal criminal law, "Rehnquist next sought to determine whether the Justice Department could prosecute Fortas for violating that law while he remained on the Court." Rehnquist found no precedents that "fit the present case exactly." But he did find that "in 1790 the First Congress, which included among its members James Madison and other drafters of the Constitution, had passed a law making it possible to prosecute Federal judges for bribery." In addition,

Rehnquist found that six years later (1796), the third attorney general of the United States had "held that a judge could be called to account for unlawful behavior by criminal indictment as well as by impeachment." Shogan reports that "Rehnquist believed that Attorney General Lee's conclusion was well grounded enough for Attorney General Mitchell to follow some 170 years later. On May 1 Rehnquist sent Mitchell a memorandum advising him that if the department had the evidence, it could prosecute Justice Fortas."[24]

Shogan had no reason to examine the basis of Rehnquist's advice, but it is easy to do so. Most striking is what Rehnquist apparently did *not* tell Mitchell: The 1790 bribery law was not necessarily designed to prosecute judges while in office; rather it provides a remedy after they had been removed by impeachment. The language and history of the Constitution clearly suggest that Congress, not the Executive Branch, is responsible for policing "good behavior" of Supreme Court justices.

Nonetheless, Rehnquist's advice gave Mitchell the solace and authority he needed. Mitchell was just getting warmed up. Before the *Life* story hit the streets he had his press man, Jack C. Landau, obtain a copy of the magazine. (Landau sent a U.S. marshal to New York to pick it up.) Shortly before publication Jack Landau was working his Rolodex, frantically calling reporters who covered the Justice Department and the Supreme Court to give them a heads-up on the coming story. As Shogan observed, this action "put the Justice Department in the dubious position of promoting *Life*'s exposé."[25]

The *Life* story was front-page news. Mitchell, proud of his handiwork, boasted of it at a White House staff meeting on Tuesday, May 6 (before meeting with the Republican leadership), and revealed his further plans for the high court. These were duly noted by presidential aide Patrick Buchanan, who dashed off a memo to the president reporting that the "Attorney General has hinted this morning that this scandal is only a part of what may soon be revealed about Fortas and other 'judges and justices.'"[26] Mitchell was bolstered by Fortas's failure to respond to the *Life* story. His lack of response prompted *The Washington Post* to call for his resignation.[27] Members of the House and Senate quickly joined the *Post* to form a chorus.[28]

Although William Lambert denied that the Nixon administration leaked the Fortas story to *Life*,[29] everyone believed (correctly) that the administration was responsible. Both Republicans and Democrats on Capitol Hill assumed that Nixon and his men were orchestrating the ouster of Fortas.[30] This truth was all but publicly confirmed when it was soon leaked that John Mitchell made a secretive visit to Chief Justice Warren's chambers to discuss Fortas.

On May 7, Mitchell's long black limousine pulled quietly into the basement garage of the Supreme Court Building, and the attorney general was whisked through the building for a confidential session with the chief justice. Mitchell had not met Earl Warren before the White House dinner a few weeks earlier, but the glow of good feeling still radiated from that evening.

While there was incipient talk of impeaching Fortas in the House of Representatives, Mitchell hoped to enlist Earl Warren—and the others on the Court—to persuade Abe Fortas to resign. To bolster his case, Mitchell carried documents that the Department of Justice had just received from the Internal Revenue Service, which had subpoenaed the Louis Wolfson Foundation. These showed that Fortas had agreed to more than a one-time payment of $20,000 from Wolfson: rather, the Wolfson Foundation had arranged to pay Fortas $20,000 a year for life, and should he predecease his wife, the foundation would pay Mrs. Fortas as long as she might live. At the time this was not an unusual arrangement. Justice William O. Douglas had a similar agreement with a foundation, and one of the judges Mitchell was reviewing for promotion to the Supreme Court, Warren Burger, had long received fees for his service on the board of the Mayo Clinic. Many justices received handsome fees for lectures. Mitchell mentioned other documents as well: Wolfson-Fortas correspondence in which Wolfson's case before the SEC had been discussed, and "one letter [in which] Wolfson asked Fortas's help in obtaining a presidential pardon [by having former President Lyndon Johnson request that Richard Nixon grant it]."[31] Mitchell reported that Louis Wolfson, who was now serving his prison term, was cooperating with the Department of Justice. The attorney general ended his visit with the implicit message: If Fortas resigned, the criminal investigation by the Department of Justice would end, saving Fortas and the Court any embarrassment.

Did the Justice Department have the goods on Fortas? Not even close. Mitchell's talk was pure bluff. On May 10, Wolfson met with FBI agents and Assistant Attorney General Will Wilson, who headed the Justice Department's criminal division. Wilson had been spearheading the investigation of Fortas with the avowed purpose of removing him from the Court.[32] To the chagrin of Wilson, not only did Wolfson not have any evidence of wrongdoing by Fortas, he exonerated the justice. Wolfson told the government's top prosecutor that Fortas had done nothing for him, nor had he ever hinted that he might. There had been no quid pro quo.

Mitchell's next move was political hardball. To increase the pressure on Fortas, the Department of Justice reopened an old investigation that focused on the two people closest to Abe Fortas—his wife, Carol Agger, a highly paid tax law specialist, and his former law partner, Paul Porter. A Washington, D.C., grand jury was convened to determine if documents allegedly misplaced but purportedly later found in Agger's office safe had been deliberately withheld when they had been subpoenaed in a price-fixing case several years earlier. The grand jury was exploring whether Agger or Porter had obstructed justice—a serious felony—by withholding the documents. Lyndon Johnson's Justice Department had investigated this question and found nothing improper, deciding the delay was not an effort to impede the earlier investigation. Reopening of the matter by Richard Nixon's Justice Department was purely a means to torture Fortas.

• • • •

By the time Fortas presented his plight to his brethren, he had made the decision to retire. More remarkably, he got no sympathy from his colleagues.[33] They treated him as a condemned man. Not one protested that he had broken no law. Not one acknowledged that other justices at the conference table had accepted fees from charitable foundations. Not one suggested that Fortas should stay and fight. Richard Nixon and John Mitchell had intimidated them all.

By May 14, 1969, it was over. Mitchell's bluff had succeeded beyond his wildest expectations.[34] Chief Justice Warren had his secretary call the White House. Dwight Chapin took the call and typed a note at 4:20 p.m. that he slipped to the president, who was in a bipartisan leadership meeting: "The Chief Justice needs to talk to you urgently. I have told his office that you will call at 4:45 p.m." Nixon nodded. At the appointed time he excused himself from the meeting to call Earl Warren, and learned that Abe Fortas was resigning. Nixon, who was scheduled to deliver a major speech on Vietnam to the nation on national television that evening, told Warren that he did not want anything distracting from his speech, so the White House would not announce the resignation until the next day. When the letter arrived at the White House, the chief justice had penned a note to the president, requesting that Fortas "be advised shortly before the release in order that he might inform President Johnson before he hears it on the radio." [35] This was fine with Nixon.

Haldeman informed John Mitchell of the news. At the Justice Department there was a small celebration in the attorney general's office. Mitchell summoned Will Wilson and his deputy Henry Petersen to congratulate the team that had been running the smoke machine. When Deputy Attorney General Dick Kleindienst stepped off the back elevator and into Mitchell's office, he was elated by the news. Kleindienst said the occasion called for a drink, so they opened the bar, pouring heartily to toast their success. The celebration was capped with a call from the president, congratulating them on a job well done. [36]

• • • •

The next morning, before the White House could advise Fortas that they were going to announce the president's acceptance of his resignation, a report was on the wires announcing the resignation. What happened was ironic: the *Los Angeles Times* ran a story claiming that the Justice Department believed the documents it had obtained from Wolfson showed that Fortas had been willing to assist him with his SEC investigation. It was the result of another Justice Department leak to pressure Fortas, before learning he had folded. When Fortas read the story, he was outraged; he knew such an interpretation was not possible, nor had he ever expressed such a willingness. Fortas called the Supreme Court's press office, and ordered that they release the news of his resignation immediately. Fortas couldn't have cared less that this was a breach of protocol, since his resignation had not been accepted by the president. Nor, given the treatment he was getting from the Nixon administration, did he give a hoot if releasing the announcement displeased Richard Nixon. [37]

The Fortas resignation meant that Richard Nixon now had two seats to fill on the Court: Earl Warren's center seat and the seat of Associate Justice Abe Fortas, who was leaving the Court at fifty-nine years of age. It also meant that two of the Court's most liberal justices were gone. Nixon's aggressive posture toward the high court was paying off in a big way, with the help of John Mitchell and his hard-nosed team at the Justice Department, Rehnquist among them.

Selecting a Chief Justice

Nixon's first major appointment would prove to be the easiest of all of the four seats that he eventually would fill. After looking briefly at some candidates, more as a matter of courtesy to Republican elders than in hope of finding a new chief justice, the president named his man and watched him sail through the Senate.

Shortly after his November 1968 election victory, Nixon told his attorney general designate, Mitchell, that they should consider appointing President Eisenhower's attorney general, Herbert Brownell, as chief justice.[38] This idea never progressed, however, because Brownell took himself out of the running. So did Eisenhower's second attorney general, William P. Rogers, whom Nixon did convince to take the post of secretary of state. J. Edgar Hoover's biographer, Curt Gentry, claims that it was the FBI director who took these men out of contention, because he had worked for them both and despite claiming them both as friends, he did not want them on the Supreme Court.[39] Regardless, both Brownell and Rogers withdrew and suggested a candidate that Nixon had already been considering: Warren Burger, the chief judge of the prestigious United States Court of Appeals for the District of Columbia.

Nixon also had considered former New York governor Thomas Dewey, the onetime Republican presidential standard-bearer. But Dewey, then in his late sixties, thought himself too old and was not interested. The rumor that Nixon was considering elevating Associate Justice Potter Stewart prompted Stewart to make a trip to the White House to tell Nixon that it was unwise to elevate a sitting justice to chief justice as President Johnson had tried to do with Fortas. In fact, Nixon was not considering Justice Stewart, for Nixon was less than impressed with Stewart as a jurist.

Warren Burger became the leading contender early. He was energetically seeking the job. He was an able politician who realized that his judicial philosophy was exactly what Richard Nixon sought. Burger had learned this in 1967, when he received a letter from Nixon complimenting him on a "law and order" article he had written for *U.S. News & World*

Report. The article was accompanied by a picture of the white-haired jurist, a man who looked like a chief justice from central casting. Nixon referred to and quoted from the Burger article often during his 1968 campaign. Following his inauguration, the new president requested that Judge Burger come to the White House to administer the oath of office to his new cabinet appointees, and after the swearing-in ceremony, Nixon had Burger join him in the Oval Office for a conversation. Nixon asked Burger, who was broadly familiar with the legal community, if he would give John Mitchell his suggestions for men who should be considered for federal judgeships, including the Supreme Court. The president said he did not care if they were Republicans or Democrats—so long as they were solid conservatives.[40] Burger was flattered, and pleased to assist.

Among the names that Burger initially suggested to John Mitchell were G. Harrold Carswell, a forty-nine-year-old judge on the United States District Court for the Northern District of Florida, and Burger's longtime friend Judge Harry Blackmun, a sixty-year-old Federal appeals court judge sitting in the Eighth Circuit. Burger's recommendations were added to a master list that was being prepared by Rehnquist.[41] The list also included a recommendation made personally to Mitchell by Senator Ernest Hollings (D-SC) for Judge Clement Haynsworth, a judge in his mid-fifties on the United States Court of Appeals for the Fourth Circuit; and a candidate being urged by Senator Harry Byrd (D-VA), Lewis Powell, a sixty-one-year-old Democrat from Virginia and the former president of the American Bar Association (ABA).[42]

While the media attention was still focusing on the resignation of Abe Fortas, Mitchell asked Judge Burger to come to his office at the Justice Department to review possible candidates to fill the Fortas seat. Mitchell also requested that Kleindienst join the meeting, which Kleindienst later described:

> I had never met Warren Burger, but I had argued an appeal before him two or three years before. When I walked into Mitchell's office I easily recognized his distinguished features and warm manner. He laughed when I reminded him of the case that I had argued before him. . . .
>
> Mitchell and Burger then spent the next hour or two going over a long list of judges, lawyers, and professors. Burger was familiar with almost every person on the list. He knew most personally and commented specif-

ically about the judicial philosophy of nearly all. What impressed me even more, however, was the absence of negative remarks about the persons he discussed. He sought only to point out the positive qualities of each. Not once did he so much as hint that he should be included on the list under consideration. His conversation with Mitchell was impressive and objective.

When Judge Burger departed, Mitchell turned to me and asked, "What did you think of that?"

"Unbelievable."

"I'm glad you think so. He's going to be the next chief justice."[43]

Mitchell did not select Burger, but there was no doubt in his mind how he became chief justice. "Burger's the first guy to run for the job of Chief Justice—and get it," Mitchell wryly observed to several aides.[44] Nor is there any doubt, as recorded by Supreme Court historian Henry Abraham, that "Nixon's choice of Judge Burger was one of those rare examples of an indisputably bona fide personal choice by a chief executive [as] chief executive. . . . By his own assertions, he considered his selection of Burger to be 'the most personal of [my] Presidency to date.'"[45]

On May 21, 1969, Nixon staged a surprise announcement of his choice for chief justice. Warren Burger and his wife were secretly smuggled into the White House via the underground tunnel between the Treasury Department building beside the White House and the East Wing basement. Burger was easily confirmed by the U.S. Senate by a vote of 74 to 3 on June 9, after only three hours of mostly laudatory debate. To milk his selection for all it was worth, Nixon personally attended the swearing-in ceremony at the Supreme Court.

The First Failed Selection—Clement Haynsworth

Nixon had managed to put the Court's stewardship into new conservative hands. Yet while a chief justice is first among equals, he has but one vote. The president still had an associate justice slot to fill. This nomination would prove far more difficult. Many Senate Democrats were still seething over Fortas's rough treatment, and itching for revenge.

Although the vacant Fortas seat, which had been held by Louis D. Brandeis (1916–39), Felix Frankfurter (1939–62), and Arthur Goldberg

(1962–65) before Abe Fortas, was often considered to be the "Jewish seat," Nixon did not so view it. There were no clear political advantages for him to appoint a Jew, as his Jewish speechwriter William Safire advised him.[46] Accordingly, Nixon instructed Mitchell to find a southerner who was a "strict constructionist." The reason he wanted a southerner was clear. After appointing Burger, as historian James Simon points out, "pressure had been building . . . to name a southerner to the Court. Though he had never publicly promised a southern nominee . . . Nixon's advisors believed that he could do southerners no higher favor than to appoint one of their own to the highest court in the land."[47] Nixon understood the South, and that they held judges in great respect. He had gone to law school at Duke in North Carolina. To win in 1968, Nixon had turned to the South, and it had responded. As a result, the South had become an essential political base to his reelection in 1972.

Nixon's call for a strict constructionist had developed during his 1968 presidential campaign. He wanted a justice who believed the Supreme Court "should interpret the Constitution rather than amend it by judicial fiat."[48] When selecting Burger, Nixon told the press that a good example of a strict constructionist jurist was former justice Felix Frankfurter.[49] It was a savvy comment, since Frankfurter was held in high esteem, but it also showed the vague meaning of the term. Frankfurter had once explained that "The words of the Constitution are so unrestricted by their intrinsic meaning or by their history or by tradition or by prior decisions that they leave the individual justice free, if indeed they do not compel him, to gather meaning not from reading the Constitution but from reading life."[50]

Rehnquist, as part of his duties as assistant attorney general, was in charge of vetting candidates for the Court by analyzing their rulings and philosophy. On May 29, Rehnquist completed his analysis of the rulings of one of two leading contenders for the Fortas vacancy: Clement F. Haynsworth, Jr., the federal judge from the United States Court of Appeals for the Fourth Circuit, who lived in Greenville, South Carolina. Judge Haynsworth had been on the federal appeals court since 1957 when appointed by President Eisenhower, and had served as chief judge (i.e., the most senior active judge) since 1964. He was a Democrat, and a fifth-generation southerner. To glean his judicial philosophy, Rehnquist reviewed twelve years of Judge Haynsworth's judicial decisions in a lengthy memorandum, which was forwarded by Mitchell to the White House. Rehnquist concluded that Haynsworth was a strict constructionist, but his own frank (if not alarming) explanation of that term bears notice:

> A judge who is a "strict constructionist" in constitutional matters will generally not be favorably inclined toward claims of either criminal defendants or civil rights plaintiffs—the latter two groups having been the principal beneficiaries of the Supreme Court's "broad constructionist" reading of the Constitution. The following conclusions about Judge Haynsworth's ideas of the law in these areas appear warranted:
>
> (a) With regard to criminal law, he appears to be a "strict constructionist" quite ready to recognize the rights of society as well as those of the accused.
>
> (b) With respect to civil rights, he appears to be more of a "strict constructionist" than the present Supreme Court, but not by any means a "die-hard."51

In other words, for Rehnquist, a strict constructionist was anyone who likes prosecutors and dislikes criminal defendants, and favors civil rights defendants over plaintiffs. While simplistic, it is a very accurate description of what Nixon wanted.

The other contender for the Fortas seat was Lewis Powell, who was a partner in an influential Richmond, Virginia, law firm. Powell's philosophy was gleaned from his handling of Richmond's difficult school desegregation situation, where he had helped guide the Richmond schools to policies that fit the strictures of the Supreme Court's civil rights rulings. Powell's philosophy was also suggested by his membership on President Johnson's Commission on Law Enforcement and the Administration of Justice, which had made him an open critic of the Supreme Court's pro-criminal decisions like *Miranda* (requiring that criminals be advised of their rights). The only negative on Powell, as far as Mitchell and Nixon were concerned, was his age. At sixty-one, he was the same age as Burger, and Nixon had hoped to pair Burger with a younger man. But this became moot when Powell told John Mitchell that he no longer wished to be considered for the Supreme Court.

With Powell out, Mitchell recommended Haynsworth, who had picked up another strong supporter at the White House, special counsel to the president Harry Dent, a South Carolinian who had been working for Senator Strom Thurmond before coming to the White House. Dent was well connected with politicians throughout the South. Mitchell proceeded to complement Rehnquist's vetting of Judge Haynsworth's judicial philosophy by ordering an FBI background investigation. The only problem uncovered was an allegation by the Textile Workers' Union in 1963, accusing Judge Haynsworth of a conflict of interest when he handled a case where he held stock in a defendant's company. The charge had been resolved, however, by the chief judge of the Fourth Circuit, who had investigated and cleared Haynsworth. In addition, the matter had been referred to Attorney General Robert Kennedy, who had found nothing amiss.

However, neither the FBI, nor Rehnquist, nor anyone else in Mitchell's Justice Department did much real digging into the affairs of Judge Haynsworth. According to Curt Gentry, J. Edgar Hoover sought to please Nixon by undertaking only a perfunctory background investigation: "The [FBI's] investigation and clearance of Haynsworth took all of one day and consisted of two telephone calls: on July 1, 1969, Hoover called the SAC [Special Agent in Charge] in Columbia, South Carolina, who reported the judge was 'considered very conservative' and 'definitely in favor of law and order'; and a follow up call in which Hoover relayed this information to Attorney General Mitchell."[52] This shallow investigation would prove to be no favor to either Mitchell or President Nixon. It made for problems that could have been avoided, which Judge Haynsworth himself raised when Nixon called him on August 16, 1969, to offer him the nomination. The judge expressed concern over the prior charge of conflict of interest. Nixon dismissed it, saying he would "kill that bird" during the confirmation.[53]

But the problem was not so easily dismissed. Haynsworth was vulnerable to more than one charge of the "appearance of impropriety." Stephen Ambrose reports the ensuing events:

> On August 18, [1969,] Nixon announced his choice. It was Judge Clement F. Haynsworth. . . . This delighted the Democrats, North and South. The southerners were pleased to have one of their own named to the Court; the northerners anticipated with glee what they could do to this southern gentleman in the confirmation hearings. Haynsworth had a segregationist background, as did virtually every southerner of that time; he belonged to exclusive clubs; he was a wealthy man.
>
> When the Senate went into session in September, Birch Bayh (D-IN)

unleashed a barrage of charges against Haynsworth, centering on the allegation that he had adjudicated cases in which he had a financial interest. The Washington *Post* and the television news programs added innuendo and rumor of their own. Nixon complained, with some justification, that no rich man would ever be able to meet the standards demanded of Haynsworth. But by the end of September, [the White House] knew Haynsworth could not make it.[54]

With Haynsworth's consent, Nixon refused to withdraw the nomination, and insisted that the Senate vote. They did, on November 21, after the White House used every bit of belated muscle it could muster. Nonetheless, the Senate rejected Haynsworth, the first rejection of a Supreme Court nomination since 1930, when the Senate refused to confirm Federal Appeals Judge John J. Parker (also of the Fourth Circuit and, as fate would have it, Haynsworth's mentor).[55] Postmortem blame for the failed selection fell on John Mitchell, as Bob Haldeman recorded in his diary following the defeat:

> [White House aide Dwight] Chapin brought the news in about 1:30. [The vote to reject Haynsworth was] 55–45. P not at all disturbed, because he expected it. . . . P called Haynsworth, asked him to stay on bench, and says he will. In analyzing it, P concludes principal fault is Mitchell's. First for not having all the facts; second for coasting on assurances from [Senators] Eastland and Hollings instead of really working . . . and keeping [the White House congressional liaison people] out until too late. . . . Then at the end [Mitchell] overplayed, with excess pressure on some, which backfired, was too heavy-handed. So we learned something and politically probably come out ahead.[56]

The Democrats controlled the Senate in 1969 by a 58 to 42 margin. Haynsworth was rejected not because of his southern heritage, or his judicial philosophy; rather, he fell to residual hostility of the Democrats over Nixon's manipulation of the Court's seats. First there had been the filibuster that blocked Fortas's elevation to chief justice, and then his ouster. Nixon's advisers recognized this fact, as surely did the president.[57]

The Second Failed Selection—G. Harrold Carswell

Nixon's next choice to fill the Fortas seat has been viewed by many as the decision of a piqued president, an effort to spite the Senate with a poorly qualified nominee. Professor Henry Abraham wrote that the next appointment "was an act of vengeance—one intended to teach the Senate a lesson and to downgrade the Court." [58] In truth, Nixon's next nominee, G. Harrold Carswell, was a colossal mistake, a complete screw-up by Nixon's advisers.[59] The Carswell nomination was the result of poor staffwork. Nixon did not pick Carswell because he was angry with the Senate. It was afterward that he would be truly angry.

John Mitchell relied on two people when he recommended Harrold Carswell: Warren Burger and William Rehnquist. It was Burger who had first brought Carswell to the attention of Mitchell. Years earlier, Burger had served as the assistant attorney general in charge of the civil division in the Eisenhower administration when Harrold Carswell was the U.S. Attorney for the Northern District of Florida (1953–58). In 1958, Carswell became a Federal District Court judge in Northern Florida, where he served for almost twelve years (1958–69). At the time of his confirmation, he had been the youngest federal judge in the country at thirty-eight years of age. Burger's endorsement of Carswell resulted in his elevation to the United States Court of Appeals for the Fifth Circuit, where he was sitting when Haynsworth was rejected by the Senate. After only a few months on the Fifth Circuit, he was suddenly nominated for the Supreme Court. It was Rehnquist who vetted his decisions, and concluded that Carswell, like Haynsworth, was a strict constructionist and qualified to sit on the Court.

When Mitchell touted Carswell to the White House, he told Nixon that the fifty-year-old jurist was "too good to be true." [60] On paper Mitchell found a law and order U.S. attorney for five years, a Federal District Court judge for almost twelve, and a new appointee to the Fifth Circuit—a man who had been confirmed by the Senate on three occasions with no problem. He had been through three FBI background checks. Mitchell was not alone in endorsing Carswell. John Ehrlichman instructed his deputy Egil "Bud" Krogh to meet with Judge Carswell.

However attractive Mitchell's choice seemed on paper, Carswell proved to be a great disappointment. This deeply flawed man had failed to mention to those vetting him that other people might have good reason to believe he was a racist, even if he was not. If the Justice Department and FBI had been careless with Haynsworth, with Carswell they did even worse. "Our investigation of Carswell had been so superficial," the FBI's assistant director William Sullivan later explained, "that we never found

out that he was a homosexual."[61] While Richard Nixon was always looking for historical firsts, nominating a homosexual to the high court would
not have been on his list. (This fact did not surface until many years later,
when Carswell was arrested for propositioning a vice squad officer in the
men's room of a Tallahassee shopping mall. Only then was it learned that
"Carswell had been a known homosexual for years.")[62]

Shortly before Carswell's confirmation hearings, the news media
began to dig up additional information the FBI had missed. It was revealed that while serving as U.S. attorney, Carswell had arranged for the
transfer of a public golf course, partially constructed with federal money,
into a private club to avoid integrating the facility under the recent rulings of the U.S. Supreme Court. Similarly, he had later signed the incorporating papers for a "whites only" booster club for the Florida State
University football team. Most damning was the discovery that when
running for elective office, Carswell told an American Legion group: "I
believe that segregation of the races is proper and the only practical and
correct way of life in our states. I yield to no man in the firm, vigorous belief in the principles of white supremacy."[63] He added that "the so-called
civil rights program [would] better be called the civil wrongs program."[64]
It is possible to understand how the FBI missed this information, since it
was two decades old. But it is difficult to grasp how investigators missed
information that a newsman discovered had occurred only two months
before Carswell was nominated. When speaking to the Georgia Bar Association, Carswell opened with a story: "I was out in the Far East a little
while ago, and I ran into a dark-skinned fella. I asked him if he was from
Indo-China and he said, 'Naw, suh, I'se from outdo' Gawgee.' "[65]

During the confirmation hearings before the Senate Judiciary Committee, the American Bar Association (which ranked Supreme Court
nominees either qualified or unqualified) found Carswell qualified. Few
others did. Blacks and civil rights groups were understandably offended
by Carswell. Although he denied that he was a racist, as did his character
witnesses, the picture was less than clear. Testimony showed that as a Federal District Court judge, Carswell had expressed his dislike of northern
civil rights lawyers coming into Florida to litigate, and he was often in-
sulting, rude, and hostile toward black lawyers appearing before him in
his courtroom. Carswell's lack of legal acumen also quickly became apparent. He was less than a compelling witness in his own defense.

Shortly after his confirmation hearings ended, on March 6, 1970, the Ripon Society, an organization of moderate Republican college students, released a study undertaken by Columbia Law School students who had reviewed all of Carswell's published decisions as a Federal District Court judge. The findings were appalling. Carswell had been reversed by the Court of Appeals in a staggering 58 percent of his decisions,[66] which appeared to be more than any other federal judge. It is not clear how Rehnquist missed this unpleasantly conspicuous problem.

Despite all this, at the urging of the Nixon administration, the Senate Judiciary Committee sent the nomination to the full Senate by a vote of 13 to 4. Democratic senator Birch Bayh of Indiana, who had led the opposition against Haynsworth, headed this fight as well. On March 16, 1970, debate opened on the Senate floor with Bayh declaring that Carswell's "incredibly undistinguished career as an attorney and jurist is itself an affront to the Supreme Court. . . . I do not think that we can let our standards fall to the low level suggested by the present nominee."[67] Senator Roman Hruska of Nebraska, the ranking Republican on the Senate Judiciary Committee, was Carswell's principal defender. His opening speech described the nominee as "well-qualified and well-suited for the post . . . learned in the law . . . experienced . . . a man of integrity."[68]

Following this ringing endorsement, Senator Hruska decided to talk with reporters outside the Senate Chamber. This interview continues to echo through history. With a tape recorder rolling, Hruska was asked by a radio reporter for his response to the charge that Carswell was mediocre. The senator pulled himself up, and in a deep, melodious voice, huffed, "Well, even if he were mediocre, there are a lot of mediocre judges and people and lawyers. They are entitled to a little representation, aren't they, and a little chance? We can't have all Brandeises and Frankfurters and Cardozos and stuff like that there."[69]

On April 8, 1970, the Senate rejected the Carswell nomination by a vote of 51 to 45, with thirteen Republicans joining the Democrats.[70] Although the White House staff thought they might be able to muscle Carswell through the Senate, once a few Republicans deserted, others followed. Haldeman recorded Nixon's reactions:

Carswell day, and he went down the tubes! Too bad. As the day started we had a pretty good chance. P's immediate reaction was to decide not to submit another nomination until after the elections, and then go for Bob Byrd of West Virginia. I urged an early start to the effect that if it was obvious this Senate would not approve a Southerner, then put in a good Northern constructionist. May do that. P did feel we had not done adequate job in our Congressional group, but that main fault was Justice. He called Carswell, good brief chat. No substance except urged him to stay on Court. He will.[71]

The reference to appointing West Virginia's senator Robert Byrd tells much of Nixon's mood. This was his fantasy punishment for the Senate. Byrd was a part of the Senate's Democratic leadership, not because his colleagues loved him, but rather because they either feared or needed him. Byrd's seniority, his mastery of the parliamentary workings of the Senate, and his committee assignments gave him great power. He was a force to be reckoned with. If Nixon were to nominate Byrd, his colleagues would have a problem: they dare not vote against him, for if Byrd was not confirmed they would have to deal with his wrath; yet how could they vote for him when he was totally unqualified? Byrd had never completed his undergraduate education, although he had gone to American University's law school, where he had—over many years—completed his law work. Byrd had never passed a bar examination, never been admitted to practice anywhere, and never practiced a day of law in his life. Nixon was particularly delighted by the fact that Byrd had once been a member of the Ku Klux Klan. Nominating Byrd to the Supreme Court was the equivalent of throwing a stink bomb into the Senate.

Senior White House aide Bryce Harlow, who headed the congressional relations staff, expressed his concern about Nixon's mood following Carswell's defeat. "If you go across the way," he told another aide, referring to the president's Executive Office Building office where Nixon was brooding, "you will undoubtedly see a plume of blue smoke curling up from under the door. He is burning mad, determined to do something. What it is, I don't know, but it will be awful, just awful; and he will wind up doing severe damage to himself, as he usually does at such time."[72] Harlow, who had known Nixon since his vice-presidential days, wanted the president to take a cruise on the presidential yacht, Sequoia, to cool down. Nixon did just that, with Haldeman and Mitchell, and Haldeman later reported a "very nice cruise to Mt. Vernon, and chopper back. Long talk about plans for next appointment."[73]

While cruising the Potomac, Nixon calmed down, briefly, and decided to nominate a northern jurist—another Burger recommendation: Harry Blackmun, who had already been checked out by Mitchell and Rehnquist. Nixon was the first president since Grover Cleveland to have the Senate reject two nominees to the Supreme Court in a row,[74] so it was also decided that Nixon should make a public statement. To take maximum political advantage of the defeat, the president would portray the Democratically controlled Senate as anti-South. When he went to the White House Press Room, however, he was still angry. Haldeman described Nixon as acting like "a demon" before he went out to "really bang the Senate." Nixon stated for the cameras that he had concluded "that it is not possible to get confirmation for a judge on the Supreme Court of any man who believes in the strict construction of the Constitution, as I do, if he happens to come from the South." Therefore, he was asking the attorney general to submit the name of a northern jurist who was a strict constructionist.[75] It was an obvious misreading of the Carswell defeat, and it only highlighted the extraordinary politicization of the appointment process under Nixon—a process that involved Rehnquist as a key player.

The Blackmun Nomination

The next day, Nixon and Mitchell held a completely off-the-record meeting (which meant that while the White House staff was aware of the meeting, it was not on the president's public schedule and was unknown to the media) with Judge Harry Blackmun, the sixty-one-year-old Minnesota jurist. Before the meeting, Nixon had sought, and received, an assurance from Chief Justice Burger that Blackmun, Burger's friend since childhood and the best man at his wedding, was a strict constructionist.[76] Face to face, Nixon liked Blackmun, and his record. Mitchell supported Blackmun because he had been endorsed by two of the attorney general's best friends: Herschel Friday, a bond lawyer from Little Rock, and Friday's former partner, Pat Mehaffy, now one of Blackmun's colleagues on the Eighth Circuit Court of Appeals.

On April 13, 1970, the White House announced Blackmun's nomination to the Supreme Court. He was quickly and easily confirmed by the Senate on May 12, by a unanimous vote of 94–0.[77] Indeed, the weary Senate might have confirmed Blackmun even sooner, but Democrats were keeping an eye on a new Republican attack in the House of Representatives, where the House minority leader, Gerald Ford, was trying to impeach Associate Justice William O. Douglas.

Efforts to Remove William O. Douglas

Having successfully ousted Fortas for behavior that was not uncommon among the justices, Nixon's men were encouraged to try a repeat performance. No matter that Haynsworth and Carswell should have served as warnings. The president wanted more seats to fill. The next target was Justice William O. Douglas, a strong liberal appointed by Franklin Roosevelt. The Nixon administration had commenced investigating Justice Douglas immediately after taking office, when the "Internal Revenue Service began an audit of Douglas's tax returns only five days after the President's inauguration. At the same time, the FBI was compiling information on Douglas's connections with Las Vegas casino owner Albert Parvin. Douglas was a director of the Albert Parvin Foundation." [78] How the Nixon administration might have initiated this action remains unclear. [79] John Ehrlichman's memoir states that "From the beginning Nixon was interested in getting rid of William O. Douglas," reporting that "John Mitchell had begun to gather information about Douglas' nonjudicial sources of income, and some of it looked hopeful." [80] As his autobiography explains, Jerry Ford became interested when he learned that "Douglas was collecting an annual retainer of $12,000 for serving as the only paid officer of something called the Albert Parvin Foundation. [Ford] also heard that he'd received $4,000 from the Center for the Study of Democratic Institutions." [81]

When the Nixon administration had forced Fortas from the Court, its members had yet to find any more compromising information on Justice Douglas, but they had not abandoned hope. White House gumshoe Jack Caulfield, the former NYPD cop hired by Ehrlichman to undertake investigations for the president, was monitoring Douglas. On June 4, 1969, Caulfield reported in his idiosyncratic cop-talk that "it has been reliably determined from a confidential source" (most likely someone in the IRS) that "at least two newspapers" had task forces working on Douglas; that one newspaper had information from an IRS supervisor who had visited a Chicago bank with an "alleged custodial account for the Flamingo Hotel in Las Vegas"; and it was believed that the "subject account contains derogatory information or substantive leads showing a deeper impropriety on the part of Justice Douglas with the Parvin Foundation and/or Cosa Nostra figures." [82] But Caulfield's information never developed.

Only with the passage of time has it been discovered the lengths to which the Nixon administration went to remove Douglas. It was the FBI that was doing the primary dirty work. Justice Douglas long suspected that the FBI was wiretapping him. He was right. As Gentry notes in his biography of Hoover, it was the director who "had supplied much of the 'evidence' used against [Douglas]. They were old enemies and had been since 1939, when Douglas had first joined the Court." Most remarkable was the wiretapping: "Douglas had been wiretapped, and by the FBI, in every administration from that of Harry Truman . . . to that of Richard Nixon, when, on June 25, 1970, Hoover sent H. R. Haldeman a report on a wiretapped conversation in which Douglas's tactics in the impeachment battle were discussed." [83]

The Douglas impeachment drive was directed by the Republican minority leader, Gerald Ford—encouraged by the Nixon White House. Ford would later claim that when Justice Douglas ignored the calls to resign from the Court by two members of the House of Representatives (H. R. Gross of Iowa and John R. Rarick of Louisiana), he decided to launch his own investigation. According to Ford's biographer, James Cannon (who had Ford's cooperation), the congressman assembled "a team of part-time investigators, but they came up with nothing to justify impeachment charges." Similarly, Ford was provided nothing from the Justice Department to justify removing Douglas. [84]

Nonetheless, Ford launched his impeachment effort against Douglas on April 15, 1970. Cannon says that Ford "could never adequately explain in public or to his closest friends" why he went after Douglas, especially why he engaged in a smear campaign from the floor of the House, which was uncharacteristic of the future president. Ford charged Douglas with "fractious behavior as the first sign of senility" and argued that "his writings [appeared] in a pornographic magazine with a portfolio of obscene photographs on one side of it and a literary admonition to get a gun and start shooting at the first white face you see on the other." Ford finished his speech with, "He does not give a tinker's damn what we think of him and his behavior on the Bench" . . . "He is unfit and should be removed." [85] Gerald Ford was joined by a number of Douglas foes: forty-nine Republicans and fifty-two conservative Democrats, but it was not nearly enough to impeach the justice. Though Ford may never have been able to explain his actions, they were quite understandable to members of the Nixon administration, who believed he was doing their bidding. They were assisting him (through the FBI), and monitoring the progress of his efforts.[86] In fact, John Mitchell believed that Ford was acting at the direct request of the president.[87]

Ford's plan was to get the House to create a "select" committee to investigate Douglas, rather than using the House Judiciary Committee, which had jurisdiction of impeachments but was controlled by Democrats. The effort failed. On April 21, the House Judiciary Committee created a special subcommittee chaired by the full committee's chairman Emanuel Celler to study the impeachment charges and report back. Chairman Celler stated that the subcommittee, with three Democrats and two Republicans, would "neither whitewash nor witch hunt."[88] Executive departments and agencies from the FBI to the CIA to the Department of State provided information to Celler's subcommittee, which soon exonerated Justice Douglas, finding no basis whatsoever to impeach him. Republicans cried that the fix was in.

Efforts to remove Associate Justice William Douglas did accomplish one thing: they created an intractable resolve by Douglas never to resign while Nixon was president. Douglas summed up his feelings toward Richard Nixon in an anecdote in his memoir. Chief Justice Warren Burger had claimed that Nixon was opposed to the impeachment effort. Yet when Douglas mentioned this to Earl Warren, he "roared with laughter and said, 'If that son of a bitch is opposed to your impeachment he could stop it in one minute.'" Douglas decided "that Nixon, being an artist of dissimulation, would, if he planned to use a knife against a person, send him a message of cheer, friendship and good will."[89] Douglas knew that Nixon had done exactly that with Abe Fortas; the day Fortas had resigned, Nixon called to express his sympathy.[90]

. . . .

After the Douglas impeachment effort ended, the president, John Mitchell, and John Ehrlichman met with Chief Justice Burger for a breakfast in the Family Dining Room on the main floor of the White House on December 18, 1970. The chief justice reported that the aging justices whose health most interested Richard Nixon—Hugo Black, William Douglas, and Thurgood Marshall—were not in the best of shape, but he added that none were incapacitated and all were functioning. Burger expected no retirements soon. For the time being, Nixon had to put his Court project on hold. It had been a constant focus since the 1968 election. It would return to center stage again soon. But for now it was banished to the wings.

• • • •

The first two years of his administration had established Nixon's procedures for selecting justices. They involved five men, beginning with Nixon himself. Chief Justice Warren Burger passed names to Attorney General John Mitchell. Mitchell filtered them for strict constructionists, and added new ones of his own, with the help of William Rehnquist. John Ehrlichman kept a watchful eye on it all, calling on such White House staff as he needed. It was Rehnquist who actually did all the initial heavy lifting: he maintained the list of potential nominees; he determined whether or not a candidate was of Supreme Court quality; he performed initial litmus testing; and he made recommendations to Mitchell. If a candidate was seriously considered, Rehnquist met with him to test, vet, and size him up in person. Bill Rehnquist had become the personnel director for future justices. But he was much more.

John Mitchell had little Washington experience when he arrived. His practice as a Wall Street bond lawyer had been far removed from the business of the federal government and the Supreme Court. Therefore, he relied on experienced Washington people, like the deputy assistant attorney general, Henry Petersen, and FBI director J. Edgar Hoover, to assist him with projects such as ousting Fortas and Douglas. At the time that Mitchell was pursuing Fortas, I asked why he never consulted the one man in the Department of Justice most familiar with the Supreme Court, Erwin Griswold, who was the solicitor general (a post he had occupied for President Lyndon Johnson as well, not to mention the fact that he was a former dean of Harvard Law School). I needed to know because I had periodic dealings with the solicitor general. "My God, we can't talk to Griswold about these things," Mitchell said, wincing with chagrin when I asked. Then he explained, "While Griswold's a good Republican he doesn't understand, nor always appreciate, Richard Nixon's politics." But

Bill Rehnquist did. Today, I have little doubt that without Rehnquist's guidance and blessings, Mitchell's hardball and dubious tactics vis-à-vis the Court would never have been undertaken. Rehnquist's participation—as a former Supreme Court insider who had clerked for Justice Robert H. Jackson—gave us all solace. Yet these, and other, activities would later haunt me, after I had successfully slipped his name into serious consideration for a Court appointment (without his knowledge) during a critical point in the selection process when two new seats became available in late 1971.

PART ONE

2

THE GAMES BEGIN

September 17, 1971

THE FIVE-WEEK CHAIN OF EVENTS that ended with William Rehnquist's Supreme Court appointment began on Friday, September 17, 1971, when the first of two vacancies arose. Both seats caught the White House by surprise, myself included (over a year earlier I had moved over from the Justice Department). Throughout the summer, rumors had persisted that Justices Thurgood Marshall, William Douglas, John Harlan, and Hugo Black all were in declining health, and any one of them might resign before the new term of the Court. But the only word from the Court had been requests (which were accommodated) by Chief Justice Burger to use the president's military aircraft for his travel. By the end of the summer, those of us who thought about these things at the White House figured that all these aging justices would probably hang on until after the election, which was only a year away. I was sure there would be no more justices nominated on my watch.

After vacationing in Europe in August and early September, I had returned having made a personal decision. It was time to leave the White

House. Within a week I had two attractive job offers in hand (one as an investment banker with a major Wall Street firm and the other as the American general counsel of a European shipping conglomerate), so I went to see White House chief of staff Bob Haldeman to tell him I was leaving. He was not pleased. "John, you wouldn't have all those damn job offers if we hadn't brought you to the White House in the first place. The same offers will be there after the election, probably more. You owe it to the president to stay through the election. Then you can leave if you want."[1] Haldeman made himself quite clear. If I left, I would be burning my bridges. I stayed, and within days found myself involved in a new, high-stakes bit of palace politics.

The process, which I have reassembled, started on September 17. Haldeman waited for the president's schedule to open so he could give him the news of its beginning. Rumors had circulated anew that Associate Justices Hugo Black and John Harlan were both too ill to continue serving, and now this had been confirmed by Attorney General Mitchell, who learned of their conditions in a telephone conversation with Chief Justice Burger that morning. First, "Justice Black is going to resign at three o'clock this afternoon. He's going to tell the Court at the same time," Mitchell reported to Haldeman.[2]

Hugo Lafayette Black had been appointed to the Supreme Court in 1937 by President Roosevelt. At the time of his appointment, Black was completing his second term as a U.S. senator from Alabama. It had been a controversial appointment. Conservatives opposed him because of his unyielding support of Roosevelt's New Deal legislation, including the unsuccessful efforts to pack the Supreme Court by adding more justices. Liberals were suspicious of Black's onetime membership in the Ku Klux Klan, notwithstanding his renunciation of the Klan before he first ran for the Senate in 1926. FDR, seeking to appoint someone from the South, saw in Black a man of brilliance with compassion for little people and underdogs. Hugo Black had never finished high school; rather, at seventeen he entered Birmingham Medical School, completing the four-year program in three years. Then he went to the University of Alabama Law School, and simultaneously took an entire liberal arts curriculum while completing his law studies with high honors. Black's thirty-four years on the Supreme Court would mark him as one of the great justices, who had a profound impact on the Constitution through his rulings and writings.[3]

Black was everything that FDR had hoped, and more. He was also the epitome of a justice that Richard Nixon abhorred. He was an activist, who had voted with Earl Warren for most of the Court's most liberal decisions. To replace him with a conservative was, for Nixon, just as desirable as it had been to replace Earl Warren with Warren Burger.

Haldeman did not think the news justified interrupting the president. He was meeting with the winners of the Seventh World International Bowling Federation Tournament. Nixon had taken the champions over to his private bowling lanes in the basement of the Executive Office Building (EOB) beside the White House. Amazingly, Richard Nixon had bowled a strike while one of the champions was so nervous he had rolled a gutter-ball. A chipper president returned to the Oval Office, sans the bowlers, to spend fifteen minutes with an old friend, actress Ginger Rogers,[4] and then with the national commander of the American Legion.[5] It was close to 1:30 p.m. that Friday afternoon when Haldeman seated himself in a chair beside the president's desk, with his pad of notes from his conversation with Mitchell on his lap, to share the news with Nixon.[6] Black was not the only justice on Haldeman's mind.

"The Attorney General called to say that at three o'clock we will receive the resignation of Justice Black, today. The Chief Justice called John [Mitchell] this morning, and Black is sending you a letter saying he resigns at the pleasure of the president, he will notify the Court at the same time. Burger suggested that you sit tight on it, and not announce it because it will cause trouble. Mitchell and I both feel that you've got to announce it, because there's a lot of rumors out there, and he's telling the whole Court, so [Justice William O.] Douglas, or somebody like that, is going to let it out anyway. I think that at four o'clock, at his briefing, [White House press secretary] Ron [Ziegler] should simply say that the president has received the [resignation]," Haldeman added, then returned to his notes. "Beyond that, Burger is meeting this afternoon at four-thirty with Justice Harlan, who has been transferred from Bethesda [Naval Hospital] to another hospital because of his problem, and it is Burger's strong feeling that at that time Harlan is going to tell of his intention to do likewise."

"But we don't want [Harlan's] resignation. We've never needed a stronger, more vigorous man," the president noted. In fact, of course, it was enticing to ponder filling two new vacancies. The president immediately mentioned the name of the man who would be his first choice for one of them: Virginia congressman Richard H. Poff. Nixon had first considered placing Poff on the Supreme Court during the Haynsworth-Carswell debacle, only to discover that he could not nominate him because the Constitution forbids a member of Congress from assuming an office for which he has voted a pay raise, and the Congress had voted to increase the salaries of the justices. But that restriction no longer applied, for it was a new Congress.

"The bar will never approve him, he's never practiced law," Haldeman added flatly. When the president said nothing, Haldeman continued reading from his notes, reporting that Mitchell was "looking for guidance."

"All right, I want Poff. I don't know, I think the bar can approve him, because he's a member of the [House] Judiciary Committee."

"John [Mitchell] says we need some real thinking, particularly in the political area, where we'll get the most credit," Haldeman reported, along with the fact that Mitchell was planning a meeting on this subject with former Federal Judge Lawrence Walsh, chairman of the American Bar Association's Standing Committee on the Federal Judiciary. He then brought up another candidate. "He wanted to know whether you were still interested in William French Smith."

"Oh, yeah, for Harlan's seat, he'd be great. William French Smith would be great, a Californian. I'd love to put a Californian on. How old is he?"

Haldeman speculated that Smith was under fifty, adding that he too thought Smith would be a good choice. The conversation then turned to the fact that Nixon had never offered a Jewish nominee to fill the previously vacated seat of Justice Abe Fortas. This prompted Nixon to state that "on the Jew side there is only one" person he would consider. Haldeman guessed that Nixon's reference was to Budget Director Caspar Weinberger, who actually was Episcopalian; but he was wrong. Nixon surprised him with "[Arlen] Specter," a Philadelphia prosecutor and later the Republican senator from Pennsylvania. Nixon said, "He's strong on law enforcement, and the rest, and I might consider him, if we want to play the Jews."

The games had begun.

• • • •

That afternoon, press secretary Ron Ziegler entered the Oval Office, looking for guidance from the president in explaining the Black resignation story to the press. A scenario, mostly true, was agreed upon.[7]

Ziegler spelled it out: "As you know we received at three-thirty the letter of retirement of Hugo Black, Justice Black. I'm going to announce this at four-thirty. I am going to say that the President is informed by personal letter of the resignation of Justice Black at three-thirty this afternoon. It came in at three-thirty and you were informed after the leadership [meeting] was over, by John Ehrlichman, I'm going to say. The President accepts with deep regret, and I'm going to say he is retiring because of health reasons. I will then be asked if we anticipated this. No, we did not. I'm going to say that the Chief Justice called earlier, at three o'clock, to say that a messenger was on the way over and I'll say he arrived here at three thirty-seven."

Nixon added, "Another thing you can say is this, that the President, in his two appearances before the Court, is often reminded that the most perceptive and vigorous questioning came from Justice Black, and the President was struck by his ability for analyzing issues." Considering that Hugo Black and Richard Nixon were philosophical and political opposites, this was a very charitable and compassionate thing to say.

Soon, Nixon received word as well in a call from Chief Justice Burger.[8]

"Hi, Warren, how are you?"

"How are you?" Burger asked.

"Fine. I understand the letter is here and that therefore it will be out. Let me ask you on [a] personal basis, because I don't know how to handle this, as to whether you think that perhaps, that we ought to consider getting a dinner for him or something like that. What's your feeling?"

"Well, it will be quite awhile before he can."

"Could he do it?"

"Be present, yes. He's a very sick man, Mr. President."

"I didn't know that. Where is he, in the hospital, or—?"

"He's in the Naval Hospital."

"Uh huh."

"I suggested to John [Mitchell] yesterday, he probably hasn't gotten the message to you," Burger said.

"Oh. I've been meeting with legislative leaders today."

"I have just a note in general. This was before this had crystallized. They said it was actually written about three weeks ago, and it's been in his drawer, waiting for a date."

"Um hum. Does he take visitors?" Nixon asked.

"No."

"No visitors, huh?"

"I haven't been able to see him for ten days."

"Well, then better, my goodness. I'll drop a little handwritten note to him."

"I think that'd be nice. Now you know John Harlan has been in [the hospital] now for five weeks."

"I've heard that. But I just assumed that was the eye trouble again."

"Well, no, no. It's something much more serious."

"Oh, God."

"Much more serious."

"That's too bad."

"He has moved out of the Naval Hospital yesterday and moved to George Washington. Just in frustration, his own frustration, although he is the most uncomplaining man I think I have ever known in my life. He's had more grief and problems than one man should bear."

"Um hum, um hum," the president murmured sympathetically.

"I've told John Mitchell, my own judgment is that John [Harlan] will not be back here."

"Yeah. I'll write a note to him, I suppose."

"Yes, I think that'd be nice."

"But as far as Black, a note is the thing to do?"

"Yes, I think so."

"But he can get that okay?"

"It would be the Naval Hospital and John Harlan is at George Washington [Hospital]," the chief justice clarified.

"Sure, sure. I'll just have it personally delivered so they'll find out. All right, fine, fine, fine."

"And I told John [Mitchell] when I talked to him yesterday, and again this morning, that my judgment on the announcement thing was the longer you could keep it, right within your own bosom, the more you keep your options open. There'll be rumors, of course, you can't avoid it."

"Oh, you mean the announcement with regard to the retirement?" the president asked.

"Yeah."

"I think it's going to be, it's almost inevitable, as it's already been asked about in the press corps today. You know, they apparently got it, they must be onto it."

"Well, they will be speculating," Burger added, subtly jousting with the president.

Nixon, not wanting to debate the timing of an announcement, changed the subject while throwing a bone to the chief justice. "Let me say that, on the successor thing, and just as we had on the other basis, I will want to have a talk with you at the proper time."

"And I'll be available."

After Nixon hung up, Ziegler continued his scenario.

"How soon will a successor be announced? Well, the President has just been informed of this, he will look for the best qualified man. Next question. Does the President intend to appoint a strict constructionist? Gentlemen, the President's going to look for the best qualified man, period."

Nixon reminded Ziegler that he had already publicly stated the qualifications; but he agreed that Ziegler should state that the president would seek "the best qualified man."

"I will not limit it geographically, I will just say he will look all over the country."

"The best qualified man wherever he is," Nixon added. The president did not need to remind his press secretary that the nominee must be a conservative.

. . . .

A short time later, the president used a brief 4:30 p.m. Oval Office meeting with a new senator, Robert T. Stafford (R-VT), joined by his wife, as an opportunity to invite the press into the Oval Office and announce the resignation of Justice Black.[9] Stafford had replaced the recently deceased Senator Winston Prouty. When Senator Stafford and his wife and the press departed, Haldeman remained and Nixon returned to his desk, taking several sheets of his personal White House stationery out of his desk drawer to write notes to Justices Black and Harlan.[10] It was hard to resist running through candidates and scenarios with Haldeman, especially if there were to be two simultaneous openings.

And what if there could be *more* than two? As the president wrote, they speculated about the longevity of Justices William O. Douglas and Thurgood Marshall. At the time, neither man was in the best of health. Chief

Justice Burger was the principal source for Nixon's intelligence, and he had informed the White House that Marshall was in much worse health than was being publicly reported.[11]

Ehrlichman joined the president and Haldeman, and quickly the conversation turned to the vacancy at hand. Ehrlichman reported, "I have Mr. Justice Black's letter here if you'd like to see it. In our opinion it is effective immediately. He's a little ambiguous, I hope he writes his opinions better than that." Ehrlichman passed the letter to the president:

> Dear Mr. President:
>   Since the adjournment of Court last June I have been ill, and, more recently have been taking medication, which together have impaired my vision and my general ability to do my work with the understanding that I consider necessary for me to perform my duties as I have performed them in the past. For this reason I have decided that the time has come for me to retire.
>   By this letter I record and advise you of my decision to retire from regular active service as an Associate Justice of the Supreme Court of the United States, pursuant to 28 USC Sec. 371(b).
>
> > Respectfully yours,
> > Hugo L. Black

After reading it, Nixon told Ehrlichman that the chief justice thought they were going to get another vacancy. If that happened, Nixon said, he wanted to find "two conservatives," adding that he felt "strongly" about it. Nixon then asked Ehrlichman what the problem was with Poff; he wanted to know who was saying that "the bar won't clear him. What the hell does that mean?" Haldeman, the non-lawyer, sat silent as the two men discussed it.

"Well, that's a question you have to cope with," Ehrlichman said. "If we're going to stick with [the American Bar Association], that cuts down the list pretty substantially. It's, you know, a judgment call as to whether you want to be bound by [the bar]."

Nixon responded that Poff is "a God damn good lawyer, isn't he?"

"There's only one person, that I know of, that you're going to have to persuade on this, and that's John Mitchell."

"He doesn't want Poff?"

"He doesn't want to buck the Bar Association, because of Poff. I think he'd like to have Poff."

"Well, the bar associations, and John Mitchell, started this [screening procedure]. I think [Mitchell] should start the conversation [with the bar] that they should make one exception to their rule of practicing law, and that is ten years of service on the Judiciary Committee of the House or Senate. Now, let's just put it that way. That's my belief, and I'm going to handle it that way, and if they want to fight me on that, fine. I told Poff he should get the God damn job, but that doesn't mean he's going to take it. For Christ sake, he'd be a damn good judge."

Nixon wanted to know whether Poff ever practiced law, and Ehrlichman guessed (incorrectly) that he probably was an assistant district attorney for six months and then ran for county judge or supervisor or something and the next thing he did was get elected to Congress. In reality, Poff was in private practice for four and a half years, which he described as "a small town general practice but very intense."

"Well, let's look very, very hard at the other conservative then, whoever he is, maybe we have this fellow from California, Reagan's guy, French, you know."

The president was referring to William French Smith. Erhlichman paused for a beat, mentally reached, and got it, "Oh, yeah."

"He's a hell of a big corporation lawyer. But it's nice to have this kind of a problem."

"Sure is."

"It's a great, great change, it's a great change to the [normal activity]. It's a great moment," Nixon said, chuckling, "but we've got to have a man, one guy, that's, frankly, is between forty and fifty years of age. I think that sixty, two sixty-year-old men, would be a mistake."

"Yep, yep."

"That's got to do it. Now, that's the trouble with John [Mitchell], and the Bar Association, they're old types. I don't want old types."

"Yep, well, on my list there are two names that appeal to me, one of them probably not confirmable, and that's [Caspar] Weinberger and Spiro T. Agnew."

Nixon paused, then wondered, "Do you think that Agnew would be—?"

"I don't know, there's a strong question in my mind. But it's a hell of an intriguing possibility."

"Well, he once told me he wants to be on the Court," the president said.

Haldeman ended the brief silence when he wisecracked, "That would really rip things up."

Nixon ignored the scoff. "He'd be a damn good judge."

A more thoughtful Haldeman rejoined with the question of whether Agnew wanted the job. Nixon quickly reversed course. "I'm sure that he wants to stay Vice President."

Nonetheless, Haldeman too liked this idea. "You know, what I was just thinking, he loves this social stuff."

Nixon agreed, noting, "He likes the movie star business."

"He could do that though, from the Court," Ehrlichman pointed out, as he and Haldeman indulged in a bit of fantasy.

"A justice can lead the social life, he's got a good social thing. He's got all summer to do it, he can go to California and spend it with [celebrities]," Haldeman began.

"May to October."

"Two or three months in Palm Springs, two or three in Newport."

Abruptly, Ehrlichman turned back to the president and reality. "You'd be accused of putting him, you know, adrift in a lifeboat, and using the Court as a shelf. There are enormous negatives to it, at the same time, he is now enjoying, sort of a climate of acceptance, that is probably temporary, before the storm." Ehrlichman was referring to Agnew's political barnstorming as the administration's point man to attack the media. Eventually, Ehrlichman appreciated, Agnew's targets would have their day. "And at that time he could get so cut up that he probably never pulls this off. Of course, it, the Senate, would have a golden opportunity to do you in, by refusing to confirm your Vice President."

"Yeah. Oh Christ, it'd be awful, if we'd give 'em that chance," the president agreed.

There would never really be any serious chance of an Agnew nomination, though Nixon would continue to enjoy occasionally toying with the idea. Meanwhile, there were lots of other angles to be considered. Haldeman returned to the question of the Jewish seat. "If you end up going [without naming a Jew], with three straight—"

"If I really wanted to put Weinberger in there, I didn't need [unintelligible]."

Ehrlichman raised Weinberger's virtues. "An arch conservative, he's a good lawyer. And that's good. Also, he's from California."

Nixon finished the thought, "And also basically he's considered to be Jewish."

"Sure," said Ehrlichman.

"He isn't, I'm sure," Haldeman corrected.

"He's Episcopalian," Ehrlichman stated for the record.

Haldeman added, "Apparently he's part Jewish."

Ehrlichman claimed—strangely—that the president would get credit for placing a Jew on the Court if he nominated Weinberger. The president, however, brushed this issue aside.

"My point is, he'd be a hell of a good, ah, a great judge. He'd do a hell of a good job."

Exactly what constituted a great justice in Richard Nixon's mind would become clear throughout the coming weeks. Law and order toughness topped the list. On that there was agreement that Weinberger would be "as tough as hell." But Haldeman was not so sure about Weinberger's credentials on other matters. "He's certainly no great conservative on social issues," the chief of staff noted, but did acknowledge, "He's conservative on economic matters."

Ehrlichman offered his appraisal. "Yeah, criminal social issues, he is tough."

When Nixon stepped in, Haldeman interrupted his thoughts as he often did. "Basically, I don't want somebody that's, ah, that's—"

"Soft on welfare and civil rights, and things like that."

Ehrlichman, the president's senior domestic affairs adviser, chuckled, thinking about his own dealings with Weinberger as head of the Budget Bureau. "Boy, he's not soft on welfare on the budget side."

"No," Haldeman agreed.

"Nor on civil rights," Nixon noted. "Basically, I don't want a man on the Court that's a racist. Frankly, I just don't want [that], and I don't feel that way myself, and we've crossed that God damn bridge." However, Nixon had no interest in the other end of the civil rights spectrum. "I'm not going to put anybody in that thing that doesn't share my views on busing, period. Find out how [Weinberger] feels about busing, and let me know. Will you do that? This Smith, of course, is a liberal when it comes to social issues." Nixon would later make clear that he did not care about economic issues, only about law and order (pro) and civil rights (con). The trick would be finding a great appointment *politically* as well as philosophically.

Nixon thumped his fingers on his desk top, and added, "Is there anybody you can think of in the Senate? Want to pick up a senator? How about Robert Byrd of West Virginia? Former member of the Ku Klux Klan."

Haldeman went even further, "How about [Alan] Cranston, from California? I think he's worse." To Haldeman, apparently Cranston's assertive liberalism was more offensive than Byrd's reactionary conservatism.

"Just might do that," Nixon quipped. He thought he had been joking about Byrd, a jest about taking an influential Democrat out of the legislative arena. In fact, Nixon would return to the idea of appointing Byrd for a different reason. At the time, however, the subject had been exhausted, as was evident when Nixon suggested he name J. Edgar Hoover to the high court as a way to get rid of him. As Ehrlichman departed, the president gave him a parting instruction.

"Well, make a good judge, John."

"I'll see what we can do."

• • • •

John Ehrlichman returned to his office and called me. As his successor as counsel to the president, he would assign me the work of doing background checks on nominees.[12]

"Counselor, how's your schedule?" Ehrlichman asked. I told him I had no crisis at that moment, and Ehrlichman continued. "I just wanted to alert you to the fact that Justice Black has resigned, and the president has accepted his resignation. We also understand, but nothing is being said, that Justice Harlan is also going to resign because of his ill heath. Based on a conversation I just had with the president, your friend Dick Poff is high on the list. We're going to need to vet him. The president doesn't have a whole lot of faith in the Department of Justice, and for good reason. I understand you are the keeper of the Poff file."

"Well, my file is certainly not very complete," I answered.

"Why don't you make it complete. And coordinate with the Justice Department."

I could not have been more pleased to learn that Virginia congressman Dick Poff was under serious consideration for a seat on the Supreme Court. I had first meet Poff in 1965, shortly after graduating from law school, when looking for a job on Capitol Hill. For any lawyer interested in government, a position with the Committee on the Judiciary of the House of Representatives was a great place to work. It was a committee of lawyers, with legislative jurisdiction over a wide range of legal matters. There I worked with Dick Poff for several years, until he requested that I take a position as associate director on the National Commission on Reform of Federal Criminal Laws in 1968. Poff had been named vice chairman, and needed someone to keep an eye on the commission, which was dealing with highly political subjects like the drug laws, gun laws, capital punishment, and the federal sentencing structure.[13]

It was while watching Dick Poff handle himself for several years during legislative battles arising within the House Judiciary Committee, and then as the vice chairman of the law reform commission, that I became convinced that Richard Harding Poff would make a great Supreme Court justice. As soon as I completed my conversation with John Ehrlichman, I called Poff.

• • • •

Meanwhile, Nixon was handing Haldeman two handwritten notes for copying prior to delivery.[14] What these notes do not record is the joy at having one, if not two, vacancies to fill this close to his reelection bid.

9/17/71

Dear Mr. Justice Black

This personal note expresses my deep appreciation as a fellow lawyer for your years of service in the Court.

As I said in my statement when I received your letter of resignation— you were the best questioner of all when I appeared before the Court—

Mrs. Nixon joins me in sending many good wishes to you in this difficult time—

Richard Nixon

9/17/71

Dear John [Harlan]

I was very distressed to learn from Warren Burger of your stay in the hospital.

This note brings my very best personal wishes during what I know must be a difficult time for you.

The nation and The Court will always be in your debt for your superb public service.

RN

3

PRIORITY ONE: A SOUTHERNER

September 18

THE NEXT MORNING, Saturday, September 18, Nixon was up early, anxious to meet with John Mitchell.[1] He was thinking politically more than philosophically, and thinking of the South in particular. With the experience of Haynsworth and Carswell, Nixon knew that finding a southerner he could get through the Senate confirmation process was not easy. His opponents would fight him hard. But changing the philosophical disposition of the Court, and doing it with a son of the South, was solid politics. Although Mitchell had screwed up with Haynsworth and Carswell, the president still relied heavily on his attorney general. Nonetheless, White House insiders knew that their relationship had become strained after the Haynsworth-Carswell donnybrook.

The Nixon-Mitchell relationship began in 1966, when Mitchell's municipal bond law firm was merged with the law firm Nixon had joined, to create Nixon Mudge Guthrie Alexander & Mitchell. As law partners, they had been equals. Former Vice President Nixon soon discovered in John

Mitchell a man who knew state and local politicians throughout the country—and they became friends. Mitchell was one of the first to encourage his partner to run for president again, and Nixon recruited the taciturn, pipe-puffing Mitchell to be his campaign manager. After Nixon's victory, Mitchell was ready to return to the practice of law, but the president-elect leaned heavily on his partner to join his new administration in Washington as his attorney general. The partnership had continued in Washington, with Nixon giving Mitchell greater authority and access than any other member of his cabinet. The deference and mutual respect these men shared for one another was apparent in the recordings of their private meetings. While Bob Haldeman and John Ehrlichman were staffmen, John Mitchell was an adviser—although he would gradually become just another staffman.

As good as the Nixon White House staff was at preparing options and recommendations for the president, Nixon had assigned the task of recommending Supreme Court nominations to Mitchell. Accordingly, Mitchell had met with William Rehnquist at noon on Friday, September 17, to give him the news, and review Rehnquist's latest list of potential candidates. Needless to say, since Rehnquist was the radar operator for potential justices, he was on no one's screen himself.

Bob Haldeman arrived in the Oval Office shortly after 10:00 a.m., and Nixon began talking about the Court appointments, preparatory to his conversation with Mitchell.[2] Nixon was thinking aloud, as he often did with Haldeman: "On this Court thing, in the event that we get Harlan along with Black, William French Smith is the best choice. He's best in the sense that he's known as a power and vigor in the law, isn't he?"

"He gives that impression."

"Pretty God damn high, I mean, that's what I hear."

Nixon compared William French Smith to Justice John Harlan, who had been a senior partner in a prestigious Wall Street law firm before being appointed to the bench in 1955 by President Eisenhower. Nixon and Haldeman assumed (correctly) that Smith was close to Reagan. But they knew more about Smith's wife, Jean Webb Smith, than her husband. Nixon knew her before she was Mrs. William French Smith. The president told Haldeman that "she is awfully nice," and Haldeman agreed, adding that she was "the national president of the Junior League, and all that kind of stuff, and she's been very good to me." When the president reported that "she was a big supporter of ours," Haldeman observed, "bet she'd like to come back to Washington."

The president again mused about Weinberger. "I think also, I must say, that Weinberger—"

"I think he's [solid]," Haldeman completed the thought.

"Weinberger's a definite possibility in my view, for the reason that, basically, because I know he'd be a good judge. Now, I don't know whether he's much of a political asset."

"As long as he met your [standard] on busing, and he would."

"Cap is an honest man."

"Oh, he's an honest man, and he's also loyal."

"Yeah."

Presidential aide Steve Bull entered the office to tell the president that Mitchell had arrived at the West Entrance, and was en route to the office. Just before Mitchell walked in and Haldeman left them alone, the president reflected proudly, "Because whatever happens in the [1972] election, we will have changed the Court. I will have named four, and Potter Stewart becomes the swing man." He paused. "He's a God damn weak reed, I must say. But if we can only get him on board, we'll have the Court." As for additional vacancies, the president felt that the only likely seats were those of Justices Douglas and Marshall. Haldeman, no doubt thinking of the impeachment effort, added: "Well, Douglas, I'm sure, will just hang on just not to give you the appointment. If Douglas or Marshall were totally incapacitated on their deathbeds, they wouldn't give you the appointment until they die."

• • • •

When Mitchell entered the Oval Office, the president got right to the business at hand. "With regard to this Court thing, John, of course, you and I have got to decide who we tell, so we'll get all the input we can. But just the two of us will talk. Now, Ehrlichman says that Poff's [problem with the bar] could be surmountable. Let me give you my own thinking on it."

"Okay."

"As to where we stand, with Black out. We now do have to have a southerner. I really think it would be a slap to the South not to try for a southerner. So I'd say that our first requirement is have a southerner. The second requirement, he must be a conservative southerner."

"Yes."

"I don't care if he's a Democrat or a Republican. Third, within the definition of conservative, he must be against busing, and against forced housing integration. Beyond that, he can do what he pleases. He can screw around on, you know, economics, and et ceteras. But basically what I'd like is another Blackmun. A Blackmun or a Burger. Now, Poff fits all those things. He's conservative, but yet he's not considered to be a racist. He's young, oh, the other thing. The man must be neither old, fifty, fifty-five, if we put two sixty-one-year-old men on there, it's too many. I'd like to get a guy who can serve the Court twenty years. Now, what I had in mind on Poff is that when you have [your conversation with the bar, tell them the president has said] we cannot give them a veto power on Supreme Court nominees. Second, with regard to the Supreme Court appointments, they are an order of magnitude [higher], as opposed to the circuit courts, district courts and the rest, because they involve higher policy than all these others, and I believe that the American Bar in its wisdom should consider, should not rule out, or at least should consider, that ten years on the Judiciary Committee of either the House or Senate is the equivalent of frankly presiding over the district court in Abilene."

"I think it's above that. Because you handle all of the great constitutional questions that have come along through the Congress during that period of time."

Suddenly, Nixon switched topics. "Incidentally, I thought Martha was awful good on *Laugh-In*."

"Did you see that?" Mitchell almost giggled.

The president had tossed out the comment offhandedly, but John Mitchell had to be pleased. He truly enjoyed his wife, Martha, who had become the highest profile woman in the Nixon administration. Born and raised in Bluff, Arkansas, the daughter of a successful cotton broker, she was fun and fun-loving—and outspoken to a fault. With a southern accent as sweet as honeysuckle, the volatile Martha became a media favorite because she was like nothing official Washington had ever seen or heard. Her middle-of-the-night phone calls to reporters became legendary. When a newsperson found her, he had a story, or at least a great sound bite: "My husband would like to trade a few liberals for Russian communists," "The Vietnam War stinks," "Warren Burger's a crummy dinner partner—borrrrrring."

Martha was not one of Pat Nixon's favorites, so the president's comment was appreciated by Mitchell. Only he knew how close Martha's *Laugh-In* cameo had come to being a disastrous incident. She had performed her straight-to-the-camera jokes like a pro: "John and I have the perfect arrangement. He runs the Attorney General's Office and I run the rest of the country." But Martha had smarted, then steamed, when the show's star Lily Tomlin refused to speak to her off camera. Tomlin was making a political statement to the wrong person. Martha was ready to tell her off when an aide got her out of the studio.

Nixon's reference to Martha was brief. The president knew that she had a serious drinking problem, and made most of her outrageous statements when crocked, and he tried to avoid talking about her with his attorney general.[3] What he did not know was that from the first Martha learned of a vacancy on the Court, she had lobbied her husband to select a woman.

On that Saturday, Mitchell returned to the subject at hand by raising what would be a major problem for the president.

"We already have [Lawrence] Walsh [chairman of the American Bar Association Committee on the Federal Judiciary] coming in for this purpose."

"Yes."

"This was [scheduled] before Black's announcement yesterday, to see if we can straighten out [the bar's evaluation procedures]."

The Department of Justice used the ABA's evaluation committee when appointing federal trial and appellate judges. This practice had begun in 1954 with Eisenhower's attorney general, Herbert Brownell, and had been followed by all successive attorneys general. The twelve-man screening committee, with a representative from each of the Federal Circuits, plus an at-large chairman, interviewed the peers of those nominated for judgeships: local lawyers, members of bar associations, judges, and others who knew the character and practice of the nominee. Then the committee would confidentially advise the attorney general if they found the nominee qualified or unqualified. The focus was on character, judicial temperament, knowledge, and experience with the law. The ABA's evaluation committee had not been used by the Nixon White House with the nominations of Warren Burger, Clement Haynsworth, Harrold Carswell, or Harry Blackmun. But in the summer of 1970, with the president's consent, Mitchell had succumbed to pressures to restore the process. Now they were faced with actually using this group for a Supreme Court nomination for the first time, and it threatened to damage the prospects of Richard Poff due to his lack of practice in a courtroom.

Nixon praised Poff. "Take Poff. I've never seen him at the leadership meetings, but from every report I get, John, he's a stand-up guy with great character."

"Great character and extremely able."

"Is he? I don't know."

"Dick is great on the floor [of the House of Representatives], he's great in committees, and he's got a very good mind."

"How old is he? About fifty?"

"He's forty-eight, forty-nine."

"He's the right age. I'll tell you the way I think you've got to do it. Oh, the third thing I was going to mention, he's got to be a man who can be confirmed. I don't want to be halfway down the road, and have another Carswell, or anything like that. Now, I think, looking at that point, that Poff's a cinch for confirmation. I can't see how, you know, they [can] vote against Poff for the nomination, do you think so?"

"I don't believe so. Except he signed the Southern Manifesto,* and et cetera, et cetera, et cetera, which they could use as an issue if they wanted to. I think they've had that bit. Now, let me put another ingredient in here. I don't know whether Warren Burger when he talked to you yesterday mentioned it or not, but Harlan is right on the fringe."

"Yes. I wrote Harlan, yesterday. I wrote both of them."

Neither man was sure of the full extent of Harlan's illness. Mitchell did not believe that Harlan had "a malignancy" but he was not certain. Mitchell reported that Harlan was in "horrible pain," to the point that Burger had been unable to meet with him, but the chief justice hoped to meet with Harlan on Monday, September 27, to discern how long he

*The so-called Southern Manifesto was a congressional protest against the Supreme Court's 1954 historic school desegregation ruling in *Brown v. Board of Education* signed by virtually every member of Congress from a southern state, in both House and Senate.

might remain on the Court. The prospect of two openings meant that Nixon and Mitchell had varying scenarios to consider.

Mitchell began: "So, then, we may have a double play here, and of course what you do in the northern slot might very well help what you do in the southern slot, and vice versa."

"Well, even then, I don't want a liberal."

"Oh no, no."

"I don't want a liberal."

"Absolutely not."

"I just feel so strongly about that. I mean, when I think what the busing decisions have done to the South, and what it could do with de facto busing."

"I agree," Mitchell said.

"And forced integration of housing, I just feel that if the last thing we do, we have got to have exerted—"

"You would be going back on the commitments that you made during your presidential campaign."

Nixon then introduced an unprecedented idea. "Now can I ask you this? This is just to play an awful long shot. Is there a woman, yet? That would be a hell of a thing if we could do it."

"I think there is, if there's a woman that's credible within an age limit. There's a couple of them, as you know, up in years." John Mitchell, thanks to wife Martha, was way ahead of the president on this one. He had told Rehnquist to take a look months earlier. But he was not familiar with names at the time.

"They're old?"

"It would be very hard for people to vote against a woman."

"Oh, hell yes, [that's the point]."

Neither man was interested in discussing specific women by name, so the subject was dropped for the time being. Nixon next considered geographical angles.

"The second point, and, hold your hat on this. I don't think the easy road is New York for this, do you?"

"No."

"It isn't New York. [Justice] Brennan's from the East."

"Brennan's, of course, from New Jersey. [Thurgood] Marshall, of course, was originally from New York."

"Isn't any problem there. It seems to me to go to California. There are two names I want to pick. One, you probably don't know. There's a hell of a lawyer out there, this William French Smith. He's apparently on the Board of Regents. He's fifty years old, or so. A partner in Gibson, Dunn and Crutcher. He would pass the bar like Flynn."

"I would think so."

"And he's conservative as hell, isn't he? I heard he's a hell of a conservative, and on the Board of Regents, and they said he was one of the good guys. But I don't know."

"He has reacted that way, Mr. President, in our dealings with him on the appointments to the bench, other appointments out there. He has been acting for [Governor] Reagan in these clearances, and discussions. We've had quite a few of them. He's been solid as a rock."

"Yeah. And there's another guy whose name will surprise you totally. But who has the ability of doing the right thing, of course, and I put the suggestion because of his, what appears to be his racial background, and that's Weinberger."

"John [Ehrlichman]'s already mentioned him to me. I think the Jewish element would be a great plus."

Once again Nixon seemed unsure whether an Episcopalian with a Jewish name would garner any political advantage among Jewish voters. "He's considered to be Jewish? No?"

Mitchell did not seem to know how to respond. "He is?"

"He is half Jewish."

"I don't know if he is or isn't."

"He's Jewish. In this case, John [Ehrlichman] said, but everybody considers him to be Jewish. But the main point to make him a plus, as far as I'm concerned, is that he has the reputation of being liberal but actually he's not."

"Are you sure of that?"

The president paused, and shot back, "Hell, I know God damn, what he does around here, he is. The one thing I do want you to do, though, in terms of, well, you don't have to do this with Poff, but on the second appointment, I want you to have a specific talk with whatever man you consider. And I have to have an absolute commitment for him on busing and integration. I really have to. Go out and tell 'em that we totally respect his right to do otherwise, but if he believes otherwise, I don't want to appoint him to the Court."

Mitchell noted that it was Cap Weinberger who expanded the activities of the Federal Trade Commission when he was there. Nixon wasn't bothered by that. Mitchell ended the Weinberger discussion by commenting that he was the "right age" and that "it would not hurt to have a Jew on there to eliminate the Jewish seat question."

Mitchell then moved from California back to the South, raising a recommendation from Chief Justice Burger, who constantly supplied Mitchell with names. Clearly Burger wanted a Court to his liking, and Mitchell was amenable. "Warren Burger has a person. Thinking about these things."

"Good."

"He has a very interesting one. And, of course, I don't know about his political background, but he came up with a fellow by the name of Herschel Friday from Little Rock, which, of course, is not necessarily the best state in the world."

"It's in the South, that's good."

"Herschel's forty-nine years old. I've known him, worked with him for twenty-five years, never thought of him, actually. He's the political law partner of Pat Mehaffy, who is now on the Eighth Circuit, Blackmun's great friend, and proponent.[4] Ah, he's taught Federal Procedure in the colleges. He represented Arkansas, the city of Omaha, the Arkansas School Board, argued the school cases in the Supreme Court."

"Which side?"

"Well, for the school district," Mitchell quickly responded, which the president understood meant he was not in favor of integration. "And, he's way up and high in the American Bar, right age. Burger keeps coming back to him, after we go down the line, a few of the judges, and ages. The interesting part about this, you gave him [Chief Justice Burger] the Harlan seat."

"I didn't give the Harlan seat to anybody, Jesus."

Mitchell pressed, but the president was certain he did not give Burger the right to select a replacement for Justice Harlan. It apeared that Burger has misunderstood Nixon's remark in their prior conversation on September 17. In any event, it would not have been like Nixon to give his new chief justice an unnecessary perk. But Nixon did solicit assistance. For example, he had once told Martha Mitchell that if she found him the right female jurist for the Supreme Court, he would appoint her, and Martha had taken him seriously.

The subject of Burger's "perk" was dropped. Mitchell next assured the president that if he could get the bar straightened out, Poff would be an "easy, quick confirmation." The president told Mitchell that Herschel Friday would be "fine," if Poff didn't fly. Mitchell then suggested a couple of federal judges as alternative candidates.

"One of them is in Florida, a fellow by the name of [Paul H.] Rooney, that we appointed to the Circuit Court of Appeals."

"Rooney?"

"Rooney, to the Circuit Court of Appeals. He was well qualified by the bar. [He was a] practicing lawyer, when we appointed him. He checks out good on his opinions that he's [written] and so forth. And he is supposed to be [conservative]."

"You can't take my friend, David Dyer?" Nixon asked.[5]

"He'd be great, but Dave is, ah,—"

"Old?"

"Sixty-two now."

"Yeah."

Mitchell's response to his own question about the age issue revealed that Burger was influential in his thinking: "I think that Warren Burger has changed his thought on age of the Court. Warren will tell you this. Because here he is, faced this term with all these important cases that have been held up, held up, held up, and to lose two judges, and the possibility that he discovered about Douglas and Marshall, you know, now going too."

Nixon objected that Douglas's health was "too good" to suggest he would leave. Mitchell agreed, but homed in on Thurgood Marshall. "Marshall is the one that [is more likely], where it seems that we might [have a vacancy]."

When Nixon responded to the idea, it was with the kind of candor that he could never use in public. (Indeed, when Marshall finally did retire in 1991, President George Bush, or his aides, must have engaged in similar discussions before selecting Clarence Thomas.) "I don't know whether he'd do it, but really the only man for the black seat [Marshall's seat] is, you got to offer it to [Senator Edward W.] Brooke [R-MA]. He's the best man, but who the hell [knows], let's be thinking of that black seat though, in case it comes up, because that's going to be one that you got to go to a black."

"There are some others around. But I think we ought to offer it to Brooke."

"He'd never take it."

"I don't believe he would."

"Why the hell, he's a bigger man in the Senate. He wouldn't take the Court, it would be like being [demoted]."

"He may. Ed's work was so good, as the Attorney General [of Massachusetts]."

"Oh, yes. He is a very good man, John. He's basically a liberal, he has to be. But in terms of, you talk [unintelligible], he's one of the few blacks who really talks in an intelligent way."

Unfortunately, the rest of their conversation relating to Brooke remains unavailable to the public for "privacy reasons." Nonetheless, the available "black seat" discussion is revealing. The president next talked about an unnamed black judge of the Military Court of Appeals as "a pretty good man." Mitchell agreed, and added, "There's a good black judge from Michigan on the Sixth Circuit Court of Appeals." But the president believed he was a Democrat.

"We really need a Republican black."

Mitchell commented on the problem that that presented. "We started talking about, quote, strict constuctionists, unquote. You don't find very many of them in the black community. You know Bill Pullman from Philadelphia?"

"Yes." Nixon knew the the man.[6]

"Well, he's a fine man."

"Fine man, but he's too old, isn't he?" Nixon asked.

"You're probably right, yes."

"Yes, the one that impresses me very much is this guy that's the head of the Equal [Employment] Opportunity Commission."

"[William H.] Bob Brown, very much so."

"A good one."

"Yep. Bob Brown."

"There's a fellow that I would think [would be a good appointment for the Marshall seat]. But we're not going to put two blacks on the Court at one time." In other words, Nixon was saying that he would consider Brown for Thurgood Marshall's seat but not for the Harlan or Black seat.

Nixon concluded, "I think picking a young man is good. Second, Friday appeals to me, not only that, it sort of comes out of the blue, and Arkansas isn't a bad place to have somebody. [How about] Wilbur Mills [who's from Arkansas], no way could we pick him. I think though that on Poff, that I just feel very strongly and I wish you'd let Walsh know about these things with the Judiciary Committee."

"Very well."

"I think that the American Bar, let's put it this way, [when dealing with a nominee from] the Judiciary Committees of the House and Senate, the American Bar will be in far more trouble with the Judiciary Committees if the word gets around that the President didn't appoint him because [the bar didn't think he was qualified]. And I think that's true."

"I do too."

"I think it's true."

"One of our problems with Ed Walsh is timidity. Poff comes out of the Fourth Circuit, the fellow on Walsh's committee is this [Norman P.] Ramsey from Baltimore, who is a liberal Democrat, who's caused us all sorts of trouble.[7] And so that we've just got to find a way, a way around that. He's the one that predominately [is the problem]."

"Well, but we have, of course, the big gun here, which you're quite aware of. I can do it regardless of what the American Bar does, and [while] I think it's not good to do so, I think Walsh has got to know we're not giving them veto power. So you're really negotiating with, ah—"

"They don't want a veto."

"No, they don't. But I think it's very clear, we wouldn't want them coming in testifying against us. I think it's very important, a man from the Judiciary Committee, you know how those committees are, you know better than I."

Mitchell then groused about the makeup of the Senate Judiciary Committee. "This time around, after the '70 elections, of course, [I'd hoped] we'd get two good ones instead of the [Robert] McClorys and [Thomas F.] Railsbacks, and the rest of 'em we've had up there, completely under [Democratic chairman] Manny Celler's [control]. We've got that guy out of Denver, and [Charles] Thone, rather than some of the liberals they were putting on." Representatives McClory (R-IL) and Railsback (R-IL) had voted against a number of proposals favored by the Nixon administration.

"You know one of the things that's a shame is [that] Roman's so old, he'd have been a fine judge. [Senator] Roman Hruska, move him back ten years, God damn, he'd be a good judge."

"He would love the part, act the part, and release the right opinions."

"He'd love it."

"Oh, yes. He made some passes at me when we first got down here, about the Fortas thing, and then Blackmun—"

"Yeah, but by then he was too old, he's in his late sixties."

"And, of course, he recognized it."

"Yep. I think we've got to [find a young man and] I think we should move fast. I do not feel that we should have a buildup of people lining up in here on an appointment, saying that they want this, that and the other thing. And I think we're going to need a few days 'til we're ready to go, [and then] we should send it up, get the name over there."

Mitchell tossed out a new name. "Do you have any feelings on this [Alexander M.] Bickel for the Court?" Bickel, a Yale law professor, had done work for the Nixon White House.

"He'd be great. He's smart and all that sort of thing. But isn't he too God damn liberal?"

"He's been quite conservative on constitutional construction, I had him checked all out, you remember," Mitchell said.

"[He was against the] eighteen-year-old vote."

"Busing too, you know. He worked with Len Garment, as I recall. The one thing I'm worried about is his attitude in criminal law. I'm going to check that out along with the other."

"Check him out. One of the advantages of Bickel is that he's a scholar."

"A scholar, and he's young."

"And everybody would say, well, we finally appointed a scholar. I'd love that, it would be easier putting him in Harlan's seat. Why don't you just take a check on that. Incidentally, [Charles S.] Chuck Rhyne is really out of the question, isn't he, for this thing? He's out of the question? He wants it." Rhyne was Nixon's friend and classmate at Duke Law School, and as an appellate lawyer had frequently taken cases before the Supreme Court.

"Does he?"

"He didn't mention it to me, [but] I know damn well he does. I mean, the poor man argues more cases before that damn Court and all the rest."

"I'm not certain about Charlie's philosophy."

"You're not?" On reflection, however, Nixon was not sure himself either. But Nixon was interested in Bickel, so he returned to him, asking Mitchell about Bickel's age.

"He's in his forties."

"I'd like to see you talk to Len [Garment] about [Bickel], you might say we were chatting, tell him we've got to keep this close as possible, now what are Bickel's views."

"I talked to Len yesterday, about Judge [Harry D.] Goldman, who's up-state New York, in his fifties, and what attracted me to him, other than the fact that he's been a very good judge, was Nelson Rockefeller, who put this whole problem, on this Attica prison stuff on him."

"Oh."

"Rockefeller had to get off the hook on this investigation business, when the federal courts were beating up on him up there, so he got this Jewish judge up there [in New York], and allowed him to appoint the committee to investigate Attica. And I said, well, Nelson, you know what you're doing, you're just trying to [dump] this whole gambit over into somebody's hands to appoint this committee, and he said, I'm not wor-ried about Goldman, he said, I've worked with him, he's straight, he's conservative, et cetera et cetera. I'm going to check him out with some of the people upstate, who are doing footwork on it. That's why Len and I had this conversation about Bickel."

"If Bickel is in on the busing issue—" Nixon said, wanting to make cer-tain that any appointee be opposed to the unpopular policy.

"I want to make sure he's all right on the criminal laws."

"Oh, yes. Yes, I would be, well, it would seem to me if he's all right on busing, he damn well, pretty close to [unintelligible], on the criminal side. I don't care where he is on the economic, you know what I mean. They can be a socialist, that doesn't make any difference to me. Ah, like Frankfurter's later years, still a New Dealer but he was strict construction, right?"

"Humm."

"So a Frankfurter-type is fine, as far as I'm concerned. I really want to be God damn sure though, on the criminal side and the busing issue, housing, education. I [just don't want to put] a liberal on that Court. I can't handle that."

It was agreed that the only political gain for Nixon would come from appointing someone from the South. Unless, Mitchell wryly noted, he appointed Nelson Rockefeller and Ronald Reagan, to remove them from the political scene. At the time they were mildly concerned that either Rocke-feller or Reagan might mount a primary campaign to challenge the pres-ident in 1972.

As Nixon and Mitchell finished their conversation, Ron Ziegler entered the Oval Office to discuss what should be told to the press. As always in Washington, rumors were flying, and Mitchell's limousine was parked conspicuously on West Executive Drive. Ziegler began by noting that Nixon's long chat with Mitchell was driving reporters crazy. They knew that Mitchell did not hang around the White House to visit the staff.

"I'm getting questions heavy on what occurred with the Attorney General."

Nixon both did and did not want anyone to know what was up. He could have simply told Ziegler to tell the press they were talking about football, or even the so-called Pentagon Papers, the classified study of the American entry into the Vietnam War which had been leaked by former government employee Daniel Ellsberg and printed in the *New York Times*. But the president wanted the press focused on the Court. "I think it will settle the issue if you said, yes, the President, the President and Attorney General are conferring. What does it involve? Well, one of the questions is the Supreme Court problem. [They're] meeting on that."

"Now, the speculation is really starting to center on Poff, should I cool that, or—"

"I'd cool it, Ron," Mitchell interrupted, "because that's too far down the line."

"Well, that's what I'm concerned about."

Nixon tried again to find the right media obfuscation that would sug-gest what was going on without really telling. The president explained, "The American Bar is still [going to consider him]. Just say that the Pres-ident talked to the Attorney General, and the appointments are an open question. There are several that we considered. We must have a half a dozen names, under serious consideration. You're not going to say there are five names, I wouldn't pick a [number] like that, I say about—"

"Seven," Mitchell suggested.

"If there are seven, there are seven names under serious consideration."

Ziegler suggested a different answer. "Why don't I say it'll probably be a strict constructionist. I refer you to what the President has said on this subject previously, his position has not changed, just put it that way. I think that's a good way to do, don't you?"

"I think so," Mitchell responded.

"The other thing is that he will be a southerner. He'll be the best man, be the best qualified," Nixon insisted.

Ziegler wanted to know if Poff was under consideration. Mitchell told Ziegler not to get specific, and the president agreed. Ziegler was to tell the press that this is a "very important decision" and the president will "take his time, the time necessary to find the best man possible." Mitchell added that "under the scenario we have with the American Bar we submit more than one name," and while "it doesn't go out publicly when we submit it, of course, but when we start this you have a lot of speculation." Ziegler reported it had already started: "Lyle Dennison has a story this morning." (Dennison, a reporter with the *Washington Evening Star*, was correctly speculating that Poff was the leading candidate.) The president realized that time was short.

"I would say, John, we've got to get this, a name ready by the middle of the following week, ten days."

Mitchell sighed, and agreed. The rush would not be without its costs. Mitchell soon excused himself as Haldeman, Ehrlichman, and Charles Colson entered the Oval Office. Mitchell sensed a bull session, and he was not interested in participating. Instead, he returned to the Department of Justice, and reported to Rehnquist, who would have much work to do.[8]

4

———

THE PUSH FOR POFF

September 20

EVEN WITH A SINGLE Supreme Court seat, it is rare that the president seizes on a leading candidate immediately and watches that person sail through to confirmation. With two openings—something that has only occurred on a handful of occasions—it is impossible to avoid a messier process. Interest groups lobby; candidates need to be fitted into pairs; and the confirmation process can become more difficult. Nixon did not yet have a second opening, but he believed one was coming. Meanwhile, he had one candidate in mind, but needed to consider and vet others. Even his main candidate had to be checked, while backups were developed.

As Lyle Dennison's *Evening Star* column suggested, the media had quickly seized on Richard Poff as the frontrunner. The White House staff enjoyed the *Wall Street Journal's* column on Monday morning, September 20, which described Poff as being "respected by Northern liberal Democrats with whom he serves on the House Judiciary Committee. Moreover, because he is a member of Congress and because he isn't identified with Deep South racism, it appears unlikely that the Senate would refuse to confirm him." The *Journal* also noted: "Other names being mentioned for the vacancy include John D. Ehrlichman, Mr. Nixon's assistant for domestic affairs." [1]

Ehrlichman's name provoked jesting at the morning White House staff meetings, in the form of charges that he had leaked his own name, which everyone but Ehrlichman enjoyed. Ehrlichman's sensitivity, if anything, suggested that the charges might have been true. He just might have been floating his own campaign for a seat on the Court.

The president, always concerned about leaks, told Haldeman first thing, "The more I think about it, I don't think you ought to discuss [these Court appointments with anyone]. For example, I wouldn't raise it with any staff people. I would minimize, only say to John Ehrlichman." [2]

The first press problem, however, was not a leak. To the contrary, it was from what Ron Ziegler had said—or more accurately, failed to say—when talking about the president's search for the Court. By midmorning, Ziegler had made a beeline to the Oval Office for guidance. [3]

"Mr. President, first of all, the, the Women's National Caucus has taken me on a little bit on this Supreme Court thing, because I said that, ah, ah, you were looking for the best man."

"Oooooh."

Nixon's response caused Haldeman to burst out with laughter. This, in turn, caused Ziegler to laugh, but only briefly, for the press had been on him hard with questions about the president excluding women. Indeed, earlier that day, Senators Birch Bayh of Indiana and George McGovern of South Dakota (who had announced his candidacy for president) called on the president to name a woman.

Ziegler elaborated. "But I don't want this [to be misunderstood]. So I talked to the Attorney General, [and] here's what I propose to say, when I'm asked."

"[Say we're going to] consider this," the president said flatly.

"I'm going to say, right, I'm going to say that seven [people] that [were] focused on the other day, that is not a closed number. That women are not ruled out, as a matter of fact, the President told me [several of those being considered] are women, okay? You've already appointed—"

"If they will look through our appointments they will find—"

"Right."

"If a woman is qualified, she should be appointed to the Supreme

Court. If any woman's had that much experience," Nixon said as if addressing the press directly.

"Right. But I don't want to say that, I'll just say this, that women are not ruled out. Ah, then, one other point."

"All right."

"There seems to me a misconception that you said at one point that you'd only appoint people who were sitting on the bench, where I've gone on the record—"

"No, we did not."

Ziegler called a past interview to Nixon's attention. "As a matter of fact, in your interview with columnist Ken Kilpatrick, who wrote about it later, he says the President subsequently remarked that he was thinking solely of sitting judges, he might choose a distinguished southern, he was not thinking solely—"

"No, I [didn't limit it to sitting judges]," the president said softly as his press secretary kept talking.

". . . of a distinguished southern lawyer, or professor, that the criteria would be, he said, a public record of a legal philosophy founded in strict construction."

Nixon summarized where he stood, in a way that would be favorable to Poff. "The main thing is, first, he must be qualified in the law, and second, his philosophy. For example, Frankfurter was a law professor, as a matter of fact [he] never practiced a day of his life, and Harlan, he came up, I think, in a law firm as I recall. In other words, from outstanding lawyers, from the bar, and of course, people who've had experience that's the equivalent."

"Thank you."

"Now, I'm not going to just promote, the fact that I promoted from the bench does not mean that I'm limited to that. Of course, throughout the legal profession, the best people from the bar, they don't have to be off the bench."

"Thanks. Fine," Ziegler said, ready to move on. "I'm going to be asked, probably, about Harlan today too. I'm going to say we received a message—"

"No. And don't say a word about it."

Ziegler had the guidance he needed. He was savvy enough to know that the matter of selecting a woman for the Court was well founded. The potential of appointing the first woman ever to the Supreme Court was in the air. From the time of Justice Black's retirement, the White House rumor mill (worse than any small town) swirled with a story that the first lady had been on the president's case about placing a woman on the Court. It became more than a rumor when Mrs. Nixon did something extraordinary, as revealed by her daughter: During an informal conversation with some newswomen while en route to Newport News, Virginia, to dedicate a nuclear-powered guided-missile frigate, Julie Nixon Eisenhower reported that her mother made an uncharacteristically bold political statement that she wanted to see a woman appointed to the Supreme Court. "Don't you worry; I'm talking it up," Pat Nixon said. "If we can't get a woman on the Supreme Court this time, there'll be a next time."[4] Rumor had it that Mrs. Nixon was pushing hard.

• • • •

After Ziegler left, Haldeman went to the Oval Office to report the arrival of the much hoped for second vacancy on the Court.[5] If the first seat had been a lucky political break, the second seat was nothing short of a political windfall. It was the kind of news that caused the president to drop what he was doing to enjoy its significance. "[A] little interesting bit of news for you, you have another Court seat to fill," Haldeman reported, enjoying his own understatement.

"Harlan?" This question did not raise the obvious, given the health of those whom Nixon wished off the Court. Harlan was also a justice whom Nixon would prefer remained in place.

"The Chief Justice talked to John this morning, and, the—"

"Mitchell?"

"Yeah, Mitchell. And as for Harlan, he is going to step down, and, if you want him to, he'll hold up on it for awhile. But Mitchell's view is that he can't hold up on it for more than a couple of days, and in that context it is better to get it on the fire too, because there's so much speculation about it anyway, and it gives you the chance to work on it too."

"That's right."

"Which gives you some running room, in doing something you couldn't do with one, that you could do with two," said Haldeman, meaning that a two-opening strategy afforded the probability of getting at least one southerner through by appointing two. Any one of them might be rejected by a partisan Senate, but it would be hard to reject both merely because they were southern strict constructionists.

Haldeman asked if he was the first president with two Supreme Court nominees at the same time. The president reminded him that Lyndon Johnson had had two. "He appointed Fortas and Thornberry at the same time, both appointments were up, you recall," Nixon noted. But the president's thoughts were on the retiring justice. "Unfortunately, Harlan was a hell of a good justice," Nixon said.

While they spoke, Nixon telephoned John Mitchell.[6]

"John?"

"Yes sir," Mitchell snapped, giving Nixon the respect his office demanded.

"I think that the thing to do is to get the Harlan thing right away [i.e., secure the justice's formal resignation]."

"All right, sir."

"Now, I feel your intuition is exactly correct that we should have two so we have a double play. And also, Ziegler [was just questioned about it a] half hour ago, but not knowing that this was coming. Told me that the press was badgering whether or not Harlan, so don't let them badger about it. See, he goes out and lies about it, and that's not good."

"All right."

"Now, how does it work? When could we get it and how soon could we announce it?"

"I will have to check with the Chief Justice to find what the exact status is. I will do that directly and get the word back to you."

"If we could get it, if he wants to do it. Well, we don't want to rush him, but we could announce it at the afternoon briefing. It would be a good thing."

"All right, sir. I'll see what I can do," Mitchell assured him.

"Fine. Okay," Nixon said hopefully, though as it turned out, Harlan could not be reached for another day, so the announcement would have to wait.

• • • •

Nixon understood the seismic political consequences of sending Congressman Richard Poff's name to the Senate for confirmation. If anything, the second opening—the "double play"—accentuated the negatives for his opponents, who now had twice as much to lose with his shifting of the philosophical terrain of the Court. Nixon never wavered in his interest in Richard Poff for the Black seat. Though I, along with others, were still vetting Poff—trying to take readings and soundings that would tell us the strength of potential Senate backlash due to Poff's anti–civil rights votes—Nixon wanted him because everything he knew about Dick Poff suggested he would be doing in 1971 for Republicans what FDR had done for Democrats thirty-four years earlier with Hugo Black's nomination. Both were southerners from the ranks of Congress, and their congressional stature gave them (at least with the traditionalists) a courtesy that all but ensured confirmation. It was this kind of reaction the president was looking for when he mentioned Dick Poff to his next visitor in the Oval Office, Arthur Burns, the chairman of the Federal Reserve.

Burns always struck me as being like a character invented by Arthur Conan Doyle, with his thick white hair parted in the middle, and his meerschaum pipe always in hand or mouth. He also appeared a rumpled academic, oblivious to his own eccentricities. Before he had been appointed chairman of the Federal Reserve by Nixon in January 1970, he had served on the White House staff as the president's domestic affairs adviser. Nixon respected the judgment of this economist, who often lectured the president like a student—and the president listened. That day, in a scheduled meeting, Nixon used the opening minutes of their visit as an opportunity to test his thinking on the Court with Burns.[7]

"John Harlan is extremely sick."

Burns groaned in response.

"[He's in] the hospital. He'll resign today or tomorrow, it will be announced. So that means I will have four appointments to the Court. We've got two more to make, these two are very important now. But having two to make at one time is just a double play."

Burns mumbled, "Yeah, at one time."

"But, anyhow, it's a great opportunity."

"Great," Burns said, speaking clearly and emphatically, "What we show this time, is that the Justice Department and the FBI can do its homework on these fellows."

"That's right."

"They've got to."

"So we don't get caught, ah—"

Burns put it plainly. "They let you down!" He was referring to the Haynsworth-Carswell debacle.

The president mentioned his inclination to select Poff, but Burns had no reaction. The president dropped the subject. But Burns had made his point.

. . . .

That afternoon, I headed up to Capitol Hill to visit with Poff and pick up documents that his staff had been gathering. It seemed to me that Poff, a compact man (five foot seven, 175 pounds, once a Little-All American Linebacker at Roanoke College), was suddenly walking taller, maybe a few feet off the ground. His dream was happening. Years earlier, he said that he would rather have a seat on the Supreme Court than be president of the United States. Now, after twenty years of hard work in the Congress, it was within his grasp. While he was excited, he was also nervous.

"You can't really plan for something like this," Poff told me, as his well-organized staff buzzed about his office retrieving documents and preparing piles for him to examine. Standing beside a stack on his desk, studying a newsletter to his constituents back in the Sixth Congressional District of Virginia, he picked up a document that caught his attention. "Hell, I read some of this stuff I wrote fifteen years ago, or ten, or even five years ago, and I don't even remember writing it." Then with a smile, he added, "Some of it's not too bad, if I don't say so." Dick Poff wasn't bragging, he was too modest a man, rather he was relieved. "Listen to this, from a July 19, 1965, letter. That's when we were doing the Voting Rights Act," he said as he adjusted his half-glasses on his nose, and proceeded to read an eloquent passage in favor of civil rights.[8]

Poff understood that civil rights groups were not going to give him credit for his attitudes; rather, they would make much of his failure to support final passage of any of a number of civil rights laws. For Poff, as for most congressmen from the South, there had been no choice. If he had supported those laws, he would have been voted out of Congress. He had wanted to remain, so he had had to vote the sympathies of his Virginia constituents.

Poff had some very good news, however. The two patriarchs of the

House battles to write civil rights laws, House Judiciary Committee chairman Emanuel Celler (D-NY) and ranking Republican William McCulloch (R-OH), had told him they planned to send a telegram to the president recommending that he appoint Poff to the Supreme Court. When Poff added that Manny Celler had also told him he was prepared to go to the Senate to testify at a confirmation hearing, Poff had tears in his eyes. Celler was the most senior member of Congress, and the dean of the House of Representatives, and his liberal credentials could not be questioned. Nor could it be questioned that without Celler and McCulloch, there could ever have been a Civil Rights Act of 1964, or a Voting Rights Act of 1965. The fact that these civil rights stalwarts, two of the most respected lawyers of the House, were endorsing Poff's nomination could go a long way in blunting efforts to oppose him. Clearly Poff was not a racist, or these men would never have lent him their well-earned reputations.

"Hey, John. I want to thank you," Poff said, stopping me at the door as our visit was ending.

"This is not my doing, Dick. It's yours," I responded. "But rest assured I am going to do all I can to make it happen, because I think we'll have a better Supreme Court with you on it."

• • • •

Back at the White House, Nixon aide Pat Buchanan, then serving as one of Nixon's speechwriters, had drafted a memo to Nixon arguing the political advantages of appointing Poff. Buchanan had a special place in Nixon's White House. He had been the first person to travel with Nixon during the president's return to public life in 1967–68, and Nixon had come to greatly respect Buchanan's conservative point of view and judgment. Still, as with most staffers, Buchanan could only reach Nixon through Haldeman, who saw the memo and chose to read virtually all of its key passages to the president.[9]

"[On the Court thing,] Buchanan had a recommendation," Haldeman informed Nixon shortly before he was leaving the office for the day.

"Which one's he for? Poff?"

"He says, 'The political imperatives argue loudly for a rapid appointment of a Southern conservative to the Supreme Court.'"

"Well, I agree."

"He says, 'All the arguments are on the President's side. If a Southerner does not go on the Court, it will be the first time in a century the South hasn't had its own justice on the bench.'"

"Boy."

Haldeman continued reading: "'He can argue that the October session needs a full nine-man Court, thus hopefully preventing the delaying actions that would enable Democrats to hold the appointment off until the election. If Poff is the President's man, which is widely reported, the sooner the better. For Poff has reportedly already gone through the laborious clearances; it would be exceedingly difficult for the Democrats in the Senate to reject one of their own from the Hill.'"

"Mum, hmm."

"'Indeed, if they did, it would clearly put the Democrats in the position of an anti-Southern bias, and fix them in that posture for the coming election. The President might be able to even get a massive bipartisan House Resolution endorsing Poff's nomination to pressure the Senate. We have to move fast, fourteen months before the election, lest we allow the Democrats to use the Griffin Argument, that a new President should name the Court.' I think at fourteen months, you've got too much time to [let that happen]," Haldeman added.

"Right."

"If it were six months, that could do it."

"We've got to move, I've got to get Mitchell on this task, [as fast as possible]."

"[Buchanan] says, 'Vital for the long future of the country that the President name younger justices than Burger or Blackmun.'"

"Right."

"'So he'll have a Nixon Court into the Eighties and Nineties.'"

"Right."

"'My recommendation is that this week the President call on the press and announce Poff.'"

"Yeah."

Haldeman read on. "'Have him present for photographs, call for speedy action, and in his remarks point out that Nixon's pledge to name a Southern strict constructionist to the Court, to a new Senate, is with this nomination being fulfilled. The President believes that Poff will clearly and quickly be ratified. Poff as a legislator is a strict constructionist who believes that the nation's social problems should be worked out by elected legislators, which he is now, and not by unelected justices, which he will be tomorrow. For this he can draw on Burger's speech on the role of the judiciary at the Georgetown Center this Friday. The President should use the occasion to further outline and define what he means by a strict constructionist. If the President has Poff in mind, seems to me he can put the Senate into a box. The President can say that his prediction [is] that a new Senate with a different balance and point of view may accept a Southerner. He is confident this is going to come true. If the Senate approves Poff, they will vindicate Nixon's prediction. If they oppose Poff, no one will believe it was not an expression of anti-Southern bias. There is a golden opportunity to join in an effort in which conservatives can again rally to the President.' Perfect," Haldeman commented, before continuing.

" 'When the other Supreme Court appointment opens up, I suggest strongly that the President appoint a conspicuous ethnic Catholic, like an Italian-American jurist with conservative views. Not blacks, not Jews, but ethnic Catholics, Poles, Irish, Italians, Slovaks. We ought now to be canvassing the best legal and judicial conservative minds in the Italian-American, Irish-American, and the Polish-American communities. And the fellow ought to be a Holy Name Society Daily Communicant.' "

Haldeman paused to chuckle. "He's right about that. But I don't think he's got any."

" 'I'd be happy to draft for the President the statement accompanying the announcement, a statement that might elucidate and deepen the presidential position on strict constructionists. This is the kind of Court the whole country wants with the exception of the Eastern Establishment, and the President's political opponents.' "

Now it was the president's turn to chuckle. "He's right. You know, it's too bad we don't have an Italian, an honest Italian judge that I know of. Wish we did, wish we had a Pole. There ain't nothing in it for us Bob to appoint [a Protestant], not a God damn thing, you know, it means nothing to the Protestants, it could mean a hell of a lot to the Catholics." Buchanan's memo would resonate in Nixon's mind throughout the coming weeks.[10]

Haldeman pointed out that "Bill Smith is a Protestant."

Nixon got up to leave, agreeing. "I know. That's the problem, I agree. He's conservative, but you see, you get a conservative that's a Catholic, it's better."

• • • •

Nixon clearly agreed with Buchanan's analysis that Poff would survive Senate confirmation. It was true that Poff would enjoy some deference as a member of Congress, and also true that the Senate could not reject him merely because he was a southerner. But there remained a serious problem. Poff's inexperience as a legal practitioner might well bother the ABA's evaluation committee, whose approval loomed large. That evening, from the telephone in the Lincoln Sitting Room, the president talked about it with two of his most trusted advisers: Attorney General John Mitchell and Secretary of State William Rogers, before going to the White House theater for a screening of *The Sheepman* with his wife and daughters (not the worst movie ever shown there, but certainly a contender). The president wanted to talk with Mitchell about the reaction to the nomination of Poff from Lawrence Edward Walsh, the chairman of the American Bar Association's Committee on the Federal Judiciary, known to friends as Ed Walsh (a former Federal District Court judge who would later serve as the Iran-contra independent counsel).[11]

"Hi, John?"

"Yes, Mr. President?"

"I didn't want to interrupt you while you were talking earlier but how'd you get along with those fellows? You make it, make a sale, I hope?"

"I think so." Mitchell had hit Walsh with some facts on the historical relationship between the Justice Department and the ABA's Standing Committee on the Federal Judiciary on Supreme Court nominations assembled by Bill Rehnquist. "I really worked Walsh over pretty good."

"Well, we have to realize, John, that, you know, the House and Senate are, well at least the House is so damn strong for this fellow, we're going to have a hell of a time if we don't appoint him."

"Yeah, and [Walsh] recognizes that. I think Ed is in our camp completely."

"Well, he's worked the Hill before, you know."

"He has. He's done some yeoman service for us so—" Mitchell was referring to Walsh's efforts to help confirm lower federal court judges.

"Right."

"You know what Walsh's thought is?" Mitchell asked provocatively.

"What?"

"He says that he can get Haynsworth past the bar and confirmed in a
breeze. Isn't that interesting?"

"Really?"

"He says he has nothing but people all over the country who come up
to him about it. But I think that's a risk that we shouldn't [take]."

"God, I don't know. Well, I guess not. Look, I'll tell you why I think it's
a risk we shouldn't buy. I think it looks like a petulant president pushing
somebody again. That's the point. It's fine for Haynsworth but it's not
good for the presidency, you know."

"Well, the fact is, the change in the Senate would put it through."

"Yeah? But I just think it looks a little bit like we're just trying to prove
to these fellows that they were wrong, you know."

"Yeah, politically motivated. The program that I thought we'd get
started on, subject to your approval, of course, is he knows that we want
Poff."

"Right. Did you ever find out his age?"

"Poff, oh, he's in his forties."

"Great, great, all right, we're all right that way."

"Yeah, that's what I thought. Interestingly, actually the fact of the matter is that he has very, very little law firm experience."

Nixon laughed. "I know, I know. None! Hell, he has less than I had."

"Yeah, absolutely."

Nixon laughed again. "At least I was before the Supreme Court a couple
times and he'd never been."

"That's true. Well, with your permission what I'd thought we'd do is to
take Poff with Herschel Friday that the Chief Justice suggested. And a
couple of southern judges that are credible. And give [them] to his committee."

"Right."

"Ed's understanding is that Poff is the one that we want to concentrate
on," Mitchell said, feeling out his boss.

"That's right."

"And let them [work on it] a little while."

"Walsh could see the point of the Judiciary Committee experience as being enormously important?"

"Yes, he knows that. He agrees, now that we, you know, we're well prepared. But he agreed, and he's a good solider. He'll go out and try and sell him."

"And if he doesn't, then we can roll without him, you know, which we may have to do," Nixon threatened.

"Well, we may very well have to."

"But what we want to do is to get the Senate and House, about two-fifths of them endorsing him."

"That's right. And, John McClellan, you know, is a good old soldier. He has volunteered to start a program on behalf of Judge Poff." Senator John McClellan (D-AR) was considered one of the forces to be reckoned with in the Senate.

"Is he pro Poff?"

"Oh yes."

"Well, I think you should let him go then, if he could start a little program. And say, look, John, the bar raises these questions and if John could get a certain number of names. And I would also tell Ford in the House to let him go. Would you do that?" Nixon asked.

"Yes sir, I will."

"Give Jerry a call and say, look—"

"Because Poff's got a good mind, no question about it."

"Well, your evaluation [is important], as I told you, I've not been quite that impressed with him because I didn't really see him in action. But on the other hand, he's a young man, and he's a good lawyer and good God, that's what we need in that Court."

Mitchell reported that Ed Walsh was suggesting the president should appoint a judge who was older and more of the establishment. This provoked an immediate "no, no" from Nixon. Mitchell said that he explained to Walsh that the president had a commitment to the American people, and that Walsh understood.

"Now on the other thing, John, on the second one, if it comes." Nixon cleared his throat. "Can I urge you to see if you can find a Catholic, a good Catholic."

"Another Brennan?"

"No, Christ no, that's not what I mean."

"I do know if you went there, that'd be a nightmare. The administration went down that track beforehand."

"And they got Brennan, I know. But you don't have an honest Italian, do you?"

Mitchell laughed. "God, they're awful hard to find."

"A Pole?"

"William French Smith, he isn't [a Catholic], is he?"

"Oh, Christ no, he's a Protestant—"

"WASP."

"Rich and everything else," Nixon added.

"All right."

"Well, take a look at the Catholics, will you?"

"There's one up in Massachusetts that we've had under consideration, but that's not a very likely state—"

"State doesn't bother me."

They discussed a Massachusetts judge, about fifty-five years of age, who was hard-nosed on criminal law matters. Unfortunately, the name of this judge is unintelligible on the tape. The president continued to press his new interest in a Catholic.

"Well, you look for one, will you?"

"You think that's a good line to take?"

"I do. Politically, we are going to gain a lot more from a Catholic. If he's a Catholic conservative, [it] is better than a Protestant conservative. We really need that."

"Well, they're more engrained, I'm sure."

"Well, the point is, it'll mean more to the Catholics, that's my point, than it will to the Protestants. The Protestants expect to have things. The Catholics don't," Nixon emphasized.

"When are you going to fill that Jewish seat on the Supreme Court?"

"Well, how about after I die?"

Mitchell laughed.

Suddenly, Nixon thought of something. "Is Walsh a Catholic?" he asked, having given up on William French Smith's WASPishness.

"Yeah. [Definitely.]"

"How would he be? Too liberal?"

"You know he's fifty-seven."

"Yeah, I know. Would he be too liberal?"

"No, I don't believe so. I think Ed's changed a lot [over the years]."

"Well?"

"I'm not sure you could get him to take it."

"Oh, if you pick at the man," Nixon mused.

"You think so?"

"Hell, yes, he'd take it. In a minute. In a minute. The only thing I'd be worried about him is busing. He'd be all right on the criminal law. Now just think of that a minute."

"I will."

"Walsh, if he's a Catholic, if he isn't Catholic, forget it. Well, he's such a great lawyer. Just put it in the back of your head, will you?"

"I will indeed."

"I think I'll give Bill [Rogers] a call. He knows Walsh well. Is that all right?"

"Yeah, it's all right."

"Good."

"You'll get a kick out of this. [Rogers told me] all you have to do is find another Charles Evan Hughes."

"Yeah, okay," Nixon said, laughing. "How old is Walsh?"

"Ed's either fifty-six or fifty-seven."

"Right."

"Which isn't too bad, but you can—"

"Well, he can serve until he's seventy-five. Sure."

Nixon continued on the fact that Walsh "would be met with universal acclaim from the bar and it would fill in beautifully for Harlan. But I want to be sure that he's known as a conservative," he added, laughing again. "Is he?"

"That is something that may be on the borderline. But I think we can check on that."

"Now if there is anything tomorrow, I'll be available all day long. I've got a heavy schedule, but call me if anything develops, will you?"

"Yes sir, I will, because I expect to hear from Warren Burger maybe even later tonight."

"Fine. Well, give me a call, will you?"

"I will and I want to run by this panel, and I'm going to let Walsh get started on it."

"Good. Okay. Thank you."

. . . .

Nixon's final thoughts on the Supreme Court that night were reserved for William Rogers. Richard Nixon had a unique relationship with Rogers, his secretary of state. They had known one another since the Eisenhower administration. Throughout his presidency, Nixon would consult with Rogers about most everything except foreign policy, which the president and Henry Kissinger held between themselves. It was Rogers whom Nixon had turned to after winning in November 1968, in order to get Earl Warren to remain on the bench until June 1969. It was Rogers who had recommended his friend Warren Burger to be the new chief justice. That night, Nixon wanted to run through his latest thinking, to explain why he wanted Poff and also ruminate on another name. Their conversation revealed both how fixed Nixon was on Poff, and also how uncertain he was of where to turn for the second seat.

Nixon plunged right in.[12] "I was, you know, on the Supreme Court thing, we're thinking very strongly of Poff. Mainly because we think he would be pretty easy to confirm, you know. You go to the South, and it's very difficult to get a judge or anybody else."

"You hope they're not too old," Rogers added.

"Or too old. Poff is only forty-three or four or five or something like that. And he's been apparently a very outstanding member. John McClellan is very strong for him."

"You know I spent the weekend with the Chief Justice."

"Yeah."

"I talked to him about Poff. Sometime before you had mentioned it to me. And he seemed to me quite receptive to that and I think he's willing, as far as I know."

"Now, the American Bar, Ed Walsh has been down talking to Mitchell today. And the American Bar has this idea [that] he has to be a judge, or have years of practice, which he has not had. But, after all, he has been on the Judiciary Committee for twelve, thirteen years, which isn't bad. And that is a hell of a lot of experience, you know."

"Well, the question they are thinking is that he's got to be a judge, and you have a lot of—"

"Well, either a judge or, or practice at the bar. [Do] you know what practice at the bar [they care about in particular]?"

"Just to be frank, I really don't know."

"He practiced awhile and then ran for Congress. That's no big practice. He was a small town lawyer. Well, anyway, they're looking him over. Now let me ask you another thing."

"Can I help any with Ed Walsh?"

"Well, I think you could. I think Walsh is on the assignments. And, he's got to sell them. Now let me ask you another thing. It's a long shot. But tell me, what is Walsh, a Catholic?"

"No."

"He's not a Catholic?"

"No."

"He's married to a Catholic." Nixon was still looking for a Catholic connection.

"Is he? I'm not sure. I don't know what to tell you."

"I do think we ought to find somebody for Harlan's seat, who's also fifty to fifty-five years of age."

"Have they announced the Harlan thing yet?"

"No, no, they didn't. It's going to come in the next day or two because of Burger [who is meeting with all the justices]. Get them ready for a new term."

"Well, I think the most important thing is to get the next one confirmed. He's got to be a southerner and he's got to be somebody we can get confirmed," Roger said

"Yeah. But then we ought to follow with the Harlan appointment. Again, conservative. What is Walsh's age? About fifty-seven?"

"I have a great deal of respect for him. He'll be greatly admired," Rogers added. "Ed is also good in law enforcement. I just don't know enough about Poff to make a comment."

"Finding a southerner is damn hard."

"There are very few. You know who I wish you'd look at, Lewis Powell. If he was about ten years younger, he'd be great. But he is about sixty-three, I think," Rogers said.

Although Lewis Powell had told Mitchell in 1969 that he was not interested in the Court, he was in good health and actively practicing law with his Richmond law firm. Rogers would not be the only one to suggest him. But this evening, at least, Nixon wasn't interested.

"You really got to think about controlling that [problem with the Senate]," Rogers advised.

"I think Poff is a logical [selection] and also I think Poff can be confirmed."

"Has John [Mitchell] gone over his background very carefully to be sure there's nothing?"

Nixon laughed and said that Mitchell was just beginning to vet him. "It's a little harder though, for the Senate to go after him. Poff, he's frankly the best member of the House Judiciary Committee. Everybody says that. I've spoken to McCulloch. [It's a great opportunity]."

"Of course it is. Ah, you have a good opportunity now to take somebody who is an excellent policy person and [place them on the Court]. And not just one man, but two, two men."

"Right."

"And if Walsh fits that bill, [you should consider him]. If they consider them both together, [it will make it easier]."

"You think Walsh would, apparently, be considered to be a good sound, strong constructionist?"

"Yeah, I have no doubt of it. He would not be [another] Brennan. He's been very strong in that aspect."

"Yeah, he would."

"He was also the head of the crime commission. He feels very strongly about [these issues]."

"I'll put that in the back of my mind."

"He's a little bit more, you know, pro–civil rights than Poff would be, but not, I don't think [too much so]."

Nixon laughed, saying, "You just don't want him to be for busing."

Rogers joined in the laughter. "I don't think he is. I'll talk to him if you want me to, I know him well enough. To be sure."

"Particularly on—"

"You know, he's a good personal friend of mine, I can talk to him."

"You might [do that]. Things I feel strongly on, two subjects. First, I don't want the man to be a racist. But, you know, I don't want a fellow who is going to go hog-wild with integration, de facto segregation. Don't want him to get hog-wild. It would be dynamite."

"Well, I think—"

"I mean, dynamite not just for the country."

"I mean, that's the law. And I think Walsh would be great."

"I know Walsh would be excellent."

"Burger is just great on that, and I think Ed would be. But on the civil rights, I think you need to do [some checking]."

"Why don't you have a private chat with him."

"I'll do that, I'll do that. I've got be in New York, the fifth. I may chat with the Chief Justice on this too."

"Right."

"And I won't indicate that we have talked at all."

"You might say that it's your idea."

"Right."

"Good."

• • • •

While Nixon was pleased with Poff's southern credentials, they had nothing to do with my efforts to promote and assist the congressman. Notwithstanding Poff's Virginia roots and residence, I had never thought of him as a southerner. He did not have the typical Virginia southern accent (he told me he had lost it in the service during World War II), and having worked with him on countless issues (presidential disability, copyright revision, the vote for eighteen-year-olds, Electoral College reform, congressional term limits, reapportionment, and church-state issues, to mention a few), I knew his views were neither parochial nor particularly southern. Rather, it was his sense of fairness, balance, and proportion, his ability to see and appreciate all sides of an argument, his intellectual curiosity, and his natural inquisitiveness about unfamiliar political thoughts and problems that I found so appealing. From my point of view, Poff's prospect as a justice provoked thoughts of judicial eminence and renown. I was pushing not just another justice, but potentially a defining member of the Court. A public servant who, once removed from the confines of his elective office, would grow into a great jurist by force of his acumen, temperament, and God-given good sense. At times, I even entertained the grand thought that I might be agenting the modern likes of a John Marshall. Once there had been "John Marshall and the six dwarfs." Why not an updated "Richard Poff and the eight Liliputians"?

With hindsight, I realize I may have been letting my enthusiasms get the better of me. Nevertheless, at the time I thought that by helping Poff secure the seat he dreamed of occupying, I would watch him grow with unending personal and professional satisfaction. This was exactly the kind of opportunity that had attracted me to government service, where being in the right place at the right time gave a person the opportunity to make a difference. Little did I realize that with such fantasies I was setting myself up for a terrible disappointment. It was not with Poff but with William Rehnquist that I would prove to be in the right place at the right time to make a difference.

5

PRIORITY TWO:
TWO CONSERVATIVES

September 23–28

SO FAR, WE HAD FOCUSED too much on naming and confirming Poff and not enough on finding a second candidate. It seemed unbecoming to be thinking seriously about replacing Justice Harlan before he formally retired, particularly since he was a friend of the Nixon administration. But as soon as his letter of resignation arrived at the White House on Thursday, September 23, we felt the urgency of filling both seats.

Associate Justice John Marshall Harlan II had been appointed by Eisenhower to the Supreme Court when Justice Robert H. Jackson died in October 1954. Harlan was born for the job. He had been named after his grandfather, who had been named after Chief Justice John Marshall, and who had served on the Supreme Court from 1874 to 1888. Before Eisenhower appointed John Harlan II to the high court, he had appointed the Rhodes Scholar and Wall Street lawyer to the United States Court of Appeals for the Second Circuit.

As a lawyer, Nixon appreciated not only Harlan's legal scholarship but his philosophy of judicial restraint, which had resulted in votes that went against many of the majority holdings of the Warren Court. To note his esteem, Nixon found occasions to bring this reserved, courtly man to the White House to perform swearing-in ceremonies. On the last occasion Harlan had visited the White House, about a year before his resignation, both the president and White House staff were struck by how healthy he looked. He stood ramrod-straight, a distinguished-looking man with white hair and sharp patrician features. His quick mind did not miss a beat. Only afterward, when Justice Harlan went to Alex Butterfield's office adjacent the Oval Office to sign the commissions for the swearing in he had just done, was it discovered that he was almost totally blind. He had to get his nose within inches of the documents to execute his signature at the correct place.[1]

John Harlan had arrived on the Court at fifty-six years of age in 1955, and had stayed as long as his body and mind permitted. With his departure went the last justice born in the nineteenth century.

Shortly after 1:00 p.m. on the 23rd, Ron Ziegler went to the EOB office to tell the president that Justice Harlan's resignation had arrived. They needed to agree on how to play it.[2] Ziegler reported that "it is generally the view of those I've talked to—Haldeman and Ehrlichman—that we should announce this this afternoon."

"Sure."

"The thought is to do it about two-thirty. I'll tell the Attorney General about it." Ziegler asked the president for guidance on what he should say about a replacement for Justice Harlan. He wanted to be sure not only that he didn't contradict anything said publicly in the past week, but that he was dealing with it as the president wished. Ziegler's credibility with the media emanated from his access to the president, and general knowledge that he truly was speaking for the president.

"Strict construction," Ziegler suggested.

"Right. Strict construction," the president responded.

More to the point, Ziegler asked if he could say, "We did not expect, we did not anticipate specifically this [resignation]?"

"Well, I've been expecting this since Monday," Nixon replied.

"I don't think we have to say that. You received it today at twelve-thirty. I'm going to say [that was when I] informed you. Is that all right, sir?"

"Sure."

"Then they will ask the following questions. First, they will say, well, how far along is the President in getting the selection process, for Mr. Justice Black's replacement? [I'll] just say, well, he's continuing with his deliberation on that matter."

Nixon suggested different wording: "Well, that he recognizes the necessity for speed because of the Court now being short [two justices]. [The president understands that it takes time] both in naming the nominee and in getting the confirmation. On the other hand, he feels it's very important to appoint the best possible man, best qualified man for the [Court]."

"They'll say, do you anticipate when you'll make the appointment?"

"No, practically, I can't. No, I can't."

"Then they'll say has the President submitted the list to the [ABA regarding] Mr. Justice Black's [seat]?"

"No."

"We haven't?"

"No."

"Will the ABA be consulted?"

"Yes. But they will not have veto power."

"I was asked this morning whether or not we can consult with members of Congress [before submitting names to] the ABA. I said I just [did not know and would check]."

When Nixon responded vaguely that Mitchell may talk to members of the Senate Judiciary Committee and that he talks to leaders of the House and Senate, Ziegler moved to another issue. He mentioned that the first lady had said that she wanted to see " 'the appointment of a woman.' " He knew this unusual action would provoke a lot of press attention. It was a wonderful human interest story, something that the Nixon White House had little of. Ziegler wanted the president's guidance. "So I'll be asked about that and I'm going to simply say that—"

"Well, you can say that two years ago that [we started appointing women to the lower courts] and you can say [we will consider a woman who is] qualified like a man. Also that, in our appointments for lower courts, that we had in mind making those appointments with the possibility that one of those would be prepared for eventual appointment to the Supreme Court."

"Yes sir."

"Yeah, say he, the President doesn't discuss this with anybody. He only discusses it with the Attorney General," Nixon instructed.

Given the fact that there were now two seats to be filled, Ziegler anticipated more questions from the press on geography. Nixon explained to him that he was not really interested in geography. As proof, he suggested mentioning his appointments of Burger and Blackmun, both from Minnesota. Following a brief discussion, Nixon summed up his position.

"I'd just say that the President believes that the Court should represent all sections of the society and all sections of the country, but, on the other hand, what I mean, by George, we don't pick a man from New York to replace a man from New York."

"I think we're probably better off not getting into the geography thing at all."

"I think you're right."

"And maybe when it happens it happens."

"Right."

"If there's pressure develops from the south, we can always—"

"Diddle it around for awhile," the president added.

· · · ·

That morning, I had my first conversation with Bill Rehnquist about the new vacancies. According to my telephone logs, he called while I was out, and I was returning his call. Mitchell's log indicates that he spoke with Rehnquist several times: at 10:27 a.m. and 12:20 p.m., after which he saw him at 5:00 p.m. for about twenty minutes, only to call him again at 6:20 p.m. Both Rehnquist and I were working on vetting Richard Poff. Because I knew Poff so well, and had files on him, Bill wanted what I had that might help him. (It was not much by way of documents, rather six years of knowing the man.) At this point, the precise lines of authority in the vetting process were a little hazy. What was clear was that in the aftermath of Haynsworth and Carswell, the White House was going to monitor the process at every stage. Rehnquist's earlier passivity about Carswell in particular had struck me as surprising. I had no idea why he had not reacted after studying his opinions. How he let Mitchell and the president go forward with that nomination, without a warning, remained a mystery.

When we spoke, I learned he had just started reviewing the Poff material. "Have you ever met Poff?" I asked him.

"Well, I've just met him, but I don't know him," Rehnquist said, "but Don Santerelli certainly speaks highly of him." Santerelli had worked at the House Judiciary Committee, after I left, and he had become an associate deputy attorney general. Santerelli was a hard-line conservative and natural ally of Rehnquist. At the time he was using the District of Columbia as a laboratory to test such draconian criminal law measures as "preventive detention" and "no-knock" entries by police. Rehnquist was providing the legal justification for many of these proposed measures, for they shared similar views, which held that law enforcement was more important than civil liberties.[3]

I made my pitch. "Bill, you really should spend some time with Poff, if possible. Let me tell you what you won't find in those documents." Rehnquist was a former law clerk to Justice Robert Jackson, and I knew he would be suspicious that Poff had a liberal heart lurking beneath his southern conservative image.

"I look forward to meeting him," Rehnquist said flatly when I finished. "Listen, the reason I called is the attorney general told me that the president's anxious to get this thing moving. There's no sense our duplicating work. I understand that you are going to visit with Poff, and go over his material, and what-have-you, later this week."

"I'm doing it on Saturday, September 25th. Poff said it would be quiet in his office on Saturday. I plan to prepare a memo, for Mitchell and Ehrlichman," I assured him. This was what he had wanted to know, and so we talked about the areas I would go over. Before hanging up, I tried to go for the close. "What are your feelings about Poff for the Court?"

"From all I know, I think he'll be excellent for the seat vacated by Justice Black. But I really don't know much about him yet," Rehnquist replied.

"How about the other seat, Bill? Is it time to put a woman on the Court?"

"I certainly have nothing against a woman being appointed. But there are not a lot of women with the necessary experience."

"How about Mary Lawton?" I fished.

Rehnquist laughed. He had a delightfully droll sense of humor. Mary Lawton was one of the career attorneys in his Office of Legal Counsel. I had worked with her on numerous matters over the years, and knew that

Rehnquist respected her legal abilities. He couldn't say she was not qualified without demeaning the work of his office. "Well, I'm not sure Mary's
a strict constructionist," he retorted flatly, still chuckling.[4]

. . . .

Soon thereafter, the vetting system was formalized, giving me more
behind-the-scenes authority. Yet it simultaneously became more sensitive, and associated me indirectly with the soon-to-be-infamous White
House "Plumbers" in the persons of Egil "Bud" Krogh, a young lawyer
and assistant to John Ehrlichman, who was a veteran of the Haynsworth-
Carswell efforts, and his plumbing assistant, David Young. Krogh had
been a deputy counsel to the president under Ehrlichman, and was now a
deputy assistant to the president for domestic affairs. His principal areas
of focus in his current job were White House policy relating to the District of Columbia, transportation, law enforcement, and drug trafficking.
It was a full platter, but it was made even fuller when he was given additional responsibility for undertaking investigations that the president
had ordered into leaks of classified information. It was the team he put
together to investigate those leaks that would become known as "the
Plumbers," veterans of wiretapping and break-ins, including the burglary
that led to Watergate.[5]

By late 1971, though the public scandal had not yet broken, the
Plumbers' work was largely finished. Krogh's duties continued to expand,
however, and they came to include one that directly involved Bill Rehnquist: a project to accelerate the declassification of government documents (something that every recent administration has tried to do, yet
managed to fall behind on).

The declassification project is worth mentioning only because it was
headed by Rehnquist and thus provided the first occasion for Nixon to
meet his assistant attorney general up close. Unfortunately, the one meeting of the declassification committee with the president had given Nixon
a less than flattering impression of Rehnquist. The meeting had taken
place in the outer conference room of the president's EOB office on July 1,
1971. Committee members attended from the Defense Department, State
Department, Atomic Energy Commission, National Security Council,
and the CIA, along with Ehrlichman, Ziegler, Haldeman, and myself. The
president explained that he wanted to reduce the classification of docu-

ments to only those that truly justified the designation, and that he wanted to accelerate the declassification of materials from World War II, Korea, and the Bay of Pigs invasion. The president departed before the meeting ended, and he asked me to accompany him. In the reception area between the conference room and the president's office, Nixon stopped.

"John, who the hell is that clown?"

"I beg your pardon?"

"The guy dressed like a clown, who's running the meeting," the president repeated.

"Oh, you mean Bill Rehnquist."

"What's his name?"

"Rehnquist," I answered.

"Rehnquist," the president repeated. "Spell it," he asked, which I did. Nixon then asked, "Is he Jewish? He looks it."

"I don't think so. I think he's of Scandinavian background."

"Thanks," the president said as he turned to go into his office, observing, "That's a hell of a costume he's wearing, just like a clown."

I could not tell if the president was amused or appalled. But I was accustomed to Rehnquist's unpredictable wardrobe. That day, Rehnquist was wearing a pink shirt that clashed with an awful psychedelic necktie, and Hush-Puppies, which were seldom if ever seen in the corridors of the White House in those days. I sometimes wondered if Rehnquist was color-blind. To me, his lanky six foot three frame, large ears, bushy muttonchop sideburns, and heavy black eyeglasses weren't clownish so much as reminiscent of a character from Dickens, or maybe *Star Trek*.

Later that month, on July 24, during a meeting with Ehrlichman and Krogh, the president came back to the subject:[6]

"You remember the meeting we had when I told that group of clowns we had around here. Renchburg and that group. What's his name?"

"Rehnquist," Ehrlichman replied.

All in all, an inauspicious introduction for a future Supreme Court nominee to the commander in chief.

• • • •

Krogh's past experience had him thinking about who should be doing what in the vetting process. Although no longer directly involved, he wanted to make certain that nothing like the Haynsworth-Carswell experiences would be repeated, so he dictated a four-page memorandum for Ehrlichman's "Eyes Only."[7] Most of his recommendations were adopted by Ehrlichman, placing me in charge of day-to-day monitoring of the selection, vetting, and later confirmation process for the White House. Krogh also recommended, and Ehrlichman agreed, that former Plumber David Young, a lawyer who had once been Henry Kissinger's assistant, be assigned to assist me. Ehrlichman explained to me that I was to be his eyes and ears. "Remember you're working for the White House, not Justice," he told me. I took this to mean that Ehrlichman was still not sure of my loyalty, since I had once worked for Mitchell. When Ehrlichman said that he was assigning David Young to work with me, there was no doubt in my mind that while Young would be helpful, he would also be keeping an eye on me for Ehrlichman.

• • • •

Later on September 23, the president made an appearance before approximately five thousand members of the Economic Club of Detroit. The format was questions and answers, but the president first gave brief remarks, before fielding questions on his policy and thoughts on wage-price controls, automotive safety and emission standards, aid to exporters, the use of the highway trust fund, balancing the budget, actions for minority groups, interest rates, welfare, the stock market—and the Supreme Court:

"Now that there are two vacancies on the Supreme Court do you think it timely for a woman to become a Supreme Court Justice; or do you believe that a nominee for the Supreme Court should have substantial judicial experience, that we should in fact promote our best justices; or have you ever considered appointing Martha Mitchell?"

After the laughter died down, the president responded. "Well, answering the third part first, Martha Mitchell is not a lawyer, but that is not, incidentally, an inhibition as far as appointments are concerned because the Constitution does not require the president to appoint a lawyer to the Supreme Court. So, she should—or could—be considered, I should say, but her husband won't recommend her, so consequently that rules that out."

Again the crowd laughed. Nixon continued, and from his tone it was clear he was serious now. "Second, with regard to a woman, I believe that a woman who is qualified should be appointed to any court—district court, circuit court, or Supreme Court. I have instructed the Attorney General, as he looks over the nominees that he is going to present to me, the recommendations, to be sure that qualified women are included if they meet the general standards that we have set."

Wanting to drive home his point, he continued: "Now, with regard to the qualifications, and answering the question very seriously now, that I am looking for, I am frankly looking for judges who—and you can always judge a man who is going to make an appointment on his track record—I am looking for men who will have a similar judicial philosophy as the Chief Justice of the United States, Mr. Burger, whom I appointed, and Mr. Justice Blackmun. I believe that the Court at this time could well use two more judges, men with that judicial philosophy. I am more interested in the judicial philosophy than I am in what part of the country they come from and whether they are a woman or whether they are a man."

This was the kind of forum Nixon truly enjoyed. He became almost tutorial as he pushed on. "Now, is it a requirement, or should it be a requirement, that the judge or the nominee be one who has judicial experience? The answer is no. Mr. Justice Frankfurter was a teacher. He was one of the great judges; whether you agreed or not with his philosophy, he was a great judge. Mr. Justice Brandeis, who was one of my heroes when I was in law school, one of the great dissenters along with Holmes, was a man who was a great practicing lawyer, a labor lawyer primarily, fighting great causes, but that did not mean that he did not become one of the great judges."

Finally, he would tip his hand just a bit. "So teachers, legislators, for example, with great experience in the Judiciary Committee of the House or Senate, they are also good possibilities. That gives you an idea of where I am turning." [8]

As the reporters quickly figured out, he was talking about nobody other than Poff.

• • • •

On Friday, September 24, the Supreme Court announced that it was postponing oral arguments on major cases because of the two vacancies. This added public pressure for the president to get on with his nominations.

Burger did not want less than a full Court ruling on important cases like the constitutionality of the death penalty.[9] While the Court's term would begin in ten days (October 4) missing two justices, it would mark time waiting for nominations and confirmations. Much more interesting at the White House was the buzz that the president and Mrs. Nixon had exchanged terse words about appointing a woman on their Air Force One flight back from Detroit the preceding evening.

All I knew for certain was that as the White House vetter, I was working only on Poff. That evening, Ehrlichman called a meeting to check on my progress. "How's the Congressman from Virginia handling all the attention?" Ehrlichman inquired, as I pulled up a chair in front of his small, crescent-shaped desk in the corner of the cramped, second-floor West Wing office.[10]

"He's simply staying home. He says that when he walks into the Republican Cloakroom, off the House floor, his colleagues call him Mr. Justice Poff. He's embarrassed by it. He's not all that confident it's going to happen."

"Well, the attorney general has sent his name to the ABA, I understand. I think the president's pretty well decided that he wants Poff to have the Black seat. Did you see that letter from Jack Marsh, the former Virginia congressman who wrote the president to support Poff?"

"No," I replied.

"I'll send it over. Pretty interesting. He makes the case that with Hugo Black's departure, the Court will not have a justice with congressional experience. Black was a senator, of course. Marsh sent along a study that shows that there had never been a year in the Court's history that it didn't have at least one justice with a congressional background."

"That's a pretty persuasive argument."

"More persuasive are some of the names on that list. I can't recall them all, but I remember it included John Marshall and Joseph Story. You can't get much better," Ehrlichman said, rather professorially, as Krogh and Young entered and took seats at his desk. After greeting them, he questioned me.

"How you doing on gathering background material on Poff?"

I reported the effort Poff's staff had made, that he had a small mountain of material. Poff had good records, and his staff had a good eye for controversial matters. I summarized the civil rights–related material, and advised Ehrlichman that copies of everything had also been given to Bill Rehnquist.

"Any time bombs there, like our friend G. Harrold Carswell forgot to tell us about?"

"Other than the Southern Manifesto, and his voting record, which no doubt will kill him with I'd guess between twenty-five to thirty senators, nothing else in the civil rights area, so far."

"Tell you what I want you to do. Have Caulfield have his investigator go down to the local newspapers where Poff lives. Down in Virginia. Start digging around in the newspaper's morgue, and see what he finds." The investigator Erhlichman was referring to was Anthony Ulasewicz, a former New York City police detective he had hired before I arrived at the White House to undertake private investigations for the president.

"Poff asked me if the FBI had started investigating him yet," I said. "I told him no. He said he'd like to know before they do. He told Mitchell that too."

"I don't think it necessary to tell him we're looking at old newspapers," Ehrlichman retorted. "I'd like to see what an investigator finds first."

"I agree, John," Bud Krogh added. "Let's not flag it. Let's see what we find. That's the mistake we made with Carswell. And we can't rely on the FBI to really dig."

"I should tell you one thing I found," I continued. "A few years ago Poff introduced a bill that set forth the requirements for any person who served on the Supreme Court. It's a good bill. Unfortunately, Poff can't meet his own criteria. He said a justice should have at least five years of judicial experience."

"Oh, my, my," Ehrlichman said, taking off his glasses, screwing up his face, and rubbing his eyes. "They're going to roast him on that. But I don't think that will bother the president. I'll let him know."

• • • •

The president spent that Friday afternoon at Burning Tree Country Club, on the golf course with John Mitchell. When he returned to the White House that evening, he joined the first lady and Julie Eisenhower (who was living with her husband, David, on the third floor while he attended law school at George Washington University) for dinner on the Truman Balcony, overlooking the south lawn. After dinner, and before going to the White House theater with Julie and Mrs. Nixon to see *Wild Rovers* (a Blake Edwards western most notable for William Holden and Ryan O'Neal vomiting on each other in one scene and being covered with urine in another), the president called John Connally, his secretary of the treasury (a savvy Texas politician whom Nixon thought would make a good president), and the conversation wandered into the Supreme Court appointments.[11]

"For your information, I am going to appoint two conservatives. Is that all right with you?"

"Yes it is," Connally replied.

"We're going to put Poff in, you know, for the Senate. And the reason that they're going to put him in is that it's awful hard for these people to vote against a congressman. So that will get him in. And then for the one replacing Harlan, I told Mitchell I want a conservative. He can come from New York but he's got to be conservative. Mitchell's got a man in mind. I told Mitchell to get me two conservatives appointed. Just like, just like Burger and Blackmun. So we'll have four votes, right like that."

"Well, I just think, you know, it's a golden opportunity to change and this can last a generation."

"That's right. Both of the men we have in mind, you see, Poff is only forty-nine years old. The other guy we have in mind at the present time, he's fifty-three. So that means he's got twenty years, you see, because they can stay on until they're seventy. And, by God, I'm going to stand firm on that all the way." Nixon was referring to Herschel Friday, whom Mitchell had brought to his attention. But the president was just shooting the breeze, not truly suggesting two southerners. "You know, I always talk about the woman thing. We can't find a woman who's ready yet."

Connally laughed. "I don't know."

"Well, it would break up the Court, basically. Poor old Burger couldn't work with the woman, anyhow. But there'll come a time, maybe one or two appointments later, we'll find one that's ready. But there isn't one right now, that's ready." It wouldn't be the last time Nixon discussed appointing a woman.

. . . .

David Young, an athletically trim, prematurely balding young lawyer, was, like me, in his early thirties. He arrived in my office about 9:30 a.m.

on Saturday morning to discuss our forthcoming session with Dick Poff. As we talked, the president's helicopter lifted off the south lawn to take the president and first lady to Andrews Air Force Base for a trip to Montana, Oregon, and Washington, and on to Alaska. The president would be gone until Monday night, September 27, and he was expecting significant progress on finding nominees to fill the two Court vacancies by his return.

As White House counsel, I had developed an extensive questionnaire for presidential appointees. Young and I used this questionnaire, with appropriate modification for the fact that this was a Supreme Court appointment, as the basis for our questions for Poff. We arrived at his office in the Rayburn House Office Building shortly after 2:00 p.m., and spent the next three and a half hours cross-examining the congressman about every facet of his life and career.[12]

For example, I knew from private conversations from circa 1965 that Poff regretted as a young congressman signing the so-called Southern Manifesto. I was surprised, however, to discover he had spoken publicly on the issue in an interview he had given in 1970. The Southern Manifesto defended separate but equal schools that had been outlawed by *Brown v. Board of Education* (1954), and accused the Supreme Court of "abuse of judicial power" and "planting hatred and suspicion" between the "heretofore" friendly races. In the 1970 interview, Poff explained why he had signed it, and why he repudiated it later: "[The manifesto] came at a time when I was a very junior member of Congress." At thirty-three, he had been in his second two-year term. As he told the interviewer, "The pressures that were brought to bear on all members of Congress [to sign the manifesto] were more intense than they had been in my recollection. I can only say now that segregation is wrong today, it was wrong yesterday. Segregation was never right. But it is one of the most lamentable frailties of mankind that when one's wrong is most grievous, his self-justification is most passionate, perhaps in the pitiful hope that the fervor of his self-defense will somehow prove him right. But this doesn't make it so, and doesn't fool himself."[13]

If any issue was likely to be a problem, this was it. It called for more probing.

"Dick, I'm delighted to learn of this public statement," I said. "I'm sure the president will be delighted. But you understand, we all understand, that the Senate is going to grill the hell out of you on this subject. What is to prevent your detractors from saying you gave this interview hoping one day you might be appointed to the Supreme Court, or some other court?"

"Nothing. In fact, I'm sure they will say exactly that. But you know, and many of my colleagues in the House know, I didn't say anything in that interview that I'd not said long, long before I gave that interview."

"I agree, but—"

"Hold it just a second, John," Poff said, putting up his hand. "I knew when I made that statement that detractors might use it against me. Detractors on both sides. Those in my district who still think separate but equal should be the law. Those judging my fitness for the bench. But those words I used, I mean. So let the detractors detract. Let the chips fall. But my truth will stand."

For Poff, the far more difficult subject that we raised related to his family. Poff was a happily married man, with a married daughter expecting her first child, and two boys who were around twelve and ten. Poff explained, however, that his twelve-year-old son was adopted. Dick Poff had a troubled, if not pained, look on his face as he talked about this.

"My adopted son, Tommy, does not yet know he is adopted. We've never told him. We agreed to adopt him before he was born, but we don't know the mother. He came to us from the hospital. We wanted more children, but we had a dry spell, and no sooner had we adopted Tommy than my wife got pregnant with our youngest son, Dicky." There was an awkward silence. This was clearly an emotional issue. "I don't know when we'll tell the boy he's adopted. It's one of those things I think about when I wake up in the middle of the night, and worry about how to do it, and when to do it. But not just yet. We love him like he's ours, because he is ours. He's a wonderful child, but sensitive, and we will tell him when we think it's the right time." He stopped again, then finished the thought. "But not right now."

· · · ·

En route back to the White House, Young was going over his notes. "He's very impressive, John. I can see why you think he belongs on the Court." Young continued looking at his notes, then said, "I am struck that he actually reads the Constitution two or three times a year. He reads the

Federalist Papers. He reads the debates of the Constitutional Convention. I don't know many lawyers that do that, frankly."

"It only came up briefly today, but think about this, David. Here is a man who has actually written part of the Constitution."

"How so?" Young asked, as our car approached the south gate of the White House grounds.

"The Twenty-fifth Amendment to the Constitution. Without Poff, this amendment on presidential disability, which is necessarily one of the longest and most complex in the Constitution, would never have happened. He not only wrote much of it, but fashioned the compromises that resulted in the Congress sending it to the states for ratification." I smiled at my vetting partner, as the car pulled up to the West Wing and stopped. "David, look at it this way. We're only trying to put one of the framers of the Constitution on the Court with Poff's nomination."

• • • •

That night, at the Benson Hotel in Portland, Oregon, Richard Nixon was restless in the presidential suite. He called Haldeman's room, and asked him to come down the hall for a chat. The president was studying papers for the trip to Alaska, and his meeting with Emperor Hirohito and Empress Nagako of Japan. They talked briefly about the use of interpreters, before the president got to what was on his mind. The next afternoon, Haldeman made note of their conversation in his daily diary: "He had me into the room at the hotel in the evening and was talking about Supreme Court appointments and his feeling that he really should go for a woman judge, if we can get a good, tough conservative. He thinks this is the opportunity to score on that point, that we would make tremendous political mileage in that while many people would be opposed to it, nobody would vote against him because of it. On the other hand, a lot of people who were in favor of it would change their votes to Nixon because of such an appointment." [14]

• • • •

The next day, David and I worked in our respective offices preparing a memorandum of our session with Poff, who had come through the vetting with flying colors. Young wanted to add a personal comment to the joint memorandum. It was a good idea, since he had never met Poff before, and he could share his first impression with more objectivity than I could claim. Young wrote: "Poff impressed me as a man with a sense of quiet confidence and sincere humility. To some degree he is rough hewn but it is not affected and he is genuine in his manner and straight forward in his speech. He knows what he believes and he believes in it on the basis of his own independent and hard thought. Yet he does not appear to be afraid to pursue new ideas or to embrace them." For a last line he added: "There is no doubt in my mind that as far as personal integrity, moral uprightness, and dedication to serve his Country, this man is of the highest order."

• • • •

On Tuesday, September 28, after Nixon returned from Alaska, a minor black comedy arose over one of the president's least favorite duties: attending a funeral. Justice Black had passed away on Sunday, just eight days after retiring. By midmorning, Haldeman had heard from John Mitchell and others attending the morning staff meeting, all urging the president to attend the funeral service that afternoon. The cabinet was attending, along with all the living Supreme Court justices (both active and retired), the old Washington establishment, and former Black law clerks and friends. Haldeman met with Nixon and raised the subject gingerly.[15]

"Mitchell has now decided that you should definitely go to the funeral today. The Chief Justice thinks you should be there. Justice Harlan's going, looking forward to seeing you there. John [Mitchell's] recommendation, which has shifted since yesterday, said it is a question of respect to the Court. At a time when you've got the two nominations up."

"When is it?"

"Two o'clock."

"God damn. [Is Mitchell] the one who screwed this up?"

"No."

"You see, this is not a good idea. [It's] bad business. [As President] you can't go to funerals, Bob."

"As I [understand it], Mitchell called Moore this morning. 'Cause he'd said no, then he got to thinking about it. Now, I can talk to John, see whether he really feels—"

"I just feel that the whole business of going, I guess [is a bad idea]. Senators are going to die, presidents are going to die."

"You're clear on senators."

"He's not my man, either. I mean, I don't know Black. I don't know him."

"What do you do when Thurgood Marshall dies? Probably [have] Burger's pressure."

"Well, Burger would naturally pressure, because he wants everybody to pay attention to the Court. It's like everybody wants you to pay attention to something else."

The president mumbled and growled his displeasure. This conversation is also filled with Nixon's barely audible mutter about "God damn Mitchell," and repeated statements that he would have to deal with all sorts of "assholes." Nixon pressed Haldeman to know if there "is any speculation that I might or might not" attend. "If he [Mitchell] wants me to do it, I'll do it. [So double-check, and if he insists,] I'll go. You'll say I was concerned about the fact that I can't do senators, like [Winston] Prouty, and some people that I should of—"

"Yep."

"However, I'll make an exception on this. Don't you believe that not going, I don't think it means one God damn thing to the country, that's for sure. They don't give a shit about the courts. Well, why? Who the hell do we please?"

"The legalistic types say you got to get the confirmation through, and all that, and that may be part of what's influencing John."

The president, not convinced that attending the funeral would result in anyone voting for Poff's confirmation, declared: "They'll vote as they please." Haldeman echoed, "They'll vote as they politically want to."

After considerably more growling, Nixon commented on his potential nominees: "I don't give a God damn if the guy can read or write, just so he votes right. On this occasion, when they talk about undistinguished people, if just one of our people would have the guts, we don't have any people with guts, well, our people who have guts have no brains, but anyway. I just go down the line, now let's look. Is Brennan distinguished? Shit. Is Marshall?

"Is Whizzer White distinguished? [16] Now for Christ sakes, I mean, if in law school, those guys would have been in the middle of their class, I mean, of course, Whizzer White's, he's a Rhodes Scholar. In college, [he played football] big time."

Charles Colson, who had joined the meeting, tossed out another name. "Potter Stewart."

"Is Potter Stewart distinguished? Jesus Christ," Nixon said, causing Haldeman to laugh. The president continued, "I must say that the ones that have any brains, really, that I'd put in the same league—"

"Fortas," interjected Colson.

"And Black, and Harlan. Those are the only three. Harlan's a very able man. Black is a very able man. Fortas, was, of course, very smart, a Jew to begin with. And Warren's a dumb Swede. He was thick. [Dumb as hell.] All this bullshit about distinguished judges. Burger is more distinguished than any of them. When you compare Burger, Burger's got class. [To say that] Poff, that he's not distinguished. Shit, he's brighter than those other people, and hell, who knows how distinguished he will become."

Finally, Nixon turned to Haldeman. "Well, I'll tell you what I will do. I will go. But now, you're not going to laugh at this, you're not to tell Ziegler, you're not to tell the Secret Service, and all that, I'm just going to go to the God damn thing, I'm going to sit in the back of that church and leave. I'm not going to make this a big public parade. I just insist on that, just not going to make it a God damn [big show]. I'm only doing it for a half-assed reason anyway. I've got to go up there, television and all that—"

"There'll be television there anyway—"

"I'm not doing it for that. I'm doing it for John Mitchell. I'll go. But low key. It's a private matter, understand. It's totally private matter. I only decided at the last minute to do this. I don't want the press corps to go with me, [or] I'm not going to do it. I have a thing about funerals. I don't like them. I believe that's one thing that should not be exploited, and God damn it, I've always felt that way."

The conversation ended when the president explained that he wanted to get the selections made, and the confirmation proceedings going, so he hoped that nothing else would be "screwed up" on his schedule.

To complete the black comedy, the funeral in fact turned out to be an embarrassment to the president. By 3:00 p.m. he was back in the Oval Office, and Haldeman asked for his reaction. Haldeman had attended and had been dumbstruck when the minister verbally attacked the president and John Mitchell while delivering the eulogy, expounding on Justice Black's dislike of strict constructionists on the Supreme Court.[17]

"That Unitarian guy's really something, isn't he?" Haldeman stated.

"The minister?"

"Yeah."

"Terrible, son-of-a-bitch."

"Political."

"Also, he gave Black a hell of a lot more than his due," Nixon observed.

"Well, that they always do at funerals."

"Poor taste, whether or not I was there. You know, the service was so God damn long. That's the last. I'll do Harlan's, I'm happy to—"

"You'll have to do Harlan's now."

"But I'm not going to do any more, now, God damn it. And if that black dies, that ah, I mean, ah, Douglas—"

"Marshall."

"I'm not going to his funeral. I'm just not going to go. And I don't want the staff to think that I approve of this now, I just want you to know that I went under duress." Nixon slammed his hand down on the desk. "And after having gone, I think it was a very bad mistake."

"I agree."

"I think it was a bad mistake to have been there, it's like going to that God damn White House Correspondents thing, exactly the same. You should not put the President in the position of going where somebody [is] either cruel or sly. Ehrlichman must understand this, he must understand this. Colson, or Ehrlichman, Mitchell said this is for the fucking Court, you know. Well, God damn it, when is he going to learn that the courts are our enemy, that's what we've got to understand. What this Court has done is ruined this country."

The conversation ended with the president telling Haldeman that he "wants [Mitchell] to know that I'm pissed off about it." He also wondered if members of the Black family realized how "gauche" the funeral was.

• • • •

Later that day, the president's often mercurial mood improved when he met with Republican congressional leaders to discuss the appointments. Yet even now, eleven days after Black's resignation and five days after Harlan's, Poff's was the only name in serious contention. Nixon's discussion with the four legislators of the Republican congressional leadership—Senators Hugh Scott (R-PA) and Robert P. Griffin (R-MI), and Representatives Gerald R. Ford (R-MI) and Leslie C. Arends (R-IL)—accompanied by White House staffers Clark MacGregor, Ron Ziegler, George Shultz, and John Ehrlichman, showed just how little consensus existed on a Poff backup, let alone a second nominee.

When discussing various congressional business first, Nixon explained that he wanted to unload on the Democratic leadership, but before doing so, he wanted to get his two Supreme Court nominations confirmed. If the Senate were to delay, furthermore, it would hurt the Court.[18]

Senator Scott offered a strategy. "Well, I suggested to John Mitchell the other day that it would be salutary to send both names up together. There are reasons, there are amenities, and it would enable us to play one man off against another, which favors somebody who's for, you know, number two say, to vote for number one. We get a bit of maneuvering room when we get them both together."

Nixon, knowing he had nobody aside from Poff, responded that "You might not get them both together, but you might get them within, maybe two, three days apart."

"That's okay."

When Nixon mentioned Poff, Senator Griffin said, "On the other hand, my analysis is on Poff, we lose thirty-one votes."

Scott thought things were worse, saying, "I think we lose about thirty-six."

Griffin rejoined, "But either way, we should have a majority."

The group agreed that an effort should be made to get moderate Republicans such as Senator Charles Mathias (R-MD) behind Poff, and solicit the assistance of Judiciary Committee Chairman Emanuel Celler of New York, who had great respect for Poff's abilities.

Jerry Ford reported that they were working on their liberal colleagues. They hoped that senators like William Saxbe and Robert Taft Jr., both of Ohio, Charles Percy (R-IL), and Ted Stevens (R-AL) would support Poff. The president then brought up the fact that Dick Poff had signed the Southern Manifesto, which would be a problem for some in the Senate. Jerry Ford said that he had talked with Democratic senator Phil Hart of Michigan, who couldn't vote for Poff because of the manifesto.

Nixon then hedged. "I can't disclose that Poff is going to get it, he is being considered. But let me say that one of those two has to be a southerner. We don't have any southerners on the Court. After Haynsworth and Carswell, we ought to be able to find one. And the reason that Poff was, frankly, high in consideration, is that it is much more difficult for them to vote against a southerner who's been in the House, than it is against some damn judge."

Nobody disagreed. They only wanted to pin down the timing of both nominations.

Nixon responded, "Well, I told Mitchell that I want both names, before we send one up, I would think. But I do think we want to get it up [as soon as possible]. In other words, have one hit, and, and two days later, or three days later, hit 'em with the other. That's what we're going to do. Anybody disagree with that?"

Ford responded for the group that they thought that would work. Then the president raised the possibility of appointing a woman, which provoked a general discussion. Notwithstanding various sexist asides, the discussion was serious. The legislators recognized that Nixon was really thinking about it.

Nixon commented, "Our problem there is, we're looking. The difficulty is, you saw a list [in the newspaper], I'm sure, of twelve women who were recommended. My God, what a bag. I mean, there, were, ah—"

Someone interjected, "What a bag of hags." Laughter filled the room.

Nixon continued: "Anyway. Of course, they can't vote against the first woman, any more than they can vote against the first Negro. So they'll take a woman, provided she can read and write. On the other hand, the main problem is [the men on the Court]. You know, that life there is very tough. They live together, they talk together, they have those conferences, and the rest, and you can't convince the Chief Justice on [this question]."

Someone joked, "Would it be safe [for a woman] with Douglas over there?" Again, everyone laughed.

When the group left, Senator Griffin remained behind for a brief moment to assure the president he would support Poff. Griffin had voted against Carswell, so his support was a welcome omen.

Nevertheless, Griffin would never be tested on his pledge. Poff, sitting home alone, was doing a lot of very serious thinking. His thoughts would disappoint not only me but his Republican colleagues, who were cashing in big chips to ease his route through the confirmation process.

6

POFF GOES POOF

September 29–October 2

ANY SOUTHERNER NOMINATED to the Supreme Court by Richard Nixon was in for a confirmation fight. So no one was surprised when opposition began to form against the prospect of Richard Poff. The first to declare himself was the NAACP's Clarence Mitchell, who opposed Poff because he had never voted for any civil rights bill. Yet Poff's broad support from his colleagues, both Democrat and Republican, liberal and conservative, in the House of Representatives, was muting civil rights opposition.

When Mitchell had sent Poff's name, along with Burger's recommended candidate Herschel Friday and two southern judges who were merely camouflage, to the ABA's Committee on the Federal Judiciary for evaluation, the committee was advised that Poff was the likely selection. To bolster Poff's position, Rehnquist had prepared a brief—in the form of a ten-page letter signed by Deputy Attorney General Kleindienst—to the evaluation committee. I sent a copy of the Rehnquist-Kleindienst letter to the president.[1] It encouraged the ABA to broaden its scope in evaluating

101

Poff's qualifications, citing an article written by Justice Frankfurter, who had said that "the correlation between prior judicial experience and fitness for the functions of the Supreme Court is zero." The letter pointed out that ABA Committee litigation experience standards would have precluded Justice Frankfurter and Justice William Douglas from sitting on the high court. The last four pages focused on Poff's legislative background, which uniquely qualified him for the Court.[2] It was an excellent letter, but it ignored Poff's work with the law reform commission. The fight for Poff had begun, though it was still behind closed doors.

Nixon was fairly confident that he would win. Late morning on Wednesday, September 29, during a meeting with Bob Haldeman and Henry Kissinger, he and Haldeman talked it through.[3] The morning news of a federal court decision in Detroit upholding forced busing caused Haldeman to comment, "Wait until you get your Court, maybe you can get it turned around."

Nixon warmed to the topic. "The one other thing I must find out, and the only other one that I should see today [is Mitchell]. Check with Mitchell to see if he has anything, if he wants any further discussion with me on judges. I'm going to Florida on Thursday night. Because I think those judges have got to go, we've got to push him, Bob. We've got to push him now on this. I think just get Poff up there now."

"Ehrlichman tells me that Mitchell's theory is we're going to have a problem with Poff."

"They're going to beat him? You're not going to send Poff down?"

"Well, no. [Mitchell] wants to keep the name up and smoke out the opposition now, rather than after it gets to the Senate."

"I understand."

"And try to get that, and now they've moved it to the ABA, haven't they, so they've got that one."

"Yeah."

"And he wants to go to the Senate and get fifty-one committed votes, so that he doesn't get there and [not have the votes]. The report is they've got thirty or thirty-one committed against [Poff]."

Nixon was more cautious, but still confident. "I understand that's [not] all. And if they get thirty-five against, that's still sixty-five for."

"All you care about is fifty-one, or all I care about is fifty-one."

"We're going to get it. I talked to [Hugh] Scott about it. Scott says we can confirm him. And Scott's no tower of strength."

"Sure isn't."

Kissinger added, "He's not one for fighting a losing battle."

Turning to the subject of the second seat, Nixon commented, "I hope Mitchell picks a woman."

"He's got one, I'm going to check out because I know that she came up elsewhere, and that, young, she's my age."

"Good."

"Not so young anymore. I think she's still in California."

"What's she do?"

"She's a judge."

"What court? Superior?"

"Superior Court. And she was dean of the S.C. Law School, or something like that [and] she's gone through a remarkable practice of [law]."

"Practice [before the courts?]"

"That's what I've got to find out."

"Probably a God damn [liberal] at S.C. Those twelve that those women came up with [in the newspaper], every one was a left-winger. Every one of them."

"She's on that list."

"Was she?"

"I think so. She's not a left-wing radical at all."

"Are you sure?"

"I'm not at all sure how conservative she is," Haldeman hedged.

"I'd guess she isn't."

"She's got to be very conservative. If you're going to put a young woman on, for God sake let's put one that's [conservative]."

"No, what I meant, she doesn't have to be, frankly, a racist. That's what I'm saying."

"Well, good."

"On all of these men, southerners want a racist on that Court. I don't want any racists."

Haldeman laughed. "It's good to hear that. I kind of like that."

"No, no, no, no. Not a racist. I need somebody that [is conservative]. Burger is perfect. Burger is good in civil rights. Strong in law and order."

Nixon pounded his palm on the desk. "That's what I want. I think Mitchell's woman, she sounds good to me. She's been in the Justice Department twelve years, she's now a state court judge. And she's supposed to be pretty good."

"Well, they're working on those."

Commenting on why it was smart to appoint a woman, Nixon admitted his feelings and calculated the advantages. "[Burger's] totally against it, on this, Burger's totally against it. Because the Court doesn't want to deal with a woman in the Court. I am against it, frankly. But basically, politically it isn't going to lose us a vote. A lot of people will grumble and say why the Christ a woman. And, to a hell of a lot of women, it could make [believers] out of them. That's just what it gets down to. See my point. You poll the country, sixty percent of the people at least would say okay to a woman judge. On the other hand, as far as those who do vote against Nixon because he appointed a woman, is zero. But on the other hand, [how many] vote for Nixon because he appointed [a woman]? One percent, maybe ten percent, there's the point. It's like the Negro vote. It's a hell of a thing."

"More important, there's a hell of a lot more women than there are Negroes," Haldeman observed.

"That's right."

"And there's a lot more reasons for a woman to be on the Court."

"There ought to be a woman judge. Lots of women, and it's economic. I'm not for women, frankly, in any job. I don't want any of them around. Thank God we don't have any in the Cabinet. But I must say the Cabinet's so lousy we [might] just as well have a woman [there] too."

• • • •

The next day, Thursday, September 30, Nixon sat down with Mitchell to have a long talk—and to make their choices. As the second week since Black's resignation drew toward a close, with Poff successfully vetted, and the ABA report due over the weekend, it was time to fish or cut bait—something Nixon had no difficulty doing. He had delegated to Mitchell the task of choosing the second candidate, but the president himself had pushed Mitchell to find a woman. Nixon acted not because of the first lady's urgings (although they were a factor), nor because of liberal or media pressure (although Nixon was not a politician to ignore either), but rather purely for reasons of realpolitik. Appointing a woman would confound opponents, allowing a second conservative to glide through the Senate, and it would help Nixon in his upcoming 1972 election. Nixon wanted his Court to have a new southerner, and he wanted two conservatives. He was determined to succeed by selecting a fellow legislator, and a woman. It was brilliant. Machiavelli could not have plotted it better.

Mitchell got right down to business.[4] "Well, first, well, let me run through the current situation on the Court. Pressures that have been building up on Poff with the civil rights people and so forth. It became very obvious that we didn't want to get mouse-trapped by sending somebody else up with him where we might lose Poff and get the other one, in a pair operation. We have Poff now before the ABA Committee, and they will meet on Saturday and give a report on it.

"Of course [you] have heard, ah, how the House people are coming to [Poff's support]. They've got a letter down here, [signed by both] liberals and conservatives."

"Yep."

"Just yesterday, [unintelligible] came out and said he was going to be against him. I think that isn't bad, the fact that the [unintelligible] and the House support him."

"Yeah, even Mac Mathias [a pro–civil rights Republican] is, from all accounts, going around building Poff up. There are three basic problems with Poff. The civil rights manifesto and his position on that."

"How does Poff [come down on civil rights]?"

"Poff has talked on the states rights' basis on the civil rights legislation. He has not talked race at all."

"But, hell, I knew the factors."

"Well, I'm talking about the factors that are part of this [manifesto]," Mitchell said.

"But the point is that we know Poff is a deep southerner. He did what any damn southerner should do. I'd sign the damn manifesto today."

Mitchell claimed, "I think I would too, if I had an opportunity. Poff has also introduced a bill over the period of years prescribing qualifications for the Supreme Court. Of course he doesn't meet those qualifications."

"Right, that's too bad."

"And there is one other factor that is involved here. After rather an exhaustive review he, like all the other congressmen, had his name on a law firm and got money out of it without participating in the practice. But when the American Bar came through with a ruling to the effect that this was unethical, he [dropped] out of the firm. Matter of fact, he did it before it was adopted in Virginia. So he has that operation."

"Otherwise he is clean."

Mitchell brought up the issue of experience. "The question will come up obviously about his practice of law, which he has had so little of. We have filed with the committee a ten-page brief on the subject matter, which covers the writings of Frankfurter and so forth, in which they say this is not a requisite for the Supreme Court."

"Good."

"And also, of course, we have documented Poff's active participation in the Judiciary Committee, what he has done. And it's quite an impressive record."

"How long did he practice law? Five years? Or maybe none?"

"Well, it was about, oh, seven years. He did practice some law while he was in Congress, not much. He tried a couple of cases. Things like that."

"In the Congress he practiced law before the Judiciary Committee," Nixon added.

"I agree."

"We all know, John, the practice of law is nothing."

"And that is exactly the point that's made in the [letter to the ABA]."

"And so the ABA knows it too, John."

"They certainly do know it by now, if they didn't [before], because we have been beating up on them, and of course other people have too."

"Let me give you my theory on Poff, if I can, because it may help your team. I've been in [this business] long enough and I see these groups lining up, and I know you're concerned, and I'm concerned [about the opposition by these] groups. But I [think] that we ought to send Poff up, and if these bastards turn him down, a decent southerner for this job, then by God, that's it. I mean, I think we've got an issue then. It is like Haynsworth and Carswell and the rest of them. We can just say that it's not fair, you can't get a southerner in there. I just think this whole civil rights thing, that people are fed up with it."

"I agree."

"The God damn, you know, these people, like [AFL-CIO Union head George] Meany, he's a hypocrite! And these God damn senators are hypocrites, John! And I just feel that we ought to bite the bullet, send it on in, and fight. If we lose it, [okay]."

"Well, we have a double-edged problem, and probably a double-edged sword, because the Congress will raise hell, if the bar doesn't approve him and he's not sent up there."

"The House will be ready to riot," Nixon declared.

"There's a lot of people in the Senate as well."

"John McClellan was in here, yesterday. [He said] you've got to tell John [Mitchell], I want them to really race. Go, go, go all out for this man."

"Very well," Mitchell said.

"You want to enlist this southern mandate because they have never been enlisted. And just say the President [needs your help]." Nixon did not believe that southern Democratic senators had helped him in his earlier efforts to place a southerner on the Court. Now was the time to do so.

"A good likelihood is that we will have support from outside of the Senate."

"Sure. I don't think they're going to have more than forty votes against him. I think it'll be thirty-five, but that's just my guess based on a talk with Scott. Based on power and strength, and he only counts thirty-six votes against him, or thirty-seven."

"I think that's about where we come out."

"And Griffin, now Griffin's going to have a problem here with the [Bar Association]. He says he supports Poff."

"Well, I think what we ought to do, Mr. President, is to see how the ABA comes out on Saturday. [And then make a judgment.]"

"I have to get that name up there Monday. Or rather [the] reason that I'd like to [is] we've got another announcement coming too, soon. I'd like to dominate the news next week with at least one announcement on these and maybe two. Can we do it? Well, you could on him at least."

"We can on him, yes."

"The second one?" Nixon asked, hopefully.

"I think we ought to fight this battle. And come with the [other later, not] now."

"All right."

"Would you be disposed to send [Poff] up if the bar disapproves of him?"

"Oh hell yes, by all means. I've decided," Nixon said, banging on his desk. "I'm not going to wait for the bar. I'll be very glad to have the bar, but if the bar disapproves him, I then send him up. And I'll say I'm very interested in having the bar's views but I disagree with them. You think that poses a problem? Of course, that will just give the civil righters a chance to [have an issue]."

"That'll be the issue. And that's what some of our troops will use as an excuse to get out."

"Can't Walsh get his people to wheel this?"

"We have told him in no uncertain terms that this is probably the parting of the ways with the whole operation if they don't act responsibly. And Walsh is trying to do it, there is no question about it because he wants to."

"God, I hate to part with the American Bar. But it looks like it. Ah, Jesus Christ! Maybe it will be all right though, maybe for once they'll come through."

"It may be," Mitchell said soothingly. "Now, we have to also look at the context of it. This is purely an off-the-record, confidential assessment [by the bar]. And what will come about, of course, will be no public statements whether he's qualified, disqualified, or otherwise. But they will, of course, as they do on all these judges, appear and testify before the Judiciary Committee. And that's where you get it, later, down the line."

"Yeah."

"So that is a factor as to how long you can hold your troops. If the American Bar goes up and testifies that he is not qualified because of lack of practice of law, this—"

"The American Bar, of course, they're going to look awful damn small if they say that some God damn little lawyer out in Paducah who has practiced law for fifteen years is better qualified to be in the Supreme Court than somebody that's been on the Judiciary Committee in the House for fifteen years."

"No question."

"God, it's a poor case. However, the way we would [deal with it] is to say that the American Bar has an obsolete deal, and say what about Frankfurter? Under this rule he would never have been [eligible to serve on the Supreme Court]. What about Black, did he practice law?"

"He was a prosecutor for a short period of time and a local police court judge."

"All right. We could say that he could never have qualified for the Supreme Court under this [bar standard]."

"There's no question about it."

"So let's go with Poff now."

"All right, sir."

"Could we do it Monday, then?"

"We can do it anytime you wanted, Mr. President."

"Wednesday?"

"I think Wednesday would be better."

"All right."

"Because it would give us more time for a count."

"All right. Let's take it. Can we set Wednesday as a good day?" Nixon asked.

Mitchell had moved on. "Now do you feel that it's possible to get commitments in advance of this vote? Can Scott go and get them?"

"Sure. Scott and Griffin both can. Scott and Griffin and [Roman] Hruska and I think [unintelligible] can, can easily get them. Is that what you had in mind?"

"Yep."

There followed a brief discussion about getting members of the Senate to commit to Poff, with the president giving general suggestions and telling Mitchell to get hard commitments. Mitchell advised the president that his White House "troops" were "getting crazy" and "concerned about another fight" with the Senate.

"They don't want Poff?" the president worried.

"No, Clark MacGregor does want Poff. But what John Ehrlichman mentioned to me, you're going to have enough problems with your tax bills and so forth, and you don't need another war."

"I know they're going to fight us on anybody. I mean, any judge we send up there risks a God damn litmus test [from the] liberals. John, you've just got to realize that it has nothing to do with Poff, it has to do with the fact that he's a conservative."

"I believe that."

"I just will not send a God damn liberal up to that Court! Okay?"

"I agree." Mitchell suddenly switched topics. "Now, let's talk about the women for a moment. There are just two women who could fit into this category, that would fit in your philosophy. And I'm a little doubtful about one of them because we don't have all of the record. The one that, obviously because she's been on the court for so many years, has expressed her philosophy, is this Judge [Mildred] Lillie in California. She was on the Superior Court out there. She's now on the intermediate Court of Appeals. She's fifty-five years old. She is solidly backed by Reagan, the prosecutors—"

"[Los Angeles mayor Sam] Yorty."

"Yorty, et cetera, et cetera."

"A Democrat too?"

"No. I don't believe she is."

"I think she is."

"Is she?"

"She's one of those [few] conservative [Democrats] out in California. She's in the Court of Appeals in [Los Angeles]," Nixon, the Califorian, reported.

"That's right."

"At fifty-five."

"Um hum. And well recommended by all of the police officers."

"And is she considered to be a good judge?"

"Yes, so far as you can tell. Because, you know, at that level it's disposing of the cases, not writing long, theoretical opinions. And the other one, of course, is Sylvia Bacon, who's got a pretty solid record."

"Tell me about Sylvia Bacon in terms of both of them, that's not to [unintelligible]. How did Lillie do in law school; what kind of a record did she have? Was she a good student?"

"Yeah. She had a good record in law school."

"Good. How about Sylvia?"

"Sylvia Bacon, well, she went to Vassar, and then she went to the London School of Economics, and then she went to Harvard. Her record in Harvard was not too good. Ah, I don't know the circumstances. And then she came out and she got a master of laws degree here at Georgetown University, so she's had a good, solid, long educational background."

"Of course that's awfully good, whatever her record at Harvard was. That's an awfully good record, that's a good track record. Vassar."

"Yes."

"London School of Economics, everybody'll think she's a liberal," said Nixon, with his customary anti-elite bias.

"And give her some breadth. Ah, she's not [a liberal] in the criminal field, and of course—"

"You're sure?"

"I'm sure she's not in the criminal field, but I don't know what, ah, you can't guarantee what might come out of anybody. Her father's a newspaper publisher from the Dakotas. She's conservative, Republican."

"She's Republican?"

"Yes."

"How old, how old is [Sylvia], John?"

"Forty. She just turned forty in July."

"Who worked with her, did you work with her? Did you get a chance to see her work?"

"I have been in conferences with her."

"And how did she act?"

"Good."

"She's an up-and-down?" asked Nixon. This expression appears to refer to Nixon's belief that people in meetings spend too much time talking without saying anything. Both Mitchell and Nixon had low tolerance for this, particularly in formal meetings. An up-and-down was someone who made her point quickly and efficiently.

"Yep, very much so. And in fact, she's dedicated her life to the law so far. She's been on the board of law examiners here, and all these commissions, and she's got a long, long list."

"Lillie is basically the better one. Frankly, she's older. And she can serve on the Court fifteen years."

"Yes."

"Everybody's going to be there until seventy."

"Correct."

"And it'll always be a woman's seat from then on. Fifteen years is about as long as she can [serve]. [Sylvia] probably would appear to be just a little too young. I don't know, what do you think? She isn't by my standards. I wonder if something could be said, John, for appointing a woman who represents the younger generation, not only a woman, but the youngest one ever appointed. Maybe that would be the case. How old was Potter Stewart?"

"Well, Douglas was in his thirties. And I guess Potter Stewart was also."

"I'm ruled out then. Well, that God damn Douglas is no good example. The old fart, though, he looked so good at that funeral, I said, oh Jesus, he's [going to be around awhile]."

"Yeah, didn't he?"

"I think I'm going to get one of those things [a pacemaker] in my heart."

Mitchell chuckled. "What he's doing with it makes it work pretty good." *

"Now, on Sylvia Bacon—Oh, did you get to meet Mildred Lillie, by any chance?"

"No, I haven't."

"Do you know if you have any negative traits on her?"

"No. We haven't, of course, surfaced her," said Mitchell, meaning leaked her name or introduced her to the media. "It's all been a check with the people out there."

"Is she highly regarded?"

"She can't be highly regarded because she is a conservative and of course is in this intermediate court."

"Yep. But it is an appeals court?"

"Yes."

"It's pretty dang good."

"It's like the appellate division in New York."

"Right, right."

"Now, one other thought in here, Mr. President. I would believe that if you didn't go with a woman, realizing you're going to have to have a southerner, no matter how far you have to battle for it, you've got to have somebody from the South. [I'm told that] your friend [William French] Smith from California would probably be the ideal choice as a second man on the appointment to the Court."

"Would he?"

"Yeah."

"You've got an eye on him?"

"Mum hum. Just very impressive, a very impressive record."

---

*Justice William O. Douglas was married to a woman young enough to be his granddaughter.

Mitchell continued, "If you feel [you need to] go with a woman, I've mixed emotions about that."

"I know, I know. Let me tell you so that we have a total understanding on this."

"Yeah."

"I don't think a woman should be in any government job whatever. I mean, I really don't. The reason why I do is mainly because they are erratic. And emotional. Men are erratic and emotional too, but the point is a woman is more likely to be."

"Right."

"The second problem they've got is that in terms of the Court, I know that that's like living with somebody inside of a spaceship."

"Yep."

"See, you're just one little [group of] people."

"Absolutely."

"What about that poor Burger? What he'd have to go through? So from the standpoint of that, I just think we shouldn't have a woman. There should never be a woman there. In a political sense, you know, it comes right down to cold turkey. If you were to poll the country, seventy percent of the people would say, no, they don't want a woman on the Supreme Court, I am sure. However, if you were to poll the country and say if the President appoints a woman, would you vote against him for that reason?, it would be zero. On the other hand, if a woman were appointed, it could affect one or two percent, who would say because he appointed a woman, I am for him. Now it's as cold as that. [It would show everybody] that we care about women. My God, we've put a woman on the Supreme Court. There's another important fact with all this talk of whether [we will or won't]. Whatever you and I think about the woman thing, and whatever Burger thinks, and we all think alike, believe me, women's lib is here, [and] it is a growing thing. And the demand is there. And the woman's viewpoint probably ought to be on the Court. It isn't a man's world anymore, unfortunately. So I lean to a woman only because, frankly, I think at this time, John, we got to pick up every half a percentage point we can. Now there's the darn [situation in a nutshell]. We've got to make a little political [hay]. All right if she's a conservative. Now if she's liberal, the hell with it. I won't appoint any liberal [to the Court]."

"No, I think this woman will qualify."

"Lillie?" Nixon asked, to be sure.

"Lillie. Um hum."

"Would you raise her over Bacon?"

"I would for this reason, Mr. President. Bacon is young and she is an unknown in the civil rights field."

"Well, do you think Lillie is known in the civil rights field?"

"From what readings we've had to date she's just conservative period. All across the board."

"One thing about the woman conservative, these bastards can't vote against her."

"I would believe not, I don't see how. Because they all get up there [and] scream and put you in the spot thinking they're—"

"Thinking that I won't do it."

"That you won't do it, and that they're all out for it, the Bayhs and the Kennedys."

"Let me ask you to do this. There's no reason we can't have two from California. We've got two from Minnesota. If we could get another seat, other than the Black seat, I think Smith would be a hell of a fight because that's the kind of a guy that is in, you know, frankly, is in the league with a Burger. I mean, he's a real student of the law, right?"

"He is that."

"And he's a guy I'd rather appoint. But who has told you about Lillie? Is it Reagan?"

"Reagan, Younger." Evelle Younger was the top city prosecutor in Los Angeles.

"What'd Younger think of her?"

"Thinks she's just hard as nails on criminal law."

"Younger did?"

"Yeah."

"Well, Younger's a liberal, and he [Reagan] likes her."

"Oh yeah. No, Younger's not [a liberal]. Not in the criminal law."

"No, that's right. But what's he say?"

"He called me Sunday morning, after a lot of these names [of women] got out [in the newspaper]. And, of course, they were almost jumping out of the wall when they heard about [Shirley] Hufstedler [a federal judge on Ninth Circuit Court of Appeals]. That, you know, that [she might be under consideration]."

"She lefty, isn't she?"

"Lefty, Democrat, whose name has been so prominent."

"I know. Well, the names that I saw were all lefties."

"With respect to Mildred Lillie, according to all the people that have been checked, including the District Attorney's Office out there, and the U.S. Attorney's Office, and so forth, [her reputation is] just as solid as can be in the criminal law. According to the opinions that our people have read—[including] Bill Rehnquist [who] is very conservative—"

The president laughed at this understatement.

Mitchell continued, "He says that her philosophy is the same as yours. We've checked through some of the judges that have sat with her on the different courts out there, who are now up on the Ninth Circuit, conservative judges. They say that her philosophy is conservative."

"Um hum. Where'd she go to school, John? Cal, probably University of Southern Cal?"

"I'm not certain, I don't have that here, Mr. President."

"That's all right, doesn't make a difference. Law school [doesn't matter]. Reagan is for her?"

"Very much so. That's if it's a woman, then he's very strong for her."

"All right. Let's run her by. I think the Bacon one is a little too soon. Is that your [thinking]? I think that she's a better appointment, frankly, because I think she's more in tune with national politics, basically."

"I believe so and she's probably has a wider exposure to Washington and legislation and so forth."

"Yep, but isn't she just a little early?"

"I think that this would be the criticism."

"Mildred Lillie will have a hell of a time, and she's been judge for longer than I can remember, I think twenty years."

"Yep, well, she's been on the District Court of Appeals since 1958 and she sat on the Supreme Court for quite a number of years before that."

"The District Court of Appeals since '50?"

"Since '58."

"My, just think of it, that's thirteen years. All right. We go with her.

Now, let me [ask] you this. How about sending her name first? [No,] Poff should go first."

"I think so, I think otherwise we're going to get mouse-trapped."

"Good. Well, try to get Poff on Wednesday if you can. Wednesday or Thursday [October 6 or 7] at latest if you can. Could you do that for next week?"

Mitchell said he could.

The decision had been made. The president had selected Dick Poff and Mildred Lillie. He was delighted: "A conservative woman, from California. God! That will kill them!" Nixon alluded to his daughter and wife telling him that "women lib" was something that was important to women. While both men acknowledged that Chief Justice Burger was not going to be happy, Mitchell assured the president that "Warren Burger's a good soldier."

As the meeting was coming to a close, both men expressed concern about the bar committee rejecting Poff. This prompted Mitchell to suggest other southerners he believed would have no problem getting approved by the bar.

"We could get Lewis Powell confirmed in a minute."

"Why not? How old is he?"

"He's a good sixty-four, but we could get him confirmed in a minute. They couldn't possibly go against him."

"No."

"And he's got the same judicial [philosophy]."

"Just because of the age, his age problem."

"Age is the only factor."

"But he would stay for ten [years at least]."

"Or, we could go to Herschel Friday and let them take it on again. [The Senate can't reject southerners], you know, forever. And I know that the bar would, well, we could submit both of them to the bar and see how they came out."

"Well, let's hope for the best on Poff," the president said.

• • • •

On Friday, October 1, the president traveled with his family to their home in Key Biscayne, Florida, to take a break. I went to Ehrlichman's office to plan strategy for the Poff confirmation. In attendance were Bud Krogh,

David Young, Clark MacGregor (the former congressman who was now in charge of congressional relations at the White House), Dick Moore (a special counsel), Bill Timmons (MacGregor's top deputy), and Wally Johnson (the Justice Department congressional relations man). The consensus of the congressional vote counters was that Poff would have a fight but would win. At most the opposition could muster 37 votes against his confirmation, but they did not have the 34 votes to sustain a filibuster (an alternative way to block Poff) since not all opponents were sufficiently rabid.

Later that afternoon, I received an unexpected call from Congressman Poff. I was on the telephone when my secretary placed a note on my desk: "Dick Poff, says it's urgent." I completed my call and telephoned Poff immediately.[5]

"Congressman, what's up?"

"John, this is not a pleasant call for me to make. My wife and I have been talking about what this nomination is doing to our lives, and I've been doing some vote counting, and it doesn't look real good. I've decided that I should withdraw."

Pause. I was speechless, astounded. Dick Poff had never walked away from a political fight in his life. He had been in public office for twenty years. I figured that like many men I had taken through the confirmation process, he just needed a little reassurance and hand-holding. "That's a pretty grim assessment, Dick. Maybe we should talk about this."

"I'm working on a statement. If you'd meet me in my office, on the Hill, in a half hour, I'd sure be appreciative."

"You've got it. See you then," I said. This was a major development that needed to be reported immediately. I called Ehrlichman.

"Sounds like the jitters," Ehrlichman said. "Do you think you can bring him around?"

"I don't know. Poff did not make that call without a hell of a lot of thought. I'm not sure what's going on. I'll give it my best shot, and let you know," I promised.

"Tell him that the president wants him to sleep on it, will you?"

En route to Capitol Hill in a White House car, I tried to imagine why Poff would turn down this chance of a lifetime. Was he worried that the ABA evaluation committee would declare him unqualified? Did he have doubts about his own qualifications? Was there something hidden in his past that had not surfaced but might? I could not imagine. When I arrived at Poff's Rayburn Building office, I was met by a somber-looking Jack White, Poff's administrative assistant. Poff was on the telephone behind closed doors.

"What's happened, Jack?" I inquired.

"He'll have to tell you."

"Can I talk him out of it?"

"I couldn't. He's working on his statement. I think he's talking to Wally Johnson. He wants the Justice Department to stop the Bar Association from considering him."

"Damn," I said. This was not good. He was spreading the word, which made it very unlikely he would change his mind. When the light on the telephone in the reception area went off, Jack White opened the door to Poff's office, and I went in. I found Poff smiling. Actually, he looked relieved, as though a weight had been lifted from his shoulders. Poff crossed the office to shake hands, employing one of his bone-crushing grips that he enjoyed giving his friends, which only hurt if you had not fully grasped his powerful right hand. He was telegraphing his good spirits, which I had not expected.

"Sit down, John," he said as he returned to his desk. "Now, before you try to change my mind, you need to understand why you can't." Jack White left the room, closing the door behind him. "What I want to tell you, I don't want you to tell anyone. Is that agreeable? If not, I won't burden you with it."

I agreed.

Poff explained his regret at backing out at the last minute. He knew the time and trouble that many people had gone to for his nomination. He wanted me to understand that this was neither an easy nor a quick decision. In fact, he worried that Virginia Republicans would be so displeased they would try to block him from returning to the Congress.

He said that he had spent the last week counting votes in the Senate. While he had enough votes to get confirmed, he was worried about a filibuster to block his nomination. Poff said that during the Republican filibuster of Fortas in 1969, he had told Jerry Ford, who was a Michigan friend of Griffin's, that the senator was making a mistake. He was setting a precedent for Democrats to block Nixon nominees. "Little did I realize that I was talking about myself," Poff added. When I told him that I disagreed on the cloture vote count, Poff continued, "It isn't the filibuster defeating my nomination that is causing me to withdraw, although we both know a dragged-out confirmation proceeding is not going to be good for the Court, particularly with two vacancies."

Poff then got to the heart of the problem. He explained that his wife had discovered that his new high visibility as a controversial Supreme Court nominee was causing people to talk, to ask questions about his family and children, and he was certain that if he went forward, and particularly if there was a protracted filibuster, it would get worse.

"I assure you, John, I don't have anything to hide," Poff noted. "But my opponents, or people who want to hurt either me or my family for my political position, can do so."

"How so?" I asked.

"You recall when you were here with that other fellow, David Young, from the White House, I told you that Jo Ann and I had adopted one of our sons, Tommy?"

"I do."

"Well, Jo Ann and I are worried sick that if my nomination goes forward, the fact that Tommy is adopted is going to come out. It is inevitable. All our friends know it. We've never hidden it. Everyone knows but Tommy. He is a very sensitive child. We consulted a psychologist, and we were told to wait until the boy had matured more, until he was seventeen or eighteen, then to tell him. I can't risk going forward with this thing, because I don't want to do anything to hurt that boy. I love him, and would feel terrible if my ambitions hurt him."

I had no basis to tell Poff he was wrong. In fact, he was probably correct. Poff had considered telling the child, but he and his wife had rejected that solution. It was obvious to me that there was nothing more to discuss about his decision to withdraw. It was a noble, and loving, action. I only regretted that no one would know why he had taken it.

"So, how about looking over my statement? Let me show you what I've come up with," Poff said, handing me a sheet from a yellow legal pad, on which he had typed his announced withdrawal:

> I have asked the President not to consider my name for nomination to the Supreme Court.
>
> In the shadow of the ABA Committee rating and with little time remaining in this session of the Congress, it is unlikely that the Senate could conduct hearings and conclude floor debate this year.

From press reports, it is clear that the confirmation process would be protracted and controversial. I have been called a racist. I am not. I have never been. I will never be. With respect to the Southern Manifesto, my voting record and whatever I have written or said, I can only ask that all remember the temper of the times, consider the fact that the people's representative is in large part the property of the people he represents and believe the simple truth that none of my words or deeds have been motivated by prejudice, racial, religious or otherwise.

My decision is prompted by four imperatives.

It is imperative to the Supreme Court that both vacancies be filled promptly.

It is imperative to the nation there be no more confirmation battles pitched on the racial ramparts.

It is imperative to my family that they be spared the agonies of such a battle, whether the result is defeat or victory.

It is imperative to me that I make the decision that responds to those imperatives.[6]

It certainly did the job, stating his public reason but also including his private reason. However, I suggested the second paragraph be deleted. I assumed the Justice Department had warned him about the possibility of Senate stalling, but it was moot now. After a brief discussion, Poff deleted the entire second paragraph.

"Dick, I told John Ehrlichman that I was coming to visit you, and the reason for the visit. Ehrlichman said the president would ask you to sleep on this tonight. But I'd like to give the White House a copy of your announcement, and request that you hold it until tomorrow. And, indeed, that you sleep on it one more night."

"Fair enough," Poff said. I went to a telephone, dictated the statement to my secretary, and requested that she deliver it to Ehrlichman. While reading it aloud, I felt the paragraph filled with denials was overly defensive, and when I returned, I urged Poff to take all these statements out as well. Poff agreed.

I was very disappointed that evening. I knew that Poff would not change his mind in the morning, and he did not. Poff was putting on a good front, and was relieved to have made his decision, but I knew him well enough to understand that this had been a devastating, if not shattering, experience for him. I later suggested to Haldeman that the president call Poff, a gesture of support and understanding, after the news of

Poff's withdrawal shocked official Washington on Saturday, October 2. In the days that followed, editorials from newspapers like the *New York Times* praised his withdrawal, because it would spare the nation a divisive confirmation battle; conservative newspapers were appalled that a southern conservative could not be appointed the Supreme Court.

When Haldeman delivered the news to the president, who was in Florida, it angered him. Not Poff's decision, but the fact that another southerner was put off by the mere prospect of what the Senate would do to him. Haldeman noted in his diary that the president said "he's going to go for a real right-winger now, that is stronger than Poff on civil rights. . . . He wants to get someone worse than Poff and really stick it to the opposition now." Haldeman recorded that the president "came up with the idea of [Robert] Byrd of West Virginia because he was a former KKK'er, he's elected by the Democrats as Whip, he's a self-made lawyer, he's more reactionary than Wallace, and he's about 53." [7]

• • • •

The Poff exit had an ironic twist at the end, involving a disgusting a bit of journalism. Later in October, Poff learned that syndicated muckraker Jack Anderson was working on a story about the true reason he had withdrawn. Poff suspected the story had leaked from one of the few of his colleagues in the House whom he had told. So much time and effort had been spent by the Republican leadership to gather support for him that he had had to be square with the leaders. One of them might have spilled the beans. Anderson had decided that the public should know that Poff had placed his family above his career, and withdrawn to protect his adopted son. Poff pleaded that Anderson not write such a story because it revealed the very facts he sought to protect. When it became clear that Anderson was going to do it, one way or another, Poff decided he had to tell his son first. The child took it better than had been expected. Anderson's story appeared in his "Washington Merry-Go-Round" column in *The Washington Post* on November 2, 1971. [8]

A very angry Dick Poff related this story to me shortly before Anderson published. I wondered if Poff was heartsick that he had not told his son a few weeks earlier and then proceeded to fight for his seat. By the time of this conversation, his place had been filled by another.

PART TWO

7

————

TESTING HOW BYRD
MIGHT FLY

October 2–11

THE *NEW YORK TIMES* STORY on Poff's withdrawal, leaked by Ehrlichman, reported that "High administration officials said flatly that the White House had counted so heavily on Poff's successful ascension to the Court that no alternative nominee immediately came to mind when the popular conservative abruptly and publicly withdrew from consideration."[1] The story was correct. The president, and his staff, believed Poff was as good as on the Court, and we suddenly found ourselves back at the starting line. It was time to scramble. Ehrlichman, in a talk with Haldeman in Florida, had received directions from the president and summoned me to his office on Saturday morning.'"

Shortly before noon, I found Bud Krogh and David Young in Ehrlichman's West Wing office. No one was happy with Poff's decision. No one understood it, and I felt limited in what I could say. Ehrlichman asked me if Poff had withdrawn because of a financial problem. I responded that while Poff was concerned that he might have difficulty documenting his finances, nothing was amiss. "John, apparently this has been very difficult on Poff's family," I reported.[2] "He's been accused of being a racist, his children are getting flak at school, his wife has not enjoyed being in the spotlight. He is withdrawing for family reasons. For me to say anything more would breach a confidence."[3] Ehrlichman did not press me.

"Well, let me tell you fellows why I asked you to drop by. Haldeman's talked to the president. Mitchell apparently has a woman he's recommending, a judge in California. But I would like to have some alternatives," Ehrlichman stated, explaining that Mitchell was giving the president a very limited menu for selections.

"What about the Black seat?" Krogh interrupted.

Ehrlichman, who was stretched out in an easy chair with his feet up on a table, chuckled. The notepad resting on his substantial stomach gently shook. "Well, the leader of the Western world is thinking about substituting the distinguished Senator from West Virginia, Robert Byrd, for Poff."

"Is Byrd a lawyer?" a startled Young asked.

"He has a law degree, but that's all. It's not his legal acumen that attracts our president. Rather it is his past affiliation with the Ku Klux Klan, combined with the fact the United States Senate could not vote against him."

"Surely he's jesting," Young protested.

"I'm not so sure," Ehrlichman opined. "Richard Nixon likes him. He told me one time that Byrd reminded him of a mean little rooster a neighbor had when the president was a child. He said the rooster raised hell from sunup until sundown."

Ehrlichman said he wanted Young to assist me in developing additional candidates, starting with women, since "the president appears truly interested in appointing the first woman to the Supreme Court. Haldeman says he keeps coming back to it. The president thinks it could have significant political benefits in '72. And I agree with him." As for the Poff replacement, Ehrlichman's parting instruction to his legal team was "put on your thinking caps, and find a nominee who is more conservative than Poff, but can get confirmed. If there is such a creature."

· · · ·

By Monday morning, Mitchell was back from California and in his office at the Department of Justice. His first call, at 9:50 a.m., was to Rehnquist, to tell him that the president had given the nod to Mildred Lillie, and that during his own trip to California (Mitchell had given a graduation address at the Los Angeles Police Academy) he had received further positive assurances about Judge Lillie. Rehnquist was to take a close look at Judge Lillie's decisions. With Poff out of play, Mitchell said he was going to ask Herschel Friday to come to Washington, for he was now his lead candidate for Justice Black's seat.

That same day, at the White House, Young and I met. He was eager to take on the work of gathering names. This pleased me, for I had no interest in getting between Ehrlichman and Mitchell's mutual disenchantment. I suggested that David visit with Barbara Franklin, a member of the White House staff, who had been asked by Haldeman a few days earlier to come up with potential women nominees for the Supreme Court. I had just received her list.

"I don't know where Barbara got these names, but it's an interesting cross section," I said, and passed a copy of the material to Young. Barbara Franklin had listed twelve women, noting their current positions along with party affiliations, ages, and in several instances, their philosophical leanings. In addition she had sent me copies of their résumés.[4] "We can scratch the liberal Democrats," I told David. "I'm not sure why she included them. There's not a chance the president will appoint a Shirley Hufstedler." That eliminated four candidates. "The judge Ehrlichman mentioned who is under consideration is Mildred Lillie. Rehnquist is studying her opinions as we speak. So you don't need to work on her."

Young was pleased that a woman was being considered.

"Frankly, David, the most interesting of Barbara's candidates is Jewel Lafontant. She was a candidate for the Illinois appellate court last year. According to her résumé, we've already appointed her to an advisory commission on international education and cultural affairs, and the President's Council on Minority Business Enterprises, which means she can pass political muster. It's an impressive résumé, for anyone. It's even more impressive because she's a black woman."

• • • •

It was that day—October 4—that I first floated the name of William Rehnquist. I did it in a seemingly innocuous conversation, with a staffer who was not directly involved in the search. Richard Moore, who held the title of special counsel to the president, dropped by my office that afternoon. While Dick was a White House lawyer, he was not in the White House counsel's office. Dick had practiced in New York City before serving in World War II; after the war he was an assistant general counsel at American Broadcasting Corporation, then moved over to management and held several top positions with various broadcasting enterprises. Rather than retire at the end of his successful career, at fifty-six years of age, Moore had agreed to come to Washington to help his old friend Dick Nixon. His first assignment, in 1970, was at the Department of Justice. There he went to work with Mitchell, to help him with a serious public relations problem: Mitchell was perceived as a dour Nixon heavy—the suppressor of free speech and petition relating to the anti–Vietnam War movement. Moore understood the media, and so as special assistant to the attorney general he was able successfully to repackage John Mitchell into a more homogenized, pipe-puffing Wall Street lawyer who only sought to bring commonsense and order to government. With that completed, Moore moved to the White House in 1971. Moore had a full head of white hair and a grandfatherly appearance and manner in the young Nixon White House, and he floated from assignment to assignment, offering sage political and public relations advice to the White House staff.

As he settled into an easy chair in front of the long table I used for a desk, he said a friend had recommended that the president take a look at a professor at the University of Chicago Law School, a Russian-born woman who, he was told, was brilliant. Moore, who struggled with the woman's name, said he understood that Barbara Franklin had sent me her résumé. I retrieved the file, and we found her—Soia Mentschikoff.

"Barbara indicates that she's a liberal Democrat. But I don't think that's going to fly," I observed.

"No, nor do I," Moore commented, tilting his head to better focus his bifocals. "But sometimes you've got to do things just to say you've done them. Maybe she'd be good for the court of appeals." He asked for and was given a copy of the résumé. As often happened when Dick visited, he and I were soon deep in conversation. I had known Dick ever since we both were at the Justice Department. He did not like the rumblings he was hearing that the president was considering Senator Byrd of West Virginia. I decided to test a thought that had been in my mind since Ehrlichman asked for a candidate more conservative than Poff who could get confirmed.

"The president has a perfect candidate right under his nose," I said as our conversation progressed.

"Who's that?"

"William H. Rehnquist."

Moore, who occasionally stuttered or stammered when excited, was intrigued. "B-, B-, Bill, Bill Rehnquist, that's very interesting. That's even creative," he said approvingly.

"Bill Rehnquist makes Dick Poff look like an unabashed liberal," I added.

"Really?"

"Absolutely. You've talked to him?"

"Sure, while I was over at Justice. But I don't know much about his politics," Moore said.

"Bill Rehnquist makes Barry Goldwater look like a liberal. When I was in law school, I used to go up to the Senate to watch the proceedings with one of my classmates, Paul Bible, whose father was in the Senate."

"Alan Bible, from Nevada, sure."

"The most historic vote I witnessed was on the 1964 Civil Rights Act. The filibuster had been broken, and everyone wondered how Barry Goldwater was going to vote. He was running for president, and a lot of attention was on him on that vote."

"I remember it well. You and Barry Junior are longtime friends, aren't you?"

"Right, since about fourteen years of age. Barry wanted me to drop out of law school and work on his dad's presidential campaign. But I couldn't do it. Anyway, Senator Goldwater, as you will recall, voted against the Civil Rights Act. I was surprised, because I knew that he was not against blacks having their civil rights. Exactly the opposite, in fact. So after the campaign, after he'd been walloped by Lyndon Johnson, I was talking with him one night, and asked him why he voted against the '64 Civil Rights Act. He knew it was politically a bad vote. But he said he had sought the best legal advice he could get, at the time, as to whether the law was constitutional. He said he was advised that it was unconstitutional, and likely would be so found by the Supreme Court. His advice came from the most conservative lawyer he'd ever met—Bill Rehnquist."

"No kidding."

"Rehnquist is no racist. But he is far to the right of Dick Poff in his thinking on civil rights, in fact, on any constitutional issue you can think of. My files are laced with Rehnquist memos that show not only his conservatism, but its sophistication. Bill understands why he holds his conservative views."

The more we talked, the more interested Dick Moore became. When I told Moore that Rehnquist had been a law clerk for Justice Robert Jackson, after graduating at the top of his class from Stanford Law School, he agreed that the president should consider him for the high court. When Moore left my office he was carrying not only the résumé of Soia Mentschikoff but a résumé of Bill Rehnquist, which I had acquired while at the Justice Department.

In making this suggestion, I knew exactly what I was doing. Dick Moore moved about the White House, from office to office, chatting, sharing his thoughts, and always attributing his sources.[5] The White House grapevine winds around the EOB, and the West Wing, with the trellises ending in the Oval Office. I had delighted in being an agent for history with Dick Poff, but now I needed a new principal. I had believed in Poff. With Bill Rehnquist, it would be a game. If the president really wanted a young strict constructionist, I had his man. The reaction I had gotten from Dick Moore, who had an intuition to spot problems, told me I had the right candidate again.

• • • •

At 2:30 p.m. on Tuesday, October 5, John Mitchell called his old friend Herschel Friday, in Little Rock, Arkansas. Mitchell requested that Friday come to Washington as soon as possible, to meet with Bill Rehnquist and himself. Mitchell told him he was now a serious contender for a nomination to be an associate justice. Friday said he could be there Thursday. This would give him a day to inform his law partners and pull together his own thoughts.

The president, anxious to know how things were progressing, called Mitchell shortly before 4:00 p.m.[6]

"We're still on the same course, that we talked about yesterday morning, and they're getting background on [Lillie and Friday]," Mitchell told him. "One question that I had. . . . Would you feel it appropriate that we put your friend [David] Dyer into the southern [seat]?"

"Isn't he too old?"

"He's sixty-one."

"No, I think it would be appropriate."

"It might be an attractive fallback position, you know. If that came to the top and I can't think it'd be other than complimentary," Mitchell suggested.

The president gave Mitchell a name that had been mentioned to him that afternoon, by Dudley Swim, the head of National Airlines. Swim had mentioned the new president of the ABA. "Some sort of a Polish name," Nixon said.

"Leon Jaworski?"

"Jaworski." *

"I know him very well. He's a very close friend of, ah, Lyndon Johnson's."

"Oh." Nixon was not necessarily high on friends of LBJ, and he wanted to keep Mitchell on target. "Well, I hope you can sell Lillie."

"I believe that this can be done. I don't believe that anybody is going to be able to stand in the way of her," Mitchell optimistically noted.

"I hope you can sell her to the C.J. [Chief Justice Burger]. He understands that he's got to. Does [Senator John] McClellan know Friday?"

"Oh, yes. Very, very, very, very close to him."

"Right. And strong for him?"

"Yeah."

"I like that. Incidentally, you got no idea as to when you can get any name we can submit?"

"Well, I would hope that before the week is out we can have the package up there."

"Good, all right. Fine, whatever you recommend, I'll do."

Early on Wednesday morning, October 6, Senator Barry Goldwater called Nixon. At the end of their conversation, the president mentioned his Supreme Court nominations, which prompted Goldwater to mention his former adviser, Bill Rehnquist. However, Senator Goldwater could not

*Nixon would later appoint Leon Jaworski Watergate special prosecutor.

recall Rehnquist's name. Remarkably, Nixon knew the man that Goldwater was *not* identifying.[7]

"You know there is a young fellow in the Justice Department. You know, I can't think of his name. He's only forty-one or forty-two years old. Oh God, his name slips me. He comes from Arizona and Kleindienst knows him well. He's probably the greatest authority on the Constitution in the country today."

"In Justice?"

"Yeah. Ah, Bill Rensler [sic]," Goldwater said. The Senator was talking about Rehnquist but had the wrong name.

"Oh, I know Rensler well. He's an excellent man." Nixon was not much better on the name, but he seemed to know who Goldwater was talking about.

"And the papers he's done on the Constitution—"

"Are great," the president acknowledged.

"[He's respected by] every expert I know. He'd be the greatest thing [for the Court]."

"Yep. The great difficulty is that the damn bar would have a [unintelligible], because of his lack of, you know, any bar prep. But he's the right age and everything."

"I've never been one who thought that judicial experience was necessary." Nor, Nixon reassured Goldwater, did he. Goldwater continued, "Well, I know you're going to do the right thing. I wouldn't let these bastards worry you."

"They're not worrying me a bit. Not one bit," Nixon reassured him.

• • • •

On Thursday, as promised, Herschel Friday flew to Washington and met with Mitchell and others for vetting. Meanwhile, however, Nixon was pondering ways to play hardball with the Senate. The next day, in a meeting with Mitchell and Ehrlichman, he lit the fuse of his whimsical stink bomb and started it rolling toward Capitol Hill.

Ehrlichman had requested that the president convene the meeting because the president's top domestic adviser had decided to make his presence felt in the high court selection process.[8] A few minutes after 10:00 a.m., Mitchell and Ehrlichman trooped into the Oval Office, their growing weariness with and wariness of one another politely hidden. The president got right down to business.[9]

Earlier that morning, the president and Ehrlichman had been together at breakfast in the Family Dining Room with Senator Russell B. Long, the powerful Democratic senator from Louisiana. Nixon reported to Mitchell that Long had a recommendation for the high court, which could not easily be ignored. Nixon quoted Long as saying, "I've got the man for the Court." Long had told him he "ought to appoint a Democrat, you ought to appoint a senator, you ought to appoint one of these sons of bitches [they can't reject, like Bob Byrd]." Nixon continued, "And I said, Bob Byrd will go through like greased lightning."

Horrified, Mitchell sarcastically noted, "He'd go through the Senate. But with that background? Well, that and he never practiced law!"

Nixon, however, was delighting in Byrd's non-qualifications. "Never practiced law, has only been a lawyer seven years, and a member of the Ku Klux Klan probably. I don't know about the latter. The point is [it would sure] raise hell and the rest. Frankly, Byrd's tough as hell, honest, totally respected—even the liberals respect the little fellow. He's gutsy, very gutsy."

Mitchell told the president he would be accused of playing politics with the Court, not to mention placing an unqualified man there. This resulted in Nixon quipping, "I'd have to agree to put on a man who's qualified, like Thurgood Marshall with civil rights." Mitchell laughed.* The president proceeded.

"Well, anyway, and incidentally, Russell [Long] said he and [Democratic senator from Alabama] John Sparkman talked to Eastland about [confirming Bob Byrd]; he says [Chairman of the Senate Judiciary Committee James] Eastland said he agreed to take him [Byrd] and he'd go through like greased lightning."

"Sure, because that's part of the club. But I think the public—" Before Mitchell could describe his feelings about the public's outrage, the president cut him off.

"—Let's look at it from terms, sure, the country will raise hell that they put [Byrd on the Court], but let's look at it in terms of a man on the Court. He'd be the strongest man on that Court, in my opinion. You

---

*Whatever the president said during the next half minute was withdrawn as "personal."

couldn't budge that son of a bitch. He is tough. He is tough. Tough on law and order too. Tough on all the things that I want somebody to be tough on. Tough on capital punishment."

"It'd take him years to get the nuances of, to work on that Court, to be effective, I would believe," Mitchell said.

"Maybe."

"But I'm looking at it, as the criticism of the crassness of the politics."

"I know. Well, I guess it's out of the question, but I just sort of think sometimes we got to do something out of the question the way they've kicked us in the ass three times now. Incidentally, John, there have been very good editorials in the southern papers [about Poff]."

Both Nixon and Mitchell were pleased with the media reaction to Poff's withdrawal. Mitchell told the president that even the left-leaning *Village Voice* had been quoted by the television networks as saying the liberals had overreacted.

Mitchell continued: "And another point with respect to Byrd, and that is, the next time around if you want to get another one of this type, not [from] the South but [from] the border states where you have a justification for it—"

"—[Senator Howard] Baker," Nixon interrupted.

"No, I'm talking about Byrd."

Nixon then made clear to Mitchell *his* point. He wanted to give the Senate a clear message about rejecting a southern member of Congress like Poff. "[I]f you turn down one of our congressmen, we'll give them another." Although Nixon found Bob Byrd "[a cranky] little bastard, I like him. By God he's strong. He's a strong man! God, what a guy to have on that Court. He wouldn't be like Potter Stewart who came down here [to Washington] pretty clean, nice little fellow from Ohio, and goes out to Georgetown and his wife loves the parties and the rest and then comes the big case, the *Times* case,* and he goes to pieces. This is all Potter Stewart."

"I quite agree with you. I knew Byrd back in West Virginia before I ever got to Washington. There's quite a family there, you know. There's all different branches of them."

New York Times v. United States, 403 U.S. 713 (decided June 26, 1971, with Justice Stewart voting against the government effort to enjoin release of the Pentagon Papers, when Nixon's appointees Burger and Blackmun had voted for the government).

"That hurts. The Democrats in the country will think it's [Virginia senator] Harry Byrd's son," Nixon commented.

"They won't know the difference."

"Well, what would, what would the bar say? Would they just flat out disapprove him?" Nixon asked.

When Mitchell reported that Byrd had gone "to law school when he was in the Senate," the president wondered if he had practiced while in the Senate. Mitchell noted that the canons of ethics have prohibited that in recent years. Mitchell was trying hard to shut down the Byrd candidacy, but he didn't understand Nixon's thinking. It was a bluff on the president's part.

"Throw his name in," Nixon directed.

"You want to put his name in?" a disbelieving Mitchell repeated.

"Put his name in, yeah. God damn it, John, Frankfurter didn't practice law! Not a day. Did he?"

"Yes, he was in the U.S. Attorney's Office." *

"Yeah, for what? And now, what, that's the last he practiced law."

"Four years, I think it was."

"A U.S. Attorney compared with being in the United States Senate? Now which is the practice of law?"

"Mr. President, I agree with you completely, and all I have to say is—"

"Well, that's the way lawyers are. Lawyers are inbred, just like doctors, aren't worth a damn."

"I quite agree with that too. I'm getting less respect for them every day I deal with the bar."

Half-demanding, half-pleading, Nixon said, "Throw his name into the pile, will you?"

"All right."

"He's a man of enormous character, and another thing the bar should consider, that it'd be healthy to have a guy go up and go through. Got to keep moving."

Mitchell made another effort to have Nixon reconsider. "There's one

*Felix Frankfurter was assistant U.S. attorney (1906–10) in New York and a legal officer (1911–14) in the Bureau of Insular Affairs. As a professor (1914–39) at Harvard Law School, he also practiced law when appointed to special government posts. In addition Frankfurter fought for the release of Sacco and Vanzetti, and was a founder of the American Civil Liberties Union.

thing I want to point out to you. You get started down this road, the pressures are going to mount on you tremendously."

"To what, appoint more senators?"

"No, to appoint Byrd. Regardless of what the bar says, or regardless of what the public says, or regardless of what anybody says."

"To appoint Byrd?"

"Byrd. You get this started down this road, you'll have tremendous pressures to go ahead with it."

"No turning back," Ehrlichman cautioned.

"That's about it," Mitchell said, puffing on his pipe, and hoping that at least he had caused Nixon to have second thoughts. He hadn't, however.

"Yeah, well, start it. I'm going to do it," Nixon announced defiantly. "Well, I like him. I don't like [him] because of the politics at all. I don't care about the West Virginia seat and I don't care about the Senate. Damn, I know him and he's got character. I just—"

"But that's [still] what you [are] going to be hung with. The politics of it," Mitchell assured him.

"I guess so. However, can you think of anybody else who would not get hung? And so we'll give them [Herschel] Friday," the president said.

Talk of hanging brought Ehrlichman back into the conversation. Ehrlichman had obviously told the president that the White House should make its own checks on Mitchell's candidates. The president simply told Mitchell that he wanted John Ehrlichman to call Friday. Mitchell said nothing. Ehrlichman, concerned that they were going "down that same road" as they had with other southern candidates, offered a new name for consideration: "Is Howard Baker any kind of a possibility?"

"Howard Baker is a possibility," Mitchell replied.* After a brief discussion, the president returned to where he had started.

"Just put Byrd's name in [the list going to the ABA] because I would like to see what will happen," he instructed.

"All right. But I tell you that you get started down that road, you may have some tremendous pressures out of that Senate."

"I know. We can just kind of say no, that's all. We can say no because the

---

*The next 1 minute 13 seconds of conversation about Baker has been withdrawn as "personal."

bar turned him down, blame the damn bar. I don't mind the bar being blamed," Nixon said. "But you've got a couple of other good names. Maybe one of them will turn up sometime."

"I think [Herschel] Friday is going to work pretty good."

"Really?"

"The more I get into it. He's been in here yesterday and today. They're doing the tax returns and the net worth statement and so forth."

"Is he a really successful lawyer, big in the ABA?"

"Yeah."

"Burger recommended him?"

"Burger recommended him, he has the largest law firm in the state, the most successful one. He's been in the [ABA's] House of Delegates since '54."

"Has he written books or some articles?"

"He's written articles," Mitchell reported, adding, "he's taught federal practice, and so forth."

"He's sort of an Arkansas Harlan," Nixon observed.

"Yes, because he—"

"Not bad. We need a businessman." Nixon was getting interested.

Mitchell reported that the forty-nine-year-old Friday's clients included the Missouri Pacific Railroad, school boards, and the telephone company. The president noted that Arkansas was not considered a southern or right-wing state. After a brief discussion of a proposed constitutional amendment on school busing, Nixon directed the conversation back to Mitchell's timing.

"On the Court thing, you have any ideas as to when we could have a name? I have a rather significant announcement I'm going to make on Tuesday. So it can't be Wednesday and it can't be Monday." Mitchell said they could be ready by Wednesday, October 13, or any time thereafter. Nixon said he would like to have it next Thursday or Friday. Mitchell said either day was fine. Mildred Lillie would be in town on Monday.

"Incidentally, be sure she meets the Chief Justice on that day in order to help us [cushion the situation]," Nixon said.

Mitchell, puffing his pipe, shook his head.

"You don't want to? [You've not] had that horrible talk [with Burger yet]?"

"Well, no. It's going to be a very grave shock to him and whoever—"

Shouting loudly, Nixon declared: "It's a shock to me, for Christ sakes! I don't even think women should be educated!"

Mitchell replied calmly, "I would think it would better to just advise him at the time we are sending them up."

"Give him five minutes notice."

"Yeah."

"I don't want him to die," Nixon cracked.

"He is sitting and dying. He's calling maybe twice a day, you know, and I go all around the [barn] and he's trying to burrow in on it," Mitchell said.

"It has to be done," the president declared, and then repeated, "It has to be done."

"Well, he'll be a good sport," Mitchell reassured.

"Particularly [if the] woman is as conservative as I hear she is. Is her name up there at the bar now?"

"Not yet. We're going to send them up together. I would, as we mentioned the last time, Mr. President, send these two names up along with some of those southern circuit court judges and if you want Byrd to go up?"

"Put him in. Put him in."

"Put Byrd?" the still-disbelieving Mitchell asked.

"Put Byrd in. Absolutely. And also Sylvia's."

"Sylvia Bacon? We had been talking about that [unintelligible]."

"Put her name in," Nixon made clear. "I would prefer her, I don't know her [well enough], but the only thing that concerns me about her is she went to Vassar. Jesus Christ."

"Well, we don't have the track record on Sylvia Bacon in the civil liberties field that we have on this group, this Lillie."

"Well, do you think she's all right on civil liberties? Lillie?"

"Oh yes, yeah."

"She ever had a chance to rule on it or has she just spoken on it?"

"No, she's had two thousand opinions and some of them get into this area out there."

"Good."

"Rehnquist is just about as hard-nosed as anybody I know on this subject," Mitchell said.

Ehrlichman added, "He is."

"He's been through her opinions and has come—"

"Somebody suggested him for the Court the other day," the president noted.

Mitchell quickly shot down the idea. "There's no question about [his qualifications]. But what the hell do you get out of that politically?"

"Nothing."

"It'd be a great appointment, but why?" Mitchell asked.

The president agreed that Rehnquist had a first-class mind. Ehrlichman, who had known Rehnquist since they went to law school together at Stanford, presented another angle for the president to consider.

"Now, if you want to salt away a guy that would be on the Court for thirty years, is a rock solid conservative, he's it."

"Yeah," the president agreed.

Mitchell, however, did not want to waste the political opportunity. "But you don't buy anything."

"Yeah." The president had to agree with this reality as well.

So did Ehrlichman. "You don't, because he isn't a woman, he isn't a southerner, he isn't any of those other things."

"Maybe he can get a sex change," Nixon suggested.

Mitchell laughed.

"Takes too long," Ehrlichman advised.

• • • •

The story that Senator Robert Byrd was under consideration by the president became the buzz of Washington over the weekend of October 9 and 10. It was a question for the Sunday talk shows and newspapers.[10] Rather than tossing a stink bomb into the U.S. Senate, Nixon had dropped it on the street. While the effect was not as dramatic, the odor was spreading. The speculation was exacerbated by the fact that Senator Byrd had joined the president and first lady on Air Force One for a trip to West Virginia and back on Friday afternoon, October 8.

• • • •

A news summary containing the news as reported by television, wire services, syndicated columns, and news magazines was on the president's desk every morning (except weekends). Usually the president had already seen *The Washington Post*, the *New York Times*, and the *Los Angeles Times* by the time he arrived in the office, for they were delivered to the family quarters, although the news summary occasionally referred to them as well, if the president had been out of town or busy with some other matter. The news summary was actually a management tool. It not only informed the president of coverage of his administration, but the margins were made wide so he could make notes and give instructions which the staff secretary's office translated and sent to the responsible presidential aide.

Mort Allen, the staffman who prepared the summary, broke it into categories of particular interest to the president. Since late September, the news summary had contained a section entitled "Supreme Court" or "Court," and the amount of news within that category was increasing with each passing week. On Monday, October 11, Mort included the weekend news:

> CBS led Sat nite (no NBC mention) with the Byrd story from Scripps-Howard pointing out that the W[hite] H[ouse] did confirm he was under consideration but to say he'd been chosen was "way, way too strong." [CBS anchor Roger] Mudd noted Byrd has never practiced law, is one of most conservative Senators, regrets KKK membership but doesn't regret calling [Martin Luther] King a rabble-rouser. . . . [Washington Bureau, Scripps-Howard, Dan] Thomasson said appointment would raise protest rivaling those over Haynsworth and Carswell. Admin is reported not concerned over ABA's stance. And all reports say Byrd would make it. *Post* says [Senators] Griffin, Baker, and [Budget Director] Weinberger are also on the list of possible.
>
> [Senator Fred] Harris said he'd oppose Byrd but McGovern said the W. Virginian, "a man of enormous industry and personal pride," would be confirmed. . . . [Dan] Rather says black leaders around country are unsure what, if anything, to do about the possible nomination of a former KKK organizer. . . .
>
> Richard Wilson [a print journalist] says RN is determined to shape the Court as he has pledged—it'll be a big battle, but RN firmly intends to win. . . . Bill Buckley says the statesmanship and toughness of which RN is capable will be necessary to fulfill the RN Court pledges—but a liberal nominee will be felt down to the vitals of GOP morale—"a word to the wise is sufficient." *

*Haldeman frequently underlined key passages for the president's consideration, as here.

A Life poll of 65 "academic experts" ranked Warren, Black and Frankfurter as 3 of the 12 "great" justices of the total of 98 in Court history. Fortas, Harlan, Douglas and Brennan are called "near-great." No rate of
Burger or Blankman [sic] due to short terms. Vinson, Byrnes, Whittaker,
Burton and Minton among 8 called "failures."

Beside this last paragraph, Nixon had written "E—My God!" (to Ehrlichman) and circled the names of Warren and Brennan.[11]

• • • •

The president spent most of the day in his EOB office preparing for a
news conference he would spring on the press the next day, when he
would announce a Soviet Summit meeting. He interrupted his work several times, however, to call Mitchell about the Court appointments. The
first call occurred just before 9:00 a.m.[12] Having read *The Washington Post*
and his news summary, the president was chuckling over the explosion of
attention to Byrd.

"Well, it looks like a senator knows how to lobby for [a job on the
Supreme Court]."

"Somebody does." They both laughed, and Mitchell continued, "I'd say
they covered the press pretty good."

"I rode down there to West Virginia [with Byrd] and I think he was
talking about the Court, and I said, you know, Bob, you're an [unintelligi-
ble] to me. And he said he was talking to Eastland." This caused both
Nixon and his attorney general to chuckle in a conspiratorial manner.

"Yes, he had," Mitchell confirmed.

"Did you know that? I didn't."

"Yeah, Eastland had talked to us," Mitchell explained.

"And I said well, well, Bob, it's a funny thing. Smiling, I said—com-
pletely without any knowledge of what you had done—the Attorney
General and I talked about you this morning." They both laughed. "So
we're at least ahead of it. I told him what the problems were. I said he's got
Klan and all that. I said that you got the bar problem. And he said, well,
I'm convinced I can get confirmed. And boy, I just couldn't believe that.
Yet, I looked in the news summary this morning and I see McGovern says
that he's grown in stature since he's been here. What the hell do you think
they're up to?"

"I don't know."

"Want to get rid of him?"

"They probably want to get him out of that Whip job. That's what I would guess. I don't know, they might have a pretty good fight for that. But Byrd's been cooperating with you. He's been a pretty good fellow in that spot, is he not?"

"Sure. To the extent that anybody can. Well, I'll tell you one thing, John. It certainly shakes them up a little, doesn't it, though? They knocked down our friend Poff, and then Byrd comes up who has no [qualifications]"—Nixon laughed as he continued—"just became a lawyer in '63. But on the other hand, I'll tell you if it comes to that, you know, one thing, he sure is going to be tough. God, I mean, he's to the right of me, I'm afraid." Nixon laughed even harder.

"No question about that," Mitchell agreed.

"God almighty, he—"

"To the right of both of us together. Tough little cookie."

"Yeah. He is tough. [Dick] Moore talked to him too. I had to get to work, so I put Moore on him and you ought give Moore a call [to see] what he's got. He's probably talked to Moore about it too."

"Dick talked to me yesterday. And filled me in on it because Dick was a little excited to hear that somebody else, who had been on that plane, was going to be accused of leaking the story that was all over town."

"We didn't leak it. No sir."

"It's interesting, how it gets to all the press, and all the newspapers," Mitchell observed.

"I think Byrd did. That's my guess." After more talk of leaks, Nixon shifted subjects. "How's [Herschel] Friday look to you now?"

"He's looking better all of the time. We have our appellate judge friend coming in today for a session," Mitchell said, referring to Judge Lillie.

"And then you are going to send their names up after that, to the ABA?"

"Yes. As you suggested, either on, I think you said Thursday or Friday. They'll need a little time, you know, to review these things. So we'll send Mr. Byrd's name along with them unless you give different counsel."

"Oh yeah, sure, send it, send it."

"And some of those other southern judges. So, we'll put out a little smoke screen, and also [we'll send] Sylvia Bacon, I should add."

"Good. When do you think we can shoot to send a name to the Senate?"

"It'd probably be the first part of next week, I would think we could get [them ready by then]."

"Because I may do a quickie little news conference tomorrow morning, just a short one. If I am asked, I'm going to say we're going to send the names up next week. That gives us plenty of time, doesn't it?"

"Yes indeed."

After they decided they would not announce whether one or both were going up, the president observed, "Well, I'm glad to keep the game a little open on this, aren't you? I mean as, as far as Byrd's thing, let it ramble around a bit out there."

"I think it's helpful," Mitchell agreed.

"I'll bet you they're regurgitating all over the place, John, because Poff, you know, compared to Byrd, he's a flaming liberal." Nixon laughed. "Teaches them a lesson."

Nixon was still chuckling when Mitchell agreed, "It will and I think they'll be appreciative of the candidates you have. Hopefully."

"I hope the Chief Justice appreciates Mildred," the president said, and again laughed at the thought.

"Well, we still have to work out the scenario whether you want me to tell him or whether you're going to do it. We should tell him before she goes to the bar."

"Oh yeah, yeah. Well, I'll tell you, I'll be glad to join you in doing it."

"All right, sir."

"I think it's so historic that maybe we better do it that way. But I think what we ought to do is you ought to soften him up just a little and then I'll tell him that's what I want to talk to him about, that we're just going to do it."

"Good, I'll do that on that basis that we're having all of these names go up. Because he's played the game with us so well that I think we should appraise him in advance of the potential of it. And then you can put in the clincher."

"Good. Okay."

• • • •

A few hours later, the president was back on the telephone with Mitchell. The president had encountered his secretary of transportation, John Volpe, at a meeting with the minister of foreign affairs of Italy. Volpe had been pushing the president for weeks to name an Italian to the Supreme Court, and he had continued his lobbying efforts after the meeting with the Italian officials. The president wanted to warn Mitchell that he told the transportation secretary to talk to his attorney general.[13] Mitchell told the president Volpe had already given him a list of five people, but there was "no rhyme or reason for any one of them." The president chuckled as he told Mitchell it would save him an hour or more if he'd deal with Volpe. Mitchell agreed to do so, though it was likely a waste of his time.

"Did Miss Lillie come in yet?" Nixon asked.

"Yes, she's still here."

"Oh, how's she look?"

"Better all the time."

"Good, good, good. Good luck."

Mitchell reported that everything was on track.

"You know, John, it just must really make you feel happy that you will be the Attorney General to have made the first recommendation of a woman on the Court. Doesn't it just make you feel great? Doesn't it?" Mitchell could not help but hear laughter in the background. Nixon continued, laying it on. "How proud you can be back at your old college in New York."

"Yes sir, when I get with that new woman's lib, why I'll be their hero."

"John, that's Haldeman laughing in the background here."

No sooner had the president hung up than he was back on the telephone.[14] He had forgotten to ask an important question about Judge Lillie.

"Incidentally, isn't she Catholic?"

"Ah, no, I don't believe so."

"Well, she's married to an Italian now, you know."

"Yes."

"He's Catholic."

"No question about it."

"Check her religion and see if it isn't Catholic and ask her if she isn't part Italian." This caused Mitchell to laugh. "No, I think she may be," Nixon said.

"She is now," Mitchell said, then explained, "We're going to make sure that name goes out in the appropriate way."

"Yeah. Well, what is her name now?"

"Falcone."

"That's what she would be, not Mildred Lillie then?"

"That's correct."

"In other words, we'd be appointing Mrs. what?"

"Mrs. Mildred Lillie Falcone," Mitchell said.

"Not bad."

"No, I don't think so either," Mitchell agreed.

Nixon now (sort of) had his Italian, but he still had a problem. "But listen, tell her if she isn't a Catholic to get busy, get over there, God damn it, and get confirmed. Okay?" They hung up.

The president continued to prepare for his press conference. It was not long, however, before he called Mitchell again.[15] He wanted to know how Mitchell was getting along with Judge Lillie, and whether she was a Catholic.

"She is a Catholic," Mitchell reported.

"That's great. And does she got a little Italian blood?" Both laughed.

"Not according to the record, but it may be. She's sure got a distinguished-looking Italian husband, though."

"And he's a lawyer?"

"Yes."

The president was delighted, thinking this will help with the "Volpe thing." Mitchell agreed.

Mitchell was also pleased with the judge's husband. "He is just what we would want a judge's wife to be. He's a plodding mediocrity." Nixon laughed, and Mitchell added, "And rather distinguished-looking, you know the [type]."

"Is he a lawyer?"

"Yes, a lawyer and he's practiced for thirty-five years out there without great distinction. So that nobody is going to be accusing him of influencing the judge's decisions. And so far as we can see, he checks out all right. He's been in debt a little bit with some notes at the bank, but he seems to have paid them off and have a reasonably good standing in the community."

"Good."

"So far it just looks great, and she's been reversed enough by the Supreme Court in California in criminal cases to give her a good standing with the law and order people."

"Good, good, good."

"And she's got a good personality. People will see that she's not one of these frigid bitches, you know."

"That's right, I know, they're terrible. Well, this business about the Catholic thing, it's very good, married to an Italian. Okay."

"So far so good, and hopefully we will have a package for you to approve to send to the bar here in the next day or so. So that we can keep on target next week."

"Great, good."

• • • •

At this point in the process, Nixon was consumed with the politics of confirmation. He and Mitchell were warming to the advantages of appointing Mildred Lillie, and he was hoping to use Byrd as a foil to get a southerner through the Senate. Indeed, politics was threatening to overwhelm the more important question of quality, and of long-term inpact on the Court. The political moves Nixon was considering were also in danger of backfiring.

The next day, Tuesday, October 12, the president went again to his EOB office to complete preparation for his press conference at noon. He was upset with a news story that pooh-poohed the prospect that he would actually appoint Robert Byrd to the Supreme Court.[16] To keep the Byrd rumor alive, the president telephoned Ron Ziegler, at 8:40 a.m.[17] The president explained to Ziegler that "one of our boys got off the reservation on the Byrd thing and just blew a beautiful play I'm trying to make here." They had spoiled it by saying Byrd "was not under consideration" and that "he probably wasn't going to be appointed." Then the president instructed his press secretary: "You are to completely reverse that. And just say that was totally wrong. He's under very active consideration. You understand? That didn't come out of your shop anyway, did it?"

"No, sir. I didn't know how to handle the Byrd thing so I just left it loose. I talked to the Attorney General briefly about it yesterday, and the way we've been playing it [is] that he is one of those under consideration."

"He is under very active consideration," Nixon repeated. "Did you see the White House story this morning in the *Post*?" Ziegler had seen it, he said. "Yes, well, that's totally inaccurate."

"I don't know where that came from," Ziegler said.

"Well, it's one of our guys probably. You know, just trying. He's frightened to death because Byrd's been in the Klan or some damn thing. I don't know. But nevertheless, I want it, I want his name out there. Let me explain. You, of course, can understand this. Let us suppose that we were not considering him. Ron, can't you see what it's done to the opposition to have him considered. McGovern heads screaming around. All the Democratic candidates have had to determine are they for or against Byrd. He's very actively under consideration."

"Right."

"You understand?"

"Yes sir."

"We're going to make them stand up and be counted. I'd like, if you could, to get that off even before I get [to the press room for the news conference]. Is there a way you could do it?"

"Yes sir, I think so." Ziegler explained that Spence Rich had written the story. Nixon wanted Ziegler to call him in, along with the wire service reporters, and tell him he had the story on Byrd wrong. Ziegler agreed to handle it.

• • • •

Before his press conference the president called Pat Buchanan, who had first suggested he select a Catholic, and an Italian, to share his plans to select Judge Lillie.[18] He told Buchanan about his ploy with Byrd, and his delight in the reactions of the Democrats about "a racist" on the Supreme Court, commenting, "Byrd's a hell of a fellow. Do you know him?" Buchanan knew him and liked him.

"Oh Christ, I'm telling you, I think he said he gave up being a member of the Klan." Nixon laughed. "I think he still is."

Pat Buchanan laughed, not sure what to say.

Nixon continued, "No, I know, no. He's a hell of a fellow, honest, decent, hardworking and so forth. But I want to hold it up there, but we're looking for another substitute." He then took Buchanan through the qualifications of Mildred Lillie, arguing that no one was going to be able to vote against her because she was a woman. Finally, he assured his conservative aide, "as long as I'm sitting in the chair there's not going to be any Jew appointed to that Court, not because they're Jewish, because there's no Jew, Pat, that can be right on the criminal law issue."

"Yeah," Buchanan agreed.

"Have you ever known one that was?"

"No."

"They're all hung up on civil rights. So you're going to get two conservatives on this Court." After exploring potential selections, Nixon assured Buchanan there would be "One southerner. And we're going to find one. We're going to have to dig deep."

As the conversation progressed, Buchanan reported that "George McGovern is set on Sunday to say on television, 'My first choice would be a woman for the Supreme Court if I could make it. I promise you that,' and they're really going to be in a box if you've got a woman that's a strict constructionist because I don't see any way they can turn it down."

"Shit, [I hope they'll fight it]," Nixon commented.

Concerned about what the White House was doing to Senator Byrd, Buchanan asked if the senator had been clued in. "Is Byrd in on this deal, though? Does Byrd know we're going there? Is he bothered by it or what?"

"No. I don't know," Nixon admitted. "No, but my point is, it's a high honor to be considered for the Supreme Court. We're not hurting anyone. Byrd's [unintelligible] but his colleagues are going to kill him. Let us see how bad they are. Do you agree?"

"I agree. I agree about 100 percent. Do you think they will come out and say anything or will they say, well, wait and see?"

"No, they've got to come out. But I want to get the NAACP on this. [But mainly I want to] worry those sons of bitches in the Senate."

• • • •

At the press conference, after announcing his summit meeting with the Soviets, the president was asked about the Supreme Court. When was he going to make his nominations, and was Senator Byrd of West Virginia on his list?

"He is definitely on the list, and I will make the nominations next week, both," the president said.

"Sir, you are going to have a woman on there, aren't you?" All the reporters laughed because Sarah McClendon of Sarah McClendon News Service had asked the question. Sarah had been covering the White House since Franklin Roosevelt.

Before responding, the president repeated that the reports that said he had ruled out Senator Byrd, or a woman, were wrong. He continued: "Senator Byrd, as a result of several of his colleagues recommending him, is one that is being considered. And I will also say in answer to Mrs. Mc-Clendon's question that at least two women are under consideration at this time." [19]

These statements were not incorrect. But they masked part of his intentions—to nominate a southerner other than Byrd—and they failed to convey the scramble underway to settle on that southerner, and on a woman who could win confirmation.

8

GOING WITH FRIDAY
AND LILLIE

October 12–14

BY OCTOBER 12TH John Mitchell appreciated that Nixon was not serious about Byrd, and he was ready to sign off and submit Herschel Friday
and Mildred Lillie to the American Bar Association's evaluation committee. First, however, he had to face down some discussion from rival John
Ehrlichman, who was not so sure about Mitchell's choices. Ehrlichman
felt they had to be checked, and for that reason he had spoken with
Mitchell earlier in the day to explain that he wanted me, along with David
Young, to visit both Friday and Lillie. There was nothing Mitchell could
say. Both wanted to run Mitchell's choices by the president, so they
arranged to meet with Nixon after the president's press conference that
Tuesday (October 12).[1]

In the Oval Office, Mitchell explained that he was ready to submit
the names of Friday and Lillie, even though Judge Lillie lacked anything in the way of Italian heritage. The president said, "God damn it.
Can't she find an Italian grandmother or something, so we can [satisfy]
Volpe?"

Mitchell chuckled softly. "It's pretty hard, because of her birthplace in Iowa."

For Ehrlichman's benefit, the president asked Mitchell to repeat the background material he and Mitchell had reviewed on Friday and Lillie. Mitchell started with Judge Lillie, highlighting her twenty-five years on an appellate bench in California. Mitchell assured the president that although a Democrat, she was a conservative.

"Busing?" the president asked.

"She has not had busing issues, but in talking to her and reading some of her opinions in other areas, I don't think there's any doubt about—"

Nixon was not satisfied. "You've got to ask her anyway about it," the president insisted.

Mitchell's report had a new nugget on Judge Lillie, that supported her conservative credentials. "[Democratic California governor] Pat Brown considered her for the Supreme Court, the only woman he would consider, and he turned her down because she was too conservative," Mitchell said.

"God damn, that's great, all right, good. Now how about Friday? Do you know him, John?"

"No," Ehrlichman said.

"Tell us about Friday," the president instructed Mitchell, who did so. As the report was concluding, the president had a question. "John, let me ask you this. It's more important. Is he conservative?"

"No question about it in my mind," Mitchell said.

"Let me put it this way, will he follow Burger?" Nixon asked.

"I think he'll be to the right of Burger," Mitchell assured him, and commented that Democratic senator John McClellan had said that Friday was "just great."

"Is [Friday] a Democrat too?" Nixon asked.

"Yeah," Mitchell acknowledged.

"Oh Christ." The president laughed as he acknowledged that he would be putting two Democrats on the Court. "That's all right," he said.

To further document Friday's conservative credentials, Mitchell mentioned that Friday had practiced law for many years with Pat Mehaffy, who had become a federal appeals court judge. The president knew Mehaffy, a man Mitchell described as "to the right of the Sheriff of Nottingham."

For Nixon, however, this was a limited litmus test, and he wanted other evidence. "Yeah, yeah, well, understand, I want to be right. He doesn't have anything like the Klan in his background?" Membership in the nefarious Klan was not a negative to Nixon in this instance.

"No, he has nothing like that," Mitchell said. But they had checked him carefully, Mitchell explained. "Friday's wife did a very interesting thing. She's kept a scrapbook of every time his name has appeared in print from the time they were married, and Rehnquist took that thing and went all the way through it, beginning to end." If Friday had passed muster with Rehnquist's stringent view of strict constructionism, Mitchell was saying, he must be okay.

The president asked what would prove to be a telling question: "Do you think [you can get] him confirmed?"

"I believe that there would be no basis of stopping his confirmation," Mitchell answered. "Just because he's from the South, and represented a school board as a lawyer, I don't think they'd make a case against him. He doesn't have any other infirmities that you had with Haynsworth and the ethical thing."

Ehrlichman, who had remained silent as he listened to Mitchell's presentation, was not satisfied. He said flatly, "I'd like to send these two young lawyers down to comb him over in terms of his, of his personal life, and his other possible infirmities and—"

Before Ehrlichman finished the president seconded the plan, also suggesting they let the FBI do some checking. But Mitchell cautioned about using the FBI for it would spread the fact that they were under consideration. The president responded, "Let's have [Ehrlichman's] people do it. Would that be better?"

"I'd welcome that," Mitchell said. "As I told John [Ehrlichman], the better thing—"

"Don't do Lillie," the president interjected. "I don't think you have to send [Dean] out to do her, do you?"

But Mitchell wanted them both checked. While he was not concerned about Judge Lillie, he was not sure about her husband. If the Senate went looking for "an Achilles' heel," the judge's husband might be it.

"Now look, I'm not going to go for somebody like Caesar's wife. We get somebody like a Caesar's wife, we're going to have somebody that, by God, has never done a God damn thing," the president advised.

Ehrlichman, who wanted his own reading on these nominees, said that it was important that they understand all potential problems. Still, Nixon was prepared to assume the worst about the judge's husband. "Look, he's probably [a whopper].* He may have stolen something," Nixon said, unconcerned. When Ehrlichman wondered if candidates should be asked about marital infidelities, Nixon brought the discussion to a halt—with laughter. "Marital infidelity? How in the Christ did we get Douglas on the Court?" Nixon protested. And when Mitchell mentioned considering other names, like University of Chicago president Edward Levi, the president repeated his mantra: "The most important thing is we've got to have two conservatives," and he did not want anyone giving him "a Jew's name. I don't want that Levi submitted to me. God damn it, I'm not going to appoint one of these [university types]. I don't want a liberal Jew on the Court."

Mitchell said he planned to submit to the ABA's evaluation committee Mildred Lillie, Sylvia Bacon, Herschel Friday, and "whoever else" they selected as camouflage. For the latter, Nixon suggested Federal Judge Charles Clark of Mississippi.

Not unexpectedly, the president reminded Mitchell to include Senator Robert Byrd with the names he sent to the ABA. "I know they're going to turn him down. So I'd like to have that decided once and for all," he said.

Mitchell, who remained troubled with Byrd's name, tried another approach. "Let me give you one additional factor. You know, uh—"

"I know about the Klan," the president cut him off.

"Oh no," Mitchell protested. That was not what he was talking about. "When we came into office," Mitchell explained, "we kept the U.S. Attorney over in Baltimore because we had the tough cases of the Brewsters** and the Longs*** and the rest of them. Well, what happened was that when [Byrd's name] came up over the weekend, the U.S. Attorney up there [in Baltimore] called the fellow in our criminal division. He said, 'I

---

*Several persons who listened to this tape heard Nixon use the word "whopper" while one person thought he said "wop."

**Senator Daniel Brewster was indicted in 1969 on charges of accepting illegal gratuities while in the Senate; after trial, conviction, and reversal, he pleaded no contest in 1975. See *United States v. Brewster*, 408 U.S. 501 (1972).

***This appears to be a reference to Senator Russell Long of Louisiana.

want to refresh your recollection. Our friend Mr. Byrd was involved in that Brewster-Anderson-Spiegel business with the money. Here's—' "

The president interrupted, because he didn't want to hear it. This information was irrelevant because Nixon did not expect Byrd to get beyond the ABA.

Mitchell had one request. "Can I have your permission to just tell [the chairman of the ABA's committee] Ed Walsh alone that what we want to do is concentrate on Lillie and Friday?"

"Absolutely. You tell him the ones that we [picked] are those two. But I'd like to see what they say about [Byrd's qualifications]. They'll say no. But it will be interesting to know."

"Well, we can program them to say anything bad you want," Mitchell reported.

• • • •

Following a cabinet meeting, John Ehrlichman returned to the Oval Office with the president, where they continued talking about Mitchell's selections.[2] Ehrlichman did not like what he had heard about Judge Lillie's husband, but Nixon argued that if the Senate started going after husbands no president would ever get a woman on the Supreme Court. "Friday definitely sounds good," the president noted, switching topics. "I'll tell you how we got the name," he continued, and then paused to catch Ehrlichman's full attention: "Burger."

"Oh."

"He's Burger's candidate." After another pause to sign some documents, the president made it clear he was decided. "Next week I'm going to announce the Court."

"Yup."

"So that will be the big story next week. John [Mitchell] is thinking about sending the two together. The more I think about it, I think we ought to probably send one one day and one the next. Because I think the woman story is going to dominate the [news]. Nobody thinks we're going to appoint a woman. Hell, I'm against it myself, but it's got to be done. And Mitchell, he's good at [shmoozing with Burger]." When Ehrlichman gave his blessing on appointing a woman, the president noted, "Well, basically, John, if we say that the Negro viewpoint should be on the Court, why not the woman's?"

"Sure."

"There's a hell of a lot of stuff that has to do with women. I'm not for it. I don't think women should ever be allowed to vote even."

"The worst experiences I've ever had were trying cases before women judges," Ehrlichman said.

"Is that right? How did they do?"

"Just terrible."

"I've never tried a case. What do they, how are they?"

"Well, there isn't a one I ever saw that [had any] logic. And it was just frustrating as hell. So I've always steered clear of them whenever I could as a matter of practice."

It is a testament to Richard Nixon's political instincts that he spearheaded the drive for Judge Lillie, given his general attitudes about women in politics.

• • • •

"Have you talked with Herschel Friday and Judge Lillie?" Ehrlichman asked me shortly after 6:00 p.m.[3] Mitchell had called me earlier in the day, as had Ehrlichman, both instructing me to arrange visits with the putative nominees as quickly as possible. I told Ehrlichman I had booked a flight in the morning to Little Rock, Arkansas, and Herschel Friday had set aside the entire day on Wednesday, as well as the evening if necessary, to visit with David Young and me. We would fly to Los Angeles on Thursday to meet with Judge Lillie and her husband that evening, and the next day as needed. "Excellent," Ehrlichman said.

Also I told him about a memorandum Rehnquist had prepared for the attorney general about possible bases for the Senate to oppose Friday, which Mitchell had sent me. Ehrlichman requested a copy. Rehnquist had listed three problem areas: civil rights; partnership in an establishment law firm; and absence of a public career. Clearly civil rights was the most serious, but not for Rehnquist. Friday had fought desegregation for school boards throughout Arkansas, taking two cases all the way to the U.S. Supreme Court. Rehnquist found Friday's statements about civil rights "invariably in good taste," with no "evidence of personal bias, even such as the rather thin case adduced against Carswell, [that] could be proven against Friday."

Although I was not sure I agreed the case against Carswell was "rather thin," I did agree that Friday's representation of those opposed to integration should not be a basis to judge him. Rehnquist cited "Zachariah Chaffee [sic], a professor at Harvard Law School and one of the great champions of First Amendment freedom." Chaffee had said of the criticism of Charles Evans Hughes to be chief justice because of his corporate clients, that the "doctrine of guilty by association is abhorrent enough in the criminal deportation field without being extended into the relations between lawyer and client." Rehnquist was also urging the attorney general to proceed as quickly as possible to prevent the Senate from mounting a filibuster, should the confirmation hearings not bring the nomination to the floor in 1971, for 1972 was an election year. The Fortas filibuster had been justified, in part, with the claim that it was so close to the election the next president should have the selection.[4]

My mention of Rehnquist prompted me to test on Ehrlichman what I had successfully posed to Dick Moore. "You asked me for my thought on a possible nominee more conservative than Dick Poff who could get confirmed," I began.

"Right, Young came up with Wilbur Mills, but that won't sell," Ehrlichman interjected, apparently thinking I agreed with Young's recommendation. While I was aware of Young's lengthy memo to Ehrlichman on Mills,[5] I agreed with Ehrlichman. I was not sure Mills met the president's criteria, notwithstanding his southern orientation.

"No, Mills is not my candidate. John, we have within this administration the strictest of strict constructionists, he's one of the smartest, and he can get confirmed. Actually, he'd be a stealth candidate."

"Oh? Tell me."

"Your law school classmate William Hubbs Rehnquist."

Silence fell. No clever rejoinder. No quick banter. "Counselor, you've got your thinking cap pulled down over your eyes," Ehrlichman said. "Dick Moore told me you were peddling Rehnquist. Well, it's not going to happen. There's zero political benefit for the president."

"How about the benefit of putting someone with a good mind on the Court?" I argued.

But Ehrlichman wasn't interested. "Forget it. Rehnquist isn't ready for the Court." Then he told me he wanted me to telephone him after each of my sessions with Friday and Lillie. "We've had enough problems with Mitchell's picks, so let me know what he's come up with this time." To make the point that these were not pro forma visits, Ehrlichman told me my assessment was the only way to prevent the president from making a mistake.

"I'll report tomorrow evening," I said.

• • • •

On Wednesday morning, October 13, Mitchell sent his letter to the ABA. Mitchell had called Ed Walsh the preceding evening when he returned from the White House to give him the names he would include in the letter: District of Columbia Superior Court Judge Sylvia Bacon; Senator Robert Byrd of West Virginia; Judge Charles Clark of Jackson, Mississippi, who was on the U.S. Court of Appeals for the Fifth Circuit; Herschel H. Friday of Little Rock, Arkansas; Judge Mildred Loree Lillie of the California Court of Appeals in Los Angeles; and Judge Paul H. Rooney of St. Petersburg, Florida, also on the Fifth Circuit. Mitchell told Walsh to focus on Friday and Lillie.

About the time that Young and I were landing in Little Rock, the president was meeting quickly with Haldeman. He needed to do a bit of media manipulation. The president was not pleased with the focus of some speculative stories. His morning news summary had noted his focus on women, and he had called Haldeman into the Oval Office to talk about it.[6]

"Could I ask you to do something quick?" the president asked his chief of staff. "Could you have the Byrd thing floated again now? [Also], I want you to put down the woman thing. [We want that to be] a surprise. I want to be sure [this doesn't leak, and everybody must] keep [their] God damn mouth shut, since she is being considered, you know what I mean? Let whoever leaked out the fact that I was not considering Byrd leak out the fact a woman really doesn't have a chance, see what I mean? Let them float that out there, that actually the two top runners are two men. Could you get that in? Now, the second point I want to do in this PR thing. I want you to get out a story over the weekend that the strongest one advocating, pushing me on the woman side are Mrs. Nixon, and Julie and Tricia, you see? They are [in fact doing that], she's mentioned that a woman should be considered to the Court. You got anybody that we can give this sort of thing to?"

"Oh, a lot of people."

"I don't care who you give this to. Moore, Safire—no, not Safire, he'd focus on the Jew, he doesn't know how to play it, particularly when he plays it in a column. Let Moore call a wire service reporter and get it on the wire, fair enough?"

"Okay."

"He's aware of it. I ought to be sure that the fact that they're pushing for it—particularly that the kids [Julie and Tricia] are pushing for it gets out. But I want to knock down the idea [first]. Here's the reason. I don't want to get either of the people we're considering out in front. It's going to destroy them."

"Right."

"Before I get a chance to defend them, you see."

Haldeman reported that the venerable Washington columnist Mary McGrory had written "an angry" column on Byrd being under consideration. "She writes it as a great political coup for you to put Byrd in there, because he [is unqualified and] you force the Senate to confirm him. You put Byrd on and they'd have to confirm him. And you get the worst possible racist you could get on the Court, which would satisfy your desire that you screw the Senate, which you'd love to do." Haldeman chuckled with delight. "She's not far off the mark."

"Not far off the mark, if I can do it."

Both men were laughing, as Haldeman repeated, "If you can do it."

• • • •

Following a meeting with Washington mayor Walter Washington to talk about the District's drug problem, Nixon talked to Ehrlichman.[7] He was impatient and wanted to get Lillie and Friday's names announced. The only problem Ehrlichman had for the president was the likely reaction. Based on discussions during a White House staff meeting, Ehrlichman advised the president that the most likely criticism would focus on their stature, asking why he had not named a legal giant.

Nixon responded with a suggestion. "I'd like you to do one other thing if you would," the president said. "I would like to know how many years Friday has practiced. Then what I can say is that he has had more years of active practice than any present member of the Court." Similarly, with Judge Lillie, he could say she had "more service as a trial court judge in unlimited jurisdiction than all the other judges presently on the Court combined. And we need that kind of knowledge on the Court. See, now don't you think that sells?"

"Oh, no question, no question."

. . . .

Meanwhile, David Young and I had met with Herschel Friday. "He's clean as a hound's tooth," I told Ehrlichman when I called him from little Rock.[8] We had spent seven hours with Friday. "But it's not all good news," I quickly cautioned.

"Oh? How bad is it?"

"Well, if the confirmation hearings were tomorrow, Herschel Friday would make Harrold Carswell look good." I was being as frank as possible.

"How so?"

"Let me say if I needed a lawyer for a business deal in Arkansas, I would hire this man without question. He's a fine transactional lawyer. He's probably a brilliant legal technician. He knows Arkansas law and practice as well as anyone in this state, I'm sure. He's highly intelligent, and articulate. He's obviously a man of integrity. And I'm not sure I could say any of those things about Harrold Carswell."

"That's all nice to hear. But not very helpful. Now tell me what problems you've discovered."

"The problem is, John, that Herschel Friday has never had occasion to think about the issues that Supreme Court justices confront. Or for that matter the subjects most federal judges confront today. We took him through both typical and topical constitutional issues like church-state relations, rights of privacy, abortion, capital punishment, reapportionment, pre- and post-arrest procedures, First Amendment issues, Fourth Amendment issues like search and seizure and wiretapping, to name just a few off the top. Often, he didn't have a clue what we were talking about, and when he did, he didn't know how he felt about the matter because he'd never thought about it. On most constitutional issues, he doesn't know if he's conservative, moderate, or liberal. He's like a blank sheet of paper."

"My, my, my, my," Ehrlichman said. He gave a pained groan before stating the obvious. "This is not good."

"Tell me. Both David and I actually felt embarrassed for him. At one point, he said to me, 'John, you're going to have to tell me what I should say on these issues. I want to be with the president.'"

"This is not good," Ehrlichman repeated. "How did this get this far." This was a reaction, not a question. I asked Young to pick up the extension telephone and join the conversation.

Young gave Ehrlichman a fact that had surprised us both. "Mr. Friday said this was the most detailed discussion of this kind that he had had with anyone in connection with his nomination. Apparently neither Mitchell nor Rehnquist had taken him through any of these questions. I'm sorry to say, John, but I don't think the Justice Department has done this man any favors letting him progress this far," Young added.

"I agree," Ehrlichman said.

I gave Ehrlichman my assessment, that the bar would kill the nomination. "Frankly, I cannot imagine the ABA finding this man qualified to sit on the Court. Although I must tell you he's got a lot of friends in high places in the ABA, and they're lobbying for him, he told me."

"Are you saying they won't reject one of their own?" Ehrlichman asked me.

"While I don't have a clue what the bar will do, regardless of any lobbying, I am saying it would be remarkable if they found him qualified," I said. Young and I took Ehrlichman through our notes, giving him specific examples of questions that Friday could not handle, as well as some of the positive things that we had to say about the man. When we finished, I reported that we were going to meet again with Friday in the morning, before flying to California.

"Have you told Mitchell any of this?" Ehrlichman asked me.

"No, sir. Nor do I look forward to doing so."

Ehrlichman chuckled. "Well, guys, thanks for the hot potato."

• • • •

Remarkably, both the *New York Times* and *The Washington Post* had front-page, above the fold headline stories on Thursday, October 14, reporting all the names the president had submitted to the ABA. Not only did they have all the names, they had facts and photographs. I learned about the *Post* story when I called my office that morning before going to visit with Herschel Friday. My secretary read it to me. The story focused on Friday and Lillie. Because it mentioned the ABA rating on Sylvia Bacon for her judgeship in the District of Columbia and the ABA ratings of the two Fifth Circuit judges, it seemed clear that the story had been leaked by one of the members of the ABA's evaluation committee. Public reaction had been correctly anticipated by the White House staff. The *Post* story noted: "Many members of the legal community expressed disappointment that more distinguished names did not appear on the list."[9]

The first telephone call the president made when he arrived in the Oval Office was to John Mitchell.[10] Nixon was not happy.

"I was wondering [whether they were] authorized to do that?" he asked.

"To do what, Mr. President?"

"To put out the story with the pictures and so forth and the names that we had submitted to them. They've never done that before. Puts us in a hell of a spot."

"Well, the newspapers, of course, have picked up the names from the bar. And they—"

"Who at the bar would do that, John? Somebody who's working the staff, or something, I suppose?"

"Well, it would be the staff and it would probably be some of the Democrat members. You know there, there are a lot of Democrats as well as Republicans on the committee."

"Yeah, yeah. Send up a half dozen more names, would you do that? Just to keep it confused. Could you just, like send down that dean of that law school and three or four others. I don't want to limit it to this. And send down one of those Jewish [names], send Levi's name in too, would you do that, please? Get that done right away, okay? I got to do it because I just can't leave this hanging here for a week now."

"Which type of names?"

"Oh God, I don't give a damn who they are. I mean, some Jews, and liberals, and so forth, you know. Like Levi of Chicago, he'd be all right. Send him up as a name."

"Well, if you do that, of course, then the public [will think]—"

"Then, send Johnson up, that other [judge] down there."

"Frank Johnson?" Mitchell asked.

"Not Johnson but the, well, you already sent Clark, you could send that fellow from the law school down there, you could at least, you know, from Texas?"

"[Charles Alan] Wright?"

"Wright, yeah. Just pick out, if you can, John, any kind of names that are conservative enough, Powell or somebody, but I don't know."

"Well, if we do that, Mr. President, the press is going to focus on these people to the point where you will be run over with newspaper talk."

"Urging me to appoint them?"

"For not having done it."

"Well, are there any you can think of that sort just to confuse them, so we just aren't screwed here, because they are going to tear these [selections] to pieces? And, I mean, they will, you know. They'll always seize on what you've got as mediocrity and so forth and so on. That's what I'm concerned about."

"Well, if we go another route, we're going to trap ourselves into the point of—"

"The thing that I've become convinced of, the bar's broken its pick with me, the next time we have an appointment they aren't going to get a chance to look at it, John. Good God, I have more judgment, you have more judgment, as to who the hell is qualified. Now, what the hell does the bar know about it? I mean, good God, I can take a bar examination better than any of those assholes."

"I agree with you."

"That's why we're not going to give them a chance again. They have broken their pick, and I don't want you to tell them that because I know you need them for district courts and the rest. But believe me, never again do they get a crack at me. They didn't do this with Burger, you know. But now they've done it. And didn't do it with Blackmun. But they've broken their pick."

"Well, of course, those announcements were made, Mr. President, without consultation with anybody," Mitchell reminded Nixon.

"Well, we went through the bar, though."

"No, no, we did not."

"Well, that was our mistake here, then, I guess, is letting the bar have a crack at it."

"Well, every time you start a check, the word gets out as to who they are and the press is going take you on, whether it's the bar or not."

Nixon did not want to hear what his attorney general had to say. "Yeah, yeah, I think our strategy was right the other time, I mean, just not to ask the bar. They squeal. I'm really sick of the bastards anyway. They're such a bunch of sanctimonious assholes and I've told Ehrlichman to get off his ass and get me whatever his little check he's got to make. And I really think we've got to get it done now. I mean, they're really going to tear [these selections apart, they're] going to jump up and down on this now."

"Well, I expect the bar to be helpful in this picture by coming out with the solid approvals of Friday and Lillie," Mitchell said, overoptimistically.

Nixon doubted this. "When can the bar be ready and be helpful? I don't think they can."

"We haven't had an answer yet. We're pushing them and hopefully it'll be done this week."

"Can we get it by tomorrow, by chance?"

"I don't think that Walsh will be able to get his committee together by that time. It will probably be the weekend."

The president sighed in exasperation. "Well, what would be their line then, just to say that they approve two, is that what they do?"

"Yes, that's what we've asked them to do, to approve Lillie and Friday. Which I had presumed that you had concentrated on."

"Yeah, that is what we want to do. Yeah, yeah. Well, if you could push it faster. I've just told Ehrlichman that I've got to have his stuff [from Dean and Young] by tomorrow. As soon as I get it from the bar I think that we're just going to have to go with it. The mistake I think I made with Poff was to let him go up there and let them cannibalize him. I just don't want them to get killed before we get a chance to get in with the positive stuff first, you see. The first story on this is so important on these things, on any appointment, as you know. And if you could just tell [the bar] we're terribly interested to get them, to get it done, now they don't have to check too damn long on somebody like Friday that's practiced for twenty-five years, or Lillie, who's been on the bench twenty-five years. I mean, Friday and Lillie ought to be checking them, rather than them checking them."

When Mitchell started laughing, so did Nixon. Then he continued, "Would you mind pushing them on that, John?"

"I will be glad to, Mr. President."

"Well, you said you had talked to the Chief Justice?"

"Yes," Mitchell replied with a laugh. "He wrote me a three- or four-page letter which I won't bother you with, but he's talking all around the fact that, letting it be known he's not anxious to have a woman."

"I understand that, John. No more anxious than I am," the president said.

"That could be expected. However, I am sure he will take it in good grace," Mitchell counseled.

"He's got to do it. And he will do it and he's the guy to handle it. And the thing to do is for him to make it, and then he can play a great role in the history of the thing. He's a skillful man. Oh, one thing, incidentally, I have a thought. If they ever ask you, John, are these mediocre people, are they unknown and so forth, you can just smile and say, you know, I remember when the president named Mr. Burger, there were a number of editorials, snide comments that he wasn't a distinguished lawyer. I'd say everybody I think agrees he's distinguished now. And you could say, I remember that when Mr. Justice Black was appointed, and they criticized him because they said he wasn't a distinguished jurist. I'd really knock that distinguished thing down hard. If they sort of take on Friday, as the bond lawyer and all that. But, you see my point?"

"I do."

"I'm not going to let them tear these people to pieces. That's all there is to it."

After more grumbling, Nixon proposed a strategy. "I'd like to send Friday's name up first, Monday or Tuesday, and then Lillie's the next day. And when I send Friday's, I'd go out and describe him, and so forth and so on. Let him have a day's ride throughout the country. And I'd say, tomorrow I will have another announcement, after everything is complete, and then make the other. Will that satisfy you?"

"Yes, I think that will," Mitchell said. Then he returned to the press coverage. "[D]id you notice how they're playing up that she's a leading Catholic layman?"

Nixon chuckled delightedly. "I like that. Yeah."

"I'd like to see them start taking her on."

"And a Democrat. And incidentally appointed by Warren," the president had noted from the report in the *New York Times*. In fact, the *Times* had been far more informative for the president than anything Mitchell had told him. The *Times* profile noted that Judge Lillie was best known as the first woman to preside in the domestic relations court of Los Angeles; that she had moved with her mother to California from a small Iowa farm when her parents parted; that she had worked in a canning factory to earn money to go to the University of California, Berkeley; that she had been married twice, to Lillie and Falcone; and finally, in a closing note that had to please her: "In her mid-50s, she still has a bathing beauty figure."

But the president did not like the *Times* piece on Herschel Friday. "I didn't like them calling him a bond lawyer, for Christ sake," Nixon said.

"Well, that's a snide operation. As you know," Mitchell observed.

"What the hell! He does a lot of other things I found, and anyway, what's wrong with being a bond lawyer?"

"Ninety percent of his practice is in the other field." Mitchell (himself a bond lawyer) was not taking the president's bait.

"Sure, sure. Well, anyway, good luck this afternoon," the president said, referring to Mitchell's meeting with the press.

• • • •

When Ehrlichman arrived in the Oval Office at 10:18 a.m., he had done some investigating on the leak.[11] "The first wire story, I traced back on it since I talked to you, came on the Dow Jones wire out of New York. And it had all the names. And that was about six-thirty last night." This fact suggested the leak had come from the bar, from someone in New York.

The president said he had "told John [Mitchell] that I just had to have the bar's [report] by the end of the week." Then he asked, "Your people could be ready tomorrow?"

"Yes, sir, they'll be ready tonight." Ehrlichman brought the president up to date on his vetting efforts. "The boys spent seven hours with Herschel Friday yesterday. And they say he's just as clean as a hound's tooth."

"I told John [Mitchell] what I thought was a very, very low blow for the *Times* and others to point out he's bond lawyer. But John says, you know, that's ten percent of his practice."

"Yeah, that's what they told me on the phone. He has a general practice, he is the least political guy in the firm, of a fairly political firm. But he has a general practice and the bond business is a minor, it's a very minor part."

"He's a good lawyer?"

"He's a good lawyer. In fact, Dean's description of him was that he's a brilliant legal technician."

"That's all we need."

"Now, he says this. He said, 'I don't know if this man is a conservative.' He said, 'I talked to him for an hour and a half about both the crime issues and the civil rights issues,' and he said it was at the end of the day. He said, 'I've been working him over for seven hours, [and] I'm going back this morning, and hit him fresh on this.'"

"I can't do it if he's not conservative," the president insisted.

"Well, I told John [Dean] that I wanted a phone call from him just as soon as he was through down there, and then I called Mitchell and I said, how much have you talked to Herschel Friday about his convictions?"

"That's right."

"And John said, 'Well,' he said, 'I'm satisfied.' And I said, 'Well, John, here's what Dean just told me.'"

"Good, Dean, good, real good, [unintelligible]."

"And John [Mitchell] said, 'Well, I think he's wrong,' but he said, 'if there's any question in your mind, you,' he says, 'you better get him up here or we better go down there and find out,'" Ehrlichman reported.

"They thought Brennan was supposed to be a good lawyer, they really did," Nixon said, thinking back to his experience during the Eisenhower administration. "But you know because he was a Catholic, everybody said he was going to be [moderate]. He turned out to be the worst damn judge in the Court, if there is a worst one. And Friday could be his [unintelligible]. Find out about his wife. She's a member of the League of Women Voters. That could tell you something."

"All right."

"See how close he is to Fulbright.* You know what I mean now?"

"Right."

"I'm awfully glad you raised this, and then, if we don't get him, I'd go with Clark. What do you think?"

"It sounds like a safer bet."

Nixon seemed all but ready to abandon Friday and proceed with Judge

---

*Senator William Fulbright was thought to be the most liberal member of the Senate from the South.

Clark from Mississippi. But Ehrlichman, knowing he was undercutting Mitchell with this report on Friday, wanted to proceed carefully. "I don't want to close the book on Friday," Ehrlichman cautioned. "But the reason he got into this is that I badgered [Mitchell] just before you left and I said, between the two of us, I want to know this guy's philosophy."

"That's right. I'm not concerned about Lillie's conservatism," the president said.

"No, no, that's not a problem," Ehrlichman agreed. Nixon was satisfied with Lillie because of her California supporters, like Governor Reagan and Mayor Yorty, and Ehrlichman was satisfied with Lillie because of her record on the California court. Ehrlichman continued: "Now they're [Dean and Young] going to see her this afternoon. But I should hear from Dean within an hour or two, because he's going to get back, and I said, look, just open up *Miranda,* will you? And see how he reacts. He said, I did that. Said we talked about *Miranda* for forty-five minutes—"

"Shit."

"And he said, he talked all about the technical aspects of it, but he [Dean] said, I didn't feel he had his [thinking worked out]."

"What about busing? Forced integration? I've got to know," the president said. "God damn him. We're not going to have this. And I'm [not going to put a] sleeper on that Court. [If he is a liberal] he's not going to get his job."

"Well, I don't want you to close your mind to him yet, but I do raise this because I wouldn't want to leave here with you thinking that I thought he was all [right]."

"How about you taking another quick whack at"—the president paused for a moment in thought, then snapped his fingers—"Ed Clark, all right? Could you, could you have somebody [check on] him? Go down and talk to Clark, maybe he's a better judge."

"[How about] sending Krogh down to see Clark this morning?" Ehrlichman asked.

"Could you do that?"

"Sure, sure," Ehrlichman responded.

"John [Mitchell] says that Clark is from Mississippi and [elevated to the Court of Appeals only] recently, he's only been on the bench for [unintelligible], but God damn it, how can they turn him down? What do you think?"

"I don't know. I see the attractive thing about Friday, on civil rights, is that he's never been involved in a civil rights controversy except as a lawyer, professionally, and he's unassailable in terms of his personal convictions," Ehrlichman explained. "So I said to Dean, well, what are his personal convictions? And Deans says, I can't answer that. But in terms of confirmation—"

"Well, I'm not as concerned about getting him confirmed," the president said.

"And neither was John [Dean]. John says, I can get him through confirmation. Hell, I can tell him the right things to say, but how's he going to vote five years from now?"

The president, somewhat taken aback by this report, sat silently for a moment. Then he said softly, "Good."

Ehrlichman repeated that he would send Bud Krogh to visit with Judge Clark. But the president was already exploring alternatives. Maybe, he speculated, he could find another Poff, a member of Congress he could nominate. Or what about William French Smith? Ehrlichman did not like the idea of two Californians, notwithstanding the president's argument that he had appointed two Minnesotans. Still reaching, the president wanted to know about "that Oregon law school dean?"

"He's a good possibility." Ehrlichman must have known whom the president was referring to because he had recommended it. This was something between the two men, but not a name that surfaced in broader discussions.

"Two Catholics." The president sighed. "That's bad, if Lillie holds out. Have you got any other very new conservatives?"

Ehrlichman responded with a sigh of his own frustration. They searched randomly for names, but at first neither could come up with anything new. At one point, Ehrlichman laughed and said, "Well, I got a name but I don't know whether it's any good or not."

"Who is it?"

"Kleindienst," * Ehrlichman said. The conversation stopped for several beats before Nixon responded.

"He's good for me. Well, they put Whizzer White on, why not Kleindienst?"

---

*Richard Kleindienst was the deputy attorney general.

"Kleindienst was a hell of a student. He is a Harvard graduate. He had a superior law practice. He handles himself very well. He is, of course, in like a bandit with that Senate Judiciary Committee."

There was another pause in the conversation. Nixon was thinking about the Kleindienst suggestion. "They could attack him [as] mediocre but he is not," the president said.

"He is not mediocre. He is not," Ehrlichman assured him.

"And he's a Republican."

"He is president of the Federal Bar Association this year, which is a—"

"Throw his name in to John [Mitchell], okay?"

"Okay, sure."

. . . .

Ehrlichman was beginning to turn against Friday. Still, the president had gone pretty far down the road toward naming the Arkansas lawyer, and Ehrlichman had to be careful.

"Clearly Friday is a conservative in the civil rights area," I told Ehrlichman in a telephone call from the Little Rock airport, shortly before leaving for California. But that was the only area of the law for which his thoughts had been resolved, and I was not at all sure how firm those beliefs were. We had spent almost two more hours with Friday. "In fact, he was surprised at the profile in the *New York Times* that described him as a moderate during the Little Rock integration crisis. He was not displeased with the description, however."

"Any other evidence of his philosophy?"

"Well, we talked about school prayer, which was also mentioned in the *Times*. He doesn't think there should be prayer in public schools, and he advised the Little Rock School Board not to fight the Supreme Court's ban." This was bad news for Ehrlichman. Because we were rushing to make a flight to Chicago and then on to California, the conversation was brief. When Ehrlichman pressed me, I was not able to give him my assurance that Herschel Friday was a conservative. And I repeated to Ehrlichman that it was going to take a lot of work to get him ready for confirmation hearings, should the president proceed.

Now Ehrlichman was ready to make his move. He called Haldeman to request that a meeting be set up with Mitchell, himself, and the president. It was arranged and convened at 2:30 p.m. in the Oval Office.[12]

"Well, how are you doing with the judges?" the president asked Mitchell as they seated themselves around his desk.

"About the same."

"Sir, I talked to John Dean," Ehrlichman said. "He's just finished up Friday and he's on his way to L.A. He says that he spent better part of a couple hours with Friday on just philosophy, [on] a whole range of problems. *Miranda*, narcotics, juries, everything on that side that he could think of to talk about."

"Busing?" the president asked.

"Busing."

"[Forced] policy of integration?"

"All that. He said that finally, that Friday said to him, John, you're going to have to tell me what to say when I'm asked about these things."

"Oh God," the president groaned in an obvious bit of theater for Mitchell.

"[Friday] said I want to be with the President. And he said there are a lot of these things that I just don't know anything about, my practice has never brought me into them. And I just don't have any feelings on [them]. And I said, for instance, this *Miranda* thing. He says, I don't know where I stand."

For Mitchell, this had to be embarrassing. I was his young, former middle-level assistant at the Department of Justice, who was saying that once again an ill-prepared candidate had been given to the White House. Mitchell tried to bat away the *Miranda* holding, quite sure that Friday understood and was right on it.

Ehrlichman, however, had the facts and continued. "No, John [Dean] says he certainly didn't know the *Miranda* case, so they [went into the firm's law library and] took it out." After a brief discussion about the fact that Friday did not practice criminal law and therefore work with *Miranda*, Ehrlichman reported, "I backed off this and said, John, you've got to tell me what this fellow has in his gut. Is he a conservative? Down in his gut?"

"That's right," Nixon added.

"And John said, I can't tell you that he is. He said, frankly, I had the feeling that he's very intellectual about the things that he knows about. And that he's almost blank on everything else."

"Sounds like a lawyer, God," Nixon quipped.

"And I said, well, I know the President is really vitally interested in the answer to this question. Is this fellow a conservative? And I said, you've got to understand the importance of your answer to the question. He said, I understand completely the importance of the answer to the question."

"John Dean says this?" the president asked for clarification.

"Dean says this. He says you're going to have to tell the President for me that I cannot assure him that Herschel Friday is a conservative," Ehrlichman reported.

"Let me ask you another thing. Were you able to check his social attitude?" Nixon asked.

"No, I haven't had time to do that," Ehrlichman answered.

"Whether his wife likes to socialize?" Then the president turned to Mitchell. "You see, John, one thing is, you can tell a hell of a lot about people if you know what influences their wives. My wife and yours, well, [they're not as far] to the right as we are. But if he's got a social wife, she can come here [and get involved with] that God damn Georgetown set."

"Is the wife noticeable?" Mitchell asked, puzzled.

"Well, I don't care what she looks like. I just want to know is she a socialite?"

"I would say [not]," Mitchell answered.

"Think she's conservative?"

While Mitchell did not have much information about Mrs. Friday, he knew her friends, who were conservatives. Mitchell then responded to Ehrlichman's report. "Now let me point out that Bill Rehnquist got just the opposite [reading on Friday] from John Dean. And let me point out also that I've talked to John McClellan at great lengths. He is also the most blatant conservative fellow in the [Senate], and he thought that [Friday] would be just fine on the Court. . . ."

Ehrlichman countered. "I have to tell you what Dean told me. See, he went back and he gave me a report this morning. And I went back to him and was rather specific, and I also asked him to ask Friday if when he had been in Washington, if he had answered these questions. And particularly on his attitude on the criminal side. And apparently, nobody had [asked him any of these questions]."

"Bill Rehnquist tells me he did to the point where he came [to the conclusion that he was] conservative," Mitchell responded.

Nixon explained that he was concerned about appointing another Potter Stewart, who came to town a conservative but the president believed had been twisted by the Georgetown set, particularly Katharine Graham (publisher of *The Washington Post*). Mitchell did not believe there was much that could be done about that, and pointed out that he had based his selection of Friday more on what others said about him than what Friday had to say. The president wanted to know if Mitchell had asked Friday about the matters that concerned him, like busing. Mitchell had not. The president said, "I'm so concerned that I will wake up ten years from now and say I appointed that son of a bitch. See what I mean? I think with Mildred Lillie I've got no problem. I think she is strong-willed, isn't she?"

"Her track record shows it," Mitchell agreed.

Soon they were once again reaching out for other names. Friday's candidacy was teetering on the edge of an abyss. To bring focus, Mitchell finally said, "If you want to get off the hook and just make it look good, all you have to do is go to Lewis Powell." But Nixon wasn't ready to make a move, and besides, Powell was sixty-four.

At last, after going back and forth, the president concluded that "you can't always be sure but I think we've gone through the exercise" by further questioning Friday. Nixon summarized: "He has no strong convictions. I'm not worried about what he would say in committee. I'm worried how is he voting five years from now? Because he doesn't have a bedrock conviction. Now that's the question." But the president liked the fact that "he's pretty close to Burger, as you know."

On this weak evidence, Friday's candidacy was saved—for the time being. Mitchell had prevailed. Nixon finished, "Well, let's decide on it. Let's go on it. We just, we can't be sure about his beliefs. But the main thing is we just give him one hell of a [final check] when he's here, so that he understands the requisites [on the issues important to the president]. That's very important."

9

THE CHIEF JUSTICE AND
OTHER PROBLEMS

OCTOBER 14–18

I NEVER UNDERSTOOD why any president would want the prior approval of the American Bar Association's Standing Committee on the Federal Judiciary for Supreme Court nominations.[1] While there was good reason for the ABA's evaluation in nominating the many federal trial and appellate court nominees, the Supreme Court was different. Supreme Court nominees are few and should not require credentials checking by a third party, since the White House, the Senate, and the news media are certain to pay close attention to them.

In the White House Central Files I had once found a letter from a veteran federal judge, Clifford O'Sullivan, of the United States Court of Appeals, Fifth Circuit. Judge O'Sullivan described the Supreme Court as "sacred ground, to be occupied only by men who have already demonstrated that they outstandingly possess the needed high judicial qualifications." This Court was a place neither for "try-outs" nor to "be used as a proving ground or place of apprenticeship." Most striking—and irrefutable—was the belief of this seasoned lawyer (thirty-seven years of practice) and judge (twelve years on the bench) that when dealing with the Supreme Court, "political trading is not only unwise and unpatriotic, it is immoral." Judge O'Sullivan's requisite for any choice was a proven adherence to the "rule of law." [2] In short, only the best judicial minds in the nation should come into play for the Court, and these people should be conspicuous to the legal community.

If the president was looking at a person of that type of ability, he did not need a committee of Bar Association lawyers, however able and insightful they might be, to tell him if his choice had the knowledge, disposition, and experience necessary to be a justice. Persons without such proven skills would not even be considered. If the president was so foolish as to put forward an unqualified candidate, then the confirmation process would reject the nominee, and the president would pay the political price. There was no better example than G. Harrold Carswell.

In fact, in 1971 I thought that President Nixon should have broken off relations with the ABA, but only regarding his Supreme Court nominees. The ABA members could testify at a confirmation hearing, and say whatever they wished. Thus, to drop them would not have denied their input in the process. But giving any outsiders advance rejection of any candidate for any reason did not bode well.

My worries in this regard centered on Mildred Lillie. I did not think Herschel Friday would be nominated. I figured that he would withdraw from consideration, realizing he did not have the credentials. Another session like the one we had put him through in Little Rock would do it. But I hoped the situation with Judge Mildred Lillie would be different. She had great judicial qualifications. And I truly liked the idea of a woman (if not women) on the Supreme Court. It was past time.

· · · ·

On Thursday evening, October 14, Young and I arrived in Los Angeles. David had managed to embarrass me on the flight by having a group of flight attendants line up and sing "Happy Birthday." He'd overheard a conversation I'd made from the airport before boarding, and learned it was my thirty-fourth.

We met with Justice Lillie (judges on the California Court of Appeals were called justices) at her apartment in Century City, a fashionable place to live. If Warren Burger was from central casting for chief justice, Mildred Lillie presented an equally wonderful image for the first woman to sit on the Supreme Court. She was a handsome woman, large but not overweight. Motherly without being matronly. She had graying hair, a warm smile, and a strong grip. Like Burger, she had presence. We spent four and a half hours with her to find out if she had substance, or problems. When I called Ehrlichman from the hotel after our visit, I had learned all I needed to know.[3]

"What do you think?" Ehrlichman asked.

"John, she's terrific," I said, genuinely enthusiastic. I took Ehrlichman through the life and times of Lillie, the name she took when she married her first husband Cameron Lillie (who before his death in 1959 had been a law partner with Los Angeles mayor Sam Yorty). Alfredo Falcone, her current husband, had later joined our session with Justice Lillie. "This woman knows about, and has thought about, the issues that confront a Supreme Court justice," I told Ehrlichman.

"Unlike Friday," he added.

"Exactly. It was a delight to talk with her. She is articulate, well read, knows the criminal justice system from the bottom up, and the civil justice system from the top down. She's had vast experience, John. She knows her way around the Constitution. While she's had no civil rights cases, she thinks busing hurts children. She doesn't like it. She's a deeply religious woman, and very active in her community. The president will do himself proud naming her."

"What's her greatest judicial strength?" he asked at one point.

I chuckled. "She says she is best known for reorganizing the domestic relations court in Los Angeles."

"Lord, that's got to be an awful task. I'm not sure that's much of a qualification for the Supreme Court," Ehrlichman said. "But when you think about it, I'll bet being a domestic relations judge is about as tough a slot as there could be. Child custody, divorce, that's worse than police court."

"Anyway, she was there for two and a half years. Her most celebrated case was the custody fight between Ingrid Bergman and Dr. Lindstrom."

"Oh my, that was quite a case. You know it?"

"No. All I know about Ingrid Bergman is that she was terrific, and beautiful, in *Casablanca*."

"Amen." Ehrlichman then told me about a much-publicized case after Ingrid Bergman ran off to Italy with director Roberto Rossellini, leaving hubby Petter Lindstrom and daughter Pia behind. Ingrid and Roberto made movies and soon babies. "Was that the case?" he asked.

"I didn't know you were such a film buff," I responded, surprised to discover another side of Ehrlichman. He said nothing and I answered, "I don't know. Lillie said that she had not been able to find the opinion she wrote. She said she only cared about the child, but she didn't mention Pia. Justice Lillie said she often sought to get couples back together, but with Ingrid Bergman, that wasn't going to happen."

"Catholics don't much like divorce," he commented.

"Lillie's proud of her short tenure on the domestic relations court. At one point, she cracked up both David and me when she said, 'There are God knows how many little Mildred Lillie Gonzaleses running around Los Angeles.' "

We laughed, and then I went through my notes. I had two potential problems. The first was Falcone. Young and I, while believing he needed further checking, had been satisfied that his bad business judgments and practices would not cause a problem in her confirmation. When I finished, Ehrlichman raised the other problem.

"Will the ABA find her qualified?"

It was a question I had been thinking about throughout the visit. I explained to Ehrlichman that because of Dick Poff's concern about the ABA Committee, I had learned more about them—the members, and their thinking. Based on what I knew, I was troubled. This was a very reserved, make-no-waves group. "There's a real potential they'll find her either not qualified, or they'll—at best—have no opinion."

"Why is that?"

"Because she's a woman. But they'll never say that. She's very conservative on criminal law issues. She doesn't like lawbreakers, because she worked as a prosecutor. She doesn't think criminals should be freed on technicalities, particularly when guilt is overwhelming. Otherwise she's moderate. She has been reversed a good bit with her criminal holdings. The California Supreme Court is many degrees to her left, and—"

"Wonderful."

"Well, maybe not. If they focus on her reversals."

"That won't trouble the president. How bad, or good, her reversals are will depend on one's point of view. Should we review more of her holdings?"

"She estimated she had written over 1,160 opinions—"

"That's impressive," Ehrlichman interjected.

"Of the cases which she says were 'taken over' by the California Supreme Court—"

"Taken over? What does that mean?"

"That was her term for when the California Supreme Court took the case on appeal. She estimates that two-thirds have been reversed. I was struck by that being high, and she said it was about the norm for other judges. While she did not have a count, she said that very few of her cases, relatively speaking, had gone up on further appeal. And in the cases where she was reversed, typically she had upheld the trial court."

"You really think this is a problem?"

"It shouldn't be. But it may be the excuse that the bar hangs its hat on to keep a woman off the Court. If Rehnquist has not done so, someone in his shop should review all of her cases that were reviewed by the California Supreme Court. Or should I have someone in my office do it?"

"I'll have Justice do it. But as I said, I don't think her reversal rate will trouble the president," Ehrlichman decided.

"That's nice to hear. This is a woman who has worked hard all her life. She grew up on a farm doing physical labor. She earned her own way through law school as a domestic cook. And she's been in public service virtually her entire career."

"That's good. I'll keep you posted. Mitchell's going to want a full report, so you guys scurry back here as soon as you can."

• • • •

The next morning the lead item in the president's Friday, October 15, news summary really raised his dander. ABC and NBC Television news programs had both led with reports on the Court nominations. The ABC report on Herschel Friday was "relatively good" and on Mildred Lillie "very good." What caused the president to reach for his fountain pen was the NBC report: a story that the ABA wanted more names because the original six "lacked stature." In the margin the president wrote to Ehrlichman: "E—Never again do they get a shot at any judges after this performance (including District Courts)."

That afternoon, the president and first lady were going to North Carolina to participate in ceremonies honoring Reverend Billy Graham. The president would unveil a bronze plaque at the house where Graham was born. The morning was filled with important meetings. The first was on foreign trade with aides Henry Kissinger and Peter Peterson.[4] While the conversation had nothing to do with the Court, the president alluded to his ploy with Senator Byrd.

"They floated that Byrd thing out there. Well, we're not going to appoint Byrd to the Court [for] a variety of reasons. The purpose of that was to scare the hell out of the liberals, so that when we appointed somebody that was not a member of the Ku Klux Klan, [they'll say] hey!"

Peterson liked that. Laughing, he complimented the president for his deception. "That's brilliant, that's brilliant."

"You've got to do that now and then," the president said. "Then all of a sudden you come up with some other guy that's, well, a decent man, and then they don't tear him to pieces. They say, well, Christ, at least we avoided Byrd. That's what this is."

Haldeman arrived in the Oval Office at 9:37 a.m. to report that John Mitchell needed to see the president before he left because he had "a Chief Justice problem."[5]

"Is it the woman?" Nixon asked.

"I suppose that's what it has to be. He called me last night. Said it was imperative that he see you before you leave today." When the president said no more, Haldeman continued, "John Dean's been out working over Mildred Lillie and he's ecstatic. He says she's a God damn jewel. Says she's tough, able, personable, a marvelous woman. Absolutely clean. Solid conservative. Democrat. Catholic leader. Very big community type, which she is. Her husband [has had some business problems] but that's perfectly clean. There's absolutely nothing there [on the husband], Dean thinks, now."

Nixon was pleased, but still thinking about his news summary. He asked Haldeman where all the leaks were coming from about his selections. Were they coming from the American Bar, the Justice Department, the White House, or where? Haldeman assured him that "nobody here knows who you're talking about, except Ehrlichman, and you're not going to get those out of him."

"Must be out of Justice," the president speculated.

Haldeman (correctly) advised the president that it was not me. Haldeman assured him that I was "totally reliable," and that I never talked to the press on anything. I had a flat rule of never talking with the media.

"Well, I'm never going to submit anything to that God damn bar again," Nixon fumed. He addressed Mitchell's need for a meeting. "Oh, I'm really going to shit on Burger on this one. Burger has been made Chief Justice, I made him Chief Justice to fend him off, you know what I mean? He'd have never made it with anybody else in this office." It annoyed Nixon when he gave people great jobs and they immediately "start negotiating with you. Well, now God damn it, I'm just tired of this, you know."

"That's right. Put on their robes and all of sudden they think they can [deal with you] by divine right," Haldeman said, being his obsequious best.

When Mitchell, accompanied by Ehrlichman, got in to see the president, Mitchell got right to the point. "Mr. President, the topic of the conversation is that we've got Chief Justice problems." Mitchell sounded agitated.[6]

Nixon sounded disgusted. "Yeah."

"Let me give you the scenario and see where you want to go with it. On Wednesday he wrote the letter that I mentioned the other day, that talked in general terms about the strengthening of the Court. It pointed out that there was no qualified woman to be on the bench, he said that Friday was great, he reaffirmed that, and went on to the point that he thought the only way to strengthen the Court was to put on somebody who was nationally known in the judiciary. And he went back over the same bunch of names, all of them sixty-five- and sixty-nine-year-olds."

"Yeah."

"The letter was rather moderate in tone and I thought that it was just a usual pitch. But yesterday, he insisted upon coming over to the Justice Department to see me. I told him that was very unwise at this particular time to do it. He shouldn't do it. He had to. He came over and he had a handwritten letter that he read to me and it was, in effect, a letter of resignation to take place on September 18, 1972. I pointed out to him that no—"

"I, well I, I accept it."

Mitchell cleared his throat, and before he could get another word out the president addressed the resignation again.

"Right now. Right now."

"Yeah, well, we can't do that. [Though] I should thank you." Mitchell largely ignored the president's reaction and proceeded. "We had a good hour and a quarter of hard talk. I told him that there was no way that he could deliver an ultimatum to you, that if he resigned he was doing the very thing to the Court that he was trying to protect it against. I think Warren's somewhat in a state of confusion. He's been sick, you know, for about three weeks, with a fever and has been taking medicine. He's had this new term open up, et cetera, et cetera."

"Bastard."

"Yeah, that's true," Mitchell said.

"Warren Burger wouldn't be on that Court unless I had found him."

"That's absolutely true."

"There wouldn't be a chance Burger would be on that Court. I think it's great that he's there." But Nixon was not going to let Burger control his appointments. "We're not going to have that kind of thing from [anybody]. Politics to the contrary notwithstanding. It's just too bad."

"I quite agree that he cannot present you with an ultimatum of any form or shape," Mitchell concurred.

"He can't choose the people. He's acting just like Arthur Burns. We have three people on the Federal Reserve. Arthur wants to name successors. Not on your life. We'll consult him, but he isn't going to name them. That is what the [President] of the country is supposed to do."

"Well, we shouldn't even be consulting with him actually," Mitchell said, referring to Burger. "He's the one that's consulting. I haven't been consulting with him. He's the one who's had the input. At least I haven't gone around to ask who Burger [is recommending for the Court. He's coming to me]."

"Well, I didn't mean it," Nixon said, feeling he had overreacted. "But I just don't like this idea of coming in with this [threat that he'll] resign. We hear it around here all the time too. From the White House staff. Well, I'll resign unless you do this or that. Well, that's all, fine. I say, fine, resign. They'll be heroes for awhile and then forgotten. That's the way it works."

"I quite agree with you. The Court will go on. But I think this would be a hell of a time to have it happen because we will have an upheaval in the press and all the rest of it that will be carried out of proportion. You and I know that."

"I understand. This is because of the woman, is that his point?"

"Basically I believe it is." Mitchell explained: "His argument, of course, is that she's great but not distinguished and you need a distinguished judge to strengthen the Court." Mitchell cleared his throat. "Now what I would like to suggest is that when I talk to Mr. Burger tomorrow, [that I say] that this is completely unacceptable, he should go about his way. He can't be giving you ultimatums and just go back to his branch of the government and let you run the executive branch with the appointments. This is, in effect, what I told him yesterday. I think by the time he got through, he was, you know, a little off the kick. But I'm not sure."

"Well, what I meant, John, is this. Warren Burger is really one of the best appointments we've made."

"I agree with that," Mitchell said.

"We're God damn proud of that appointment. And we can't say that about a lot of the Cabinet, as you know." The president reminded Mitchell that when Burger talked about "distinguished men," he should "go back and read the editorials about him[self]. He was referred to as an undistinguished judge, with an undistinguished record. You remember? And I had to defend him."

Mitchell said he had mentioned this fact to Burger, who said that "we must have been reading different editorials."

The president soon asked Mitchell if he had seen the favorable coverage of Lillie in his news summary. He had not. "Well, what I'm getting at is, that I don't think any of those women are worth a damn. You know that."

"I agree," Mitchell said.

"But on the other hand, John, we've got a situation where there is in this country a very strong conviction for a woman." As an example, Nixon told him of John Connally's support for the idea.

Nixon told Mitchell about the ABC Television report on Mildred Lillie. ABC had interviewed people who knew Lillie. They described her as "very attractive, pleasing personality, sense of humor, bright, intelligent, conversationalist, good hostess and cook, whatever the hell that means." Mitchell laughed, and the president continued: "When asked about her legal ability, he said absolutely top legal qualifications. Schumacher went on to say she was tough, and a fair-minded judge, who did hesitate to use colorful language in some cases."

"David Schumacher, huh?" Mitchell was surprised any ABC reporter would say anything nice relating to a potential Nixon appointee.

While discussing the press, Nixon turned from Lillie to Friday and his other names. He noted the report of NBC's Carl Stern, "who said that the reason the ABA asked for more names is that the six were disappointing and lacked stature. What in the name of God? Does the ABA believe it's going to get another crack at us? Never again, including district judges. I mean this," Nixon said sternly. Then he asked rhetorically, "Can you believe the ABA put this out?" Nixon continued with Stern's report. "Stern foresaw a certain fight over Friday. At least a half a dozen lawyers are in Little Rock now looking for ways to defeat him."

"That's pure baloney," Mitchell interjected, as Nixon continued reading and summarizing.

"Friday was referred to as a segregationist. The *Arkansas Gazette* is most unhappy with the idea of Friday. Joe Rauh* says his civil rights group was carefully looking at Friday's segregationist background." Without breaking stride but with a notably lighter tone, Nixon read on: "Martha Mitchell hinted that the female RN would select is Lillie. She exclaimed, 'That's my man!' when the name of Herschel Friday was mentioned.'" Nixon and Mitchell laughed. He placed the news summary back on his desk, and stretched his legs as he turned to address Ehrlichman. "Well, here's the way I feel," he said; his tone serious again. "I think the main thing that [Burger's] got to know is first, that we're going to have a hell of a time with Friday, mind you, because of the segregationist thing. You agree, John?"

Ehrlichman agreed. "I think probably so, not because he's segregationist—"

Mitchell finished his sentence. "Because [of] the cases," referring to Friday's representation of school boards opposing integration.

Nixon picked up the thread. "The cases are all they have to hang their hat on, Rauh and that bunch. They'll get him worked over pretty good. Do we think we can confirm him?"

"Yes sir," Ehrlichman answered. And Mitchell agreed.

Ehrlichman thought it time to report my finding to the president, un-

---

*Rauh was a Washington, D.C., attorney who had once clerked on the Supreme Court and represented a number of civil rights organizations.

aware that Haldeman had already given him the gist. "John Dean called me last night about Mildred Lillie after the interview."

The president reminded them that they wanted to call her "Mildred Falcone." Ehrlichman continued, "Dean says she's the best thing since sliced bread. He really—"

"Very impressed," Nixon commented.

"And he worked over Mr. Falcone for some period of time and feels he's not great but he will not be an impediment."

"But why does he like Mildred Lillie?"

"Well, he says she has all the right vibrations on the philosophical things. On crime, on administration of justice, civil rights, she just comes down foursquare. Just couldn't be better." When Mitchell noted that she had not had civil rights cases in her court, Ehrlichman reported, "But she has all the right answers."

"We will generally find that somebody that's hard on law and order is also hard on civil rights. Right?"

"I agree," Mitchell said. "Look at all southerners. There's no southerner that I know of that's soft on civil rights. Or on crime and law and order." He cited Democratic senator Sam Ervin of North Carolina as an example.

"The best story that illustrates it is the [one about the fellow who drove Oliver Wendell] Holmes to the Court, [back in the] horse and buggy days," Nixon said. "When Holmes would get out, the fellow would say, 'Well, good morning, Mr. Justice. Do justice today.' And Holmes snapped back at him, 'That's not my job. My job is to play the game according to the rules.' And, of course, that doesn't mean that he's going to do injustice. It means that at the highest level, that justice is not individual and personal. A judge who plays the game according to the Constitution [is playing] according to the rules. That's Holmes. That was Frankfurter. And that's, by God, what we will have."

"Well, that's my speech last Friday too," Mitchell added.

"Great," the president said with a laugh. "Well, I'm sorry about the Burger thing. I knew it would come up." But he was not going to be intimidated by his chief justice. "Well, with regard to Warren, he's got to take the lead on it. And what I meant is he's got to say, if he says anything, that he welcomes the [appointment of a woman]. If he puts out some other story he can hurt himself and the Court—if it appears that Warren Burger is opposed to women. That's my point." Nixon offered a few more disparaging remarks about the reality of women in public affairs—"It's becoming like India now. And like Russia"—before returning to the problem with Burger.

"Well, I would suggest, Mr. President," Mitchell sighed, "that I just tell Warren Burger that this whole concept is unacceptable all the way around and it's not going to be discussed any further. And the conversation never happened, and that he better go about being Chief Justice in the interest of the Court and the country and stop this foolish nonsense."

But Nixon had decided that the best way to handle the chief justice was not to be tough, but rather to stroke him. He told Mitchell to tell Burger the president "thinks he's the greatest thing that's come along." To tell him that appointing a woman was "a painful thing" for the president, too. "I think we must, or I am convinced that just as the time came for a black to be on that Court, [so too] the time has come for a woman. It was hard for them to take a black, particularly a dumb black. And at least I have given them a bright woman. Now just put it that way."

Mitchell didn't seem to have a problem with this. No doubt he was happy to have ameliorated Nixon's earlier mood before the president did something he would later regret. The ensuing conversation degenerated to the president asking questions like, "Who in the hell ever thought of education for women anyway?" And Mitchell responding that they used to "teach them domestic science. That ought to be the full extent of it." To which the president told Mitchell that was no longer the case and he was "a male chauvinist pig!"

"Well, I gather that's true," Mitchell responded. The president laughed, and Mitchell continued, "But I recognize what the change is and [if] they're treated differently, they don't like it. And I'm not talking about the bra-burners and all the rest of them. I'm talking about the average house-wife."

"On paper," the president noted, "it makes a very good argument that they should have equality in all things."

• • • •

Haldeman dropped by the Oval Office after Mitchell had departed. The president explained the problem with the chief justice. The conversation is interesting because it gives Nixon's take on what he had just resolved with Mitchell.[7] "Burger's so concerned about getting distinguished people on the Court that he was going to resign in September if we don't appoint distinguished people. So what do you think of that?"

"I'd say the least distinguished one of the bunch is Friday, and that's Burger's candidate."

. . . .

When Mitchell returned to the Justice Department, he called me.[8] He wanted a private, firsthand reading on my visits. He knew that I was preparing a memorandum with Young on our visits with Friday and Lillie. But he wanted my reading as someone who had sized up the candidates and knew the Senate Judiciary Committee. I had been his congressional liaison at Justice. I gave it to him straight: I thought Herschel Friday was a great lawyer, but he would be a confirmation disaster. We would have to rehearse him with answers, and a good examiner like Democratic senator John Tunney of California on the Senate Judiciary Committee would chew him up and destroy him. Mildred Lillie would be a delight to watch before the Senate. She would manhandle them. This was a woman who had spent her entire professional life having to deal with lawyers—prosecutors and judges. There was no one on the Judiciary Committee, with the possible exception of Senator Phillip Hart (D-MI), who was a former U.S. attorney, who could go toe to toe with her—and Hart wouldn't because she was a woman, and notwithstanding her conservatism, bullying her would be a political disaster.

"Well, I suspect you're right on Friday. And Lillie too," Mitchell said as the conversation was coming to a close.

"General," I said, using a title often employed with attorneys general, "I know it is not my bailiwick, and I'm sure you've got no shortage of people giving you their two cents, but if these candidates wash out, don't overlook Rehnquist."

"Well, I understand from Ehrlichman, and Dick Moore, that you've been urging us to look at Rehnquist. No question that he'd be good. The problem, John, is there's no political positive for the president."

"I've got to disagree." I was thinking of the media. "The current candidates, rightly or wrongly, are getting hammered for being less than stellar. A former editor of the *Stanford Law Review*, with a master's degree in political science or history or whatever it is, who is a former law clerk to Justice Robert Jackson, and your constitutional lawyer, is a stellar candidate.

The political positive he gives the president is a conservative who can sit on the Court for thirty years. And the politics of a quality appointment."

"Um hum."

"While the president hasn't had many dealings with Bill, everyone over here who has respects his legal skills."

"I don't doubt that. When Ehrlichman brought up his name, I pretty much pushed it aside. Maybe I should give it further thought."

• • • •

On Sunday, October 17, both Young and I decided to go to our offices to prepare our jointly written report to Mitchell and Ehrlichman. I was surprised by the activity when I pulled in to the White House. The president's helicopter was arriving as I parked my car on West Executive Drive, and Dick Moore arrived in his car just as I did. We walked together to the EOB and noticed Secret Service agents turning on lights in the president's EOB office. To my amazement, Moore knew I had been to Little Rock and Los Angeles to vet Friday and Lillie. He explained that the president had called him from Camp David. Moore wanted my take on the putative nominees. I suggested he drop by my office, which he did about an hour later.

I told Moore I was disappointed by Friday.[9] "I assume he's Mitchell's friend," I said. Like everyone outside the inner circle, I was unaware that Friday was Burger's candidate. (Indeed, this fact has remained undisclosed for three decades.) Moore had no idea who had suggested either candidate. He knew Mildred Lillie from his years in California. Moore was disappointed that we had found no Republican woman.

"What I don't understand, Dick, is why Mitchell and Rehnquist don't dig deeper and look wider. You know if the president charged the White House with this task, we would call every judge, law school dean, and bar association in the country to find the talent. These guys wait for someone to give them a tip."

Moore agreed.

"Dick, I'm going to lobby a bit more for Rehnquist. He's got the credentials. He's been confirmed by the Senate for his current post. I think we may be wasting time with Friday and Lillie. It's time to build a bench."

"A what?"

"You know, get some backup players."

Dick was a bit depressed when he left my office. I walked down the hall with him to go find David Young. As we were parting, Moore said, "I took your idea about Rehnquist to Ehrlichman. But it didn't seem to go anywhere. Maybe we should talk to Mitchell about it. It may not have occurred to him." I said nothing of my conversation with Mitchell.

• • • •

When I read the president's news summary on Monday morning, October 18, it was clear we would have a very unhappy president. A fusillade of attacks had been launched against him before he had nominated anyone. His list of six was causing a small firestorm of protest.

The *New York Times* was questioning whether FBI checks had been made on the list of six. (They had not.) The *Times* dwelt on "Mrs. Lillie's husband who had been sued 22 times in 10 years for non-payment of debts," and on the fact that she was "also under scrutiny for her supposedly high rate of reversal by the Calif. Supreme Court." The *Baltimore Sun* had a "rare backgrounder" with Mitchell, who had been "facetious, flippant, ironic, bristling and angry" when discussing the six on the list, and had "conceded ideology, not ability, was a major consideration in Court choice." The National Women's Political Council was not pleased with the list, including the two women. The Americans for Democratic Action called those listed "a bewildering assortment of mediocrities." Reverend Jesse Jackson labeled them "racists and bigots." Senate majority leader Mike Mansfield said the list made him sorry he'd voted against Haynsworth. *New York Times* Court-watcher Fred Graham wondered "if RN is really seeking to demean the Court with a mediocrity." Even the conservative news columnist James Kilpatrick conceded that "the group wasn't really that good." *Time* magazine's Hugh Sidey called the list "appalling" and "shocking." News commentator Martin Agronsky said only two of the six were listed in *Who's Who* and the others have "no modicum of distinction." And newsman Peter Lisagor said the president was "demeaning the Court." It was a brutal rejection.

• • • •

Haldeman once told me that he believed it a vital part of his job merely to sit with the president so he could think aloud, use him as a sounding board to clarify and articulate his thoughts. Nixon appreciated it, and it was a part of the ritual between the two men. This morning, Nixon needed to sound off. He wasn't merely angry about the press; now he was also worried about the ABA.[10] "You know this problem with the [bar], I told Mitchell and Ehrlichman I'm putting [an end to sending names] through [the] American Bar. We get all those names out there, see. They get their stuff in. We can't get any of our stuff out," the president complained.

Haldeman agreed. "They're trying to make the case that [Lillie's] reversals were on legal grounds, not philosophical. But Friday they're concerned about because he turns out to be, basically, a typical pure lawyer. Pillar of the community and all that. [Apparently he's] a very fine guy but with absolutely no conviction," Haldeman said.

"Well, I think that's true, so—"

"And they're [the White House staff] afraid, you know, he's going to turn into a—"

"Potter Stewart?"

"Or worse, a Tom Wicker type," Haldeman added. Tom Wicker was a *New York Times* reporter, and a southerner considered to be a liberal by the Nixon White House. Referring to concerns expressed by the very few White House staffers with whom he was conferring about the nominations, Haldeman continued, "And they were concerned about Friday. They think you are in pretty good shape with Lillie."

"What do they mean? Concerned about his [law] firm?"

Haldeman explained, "No, not so much the firm but just about the guy himself."

"Yeah."

"How he doesn't have any [philosophical] convictions and therefore could be bad. He can take either side and play it."

"Well, Ehrlichman and Mitchell went at that for quite awhile," the president noted.

Haldeman had been told. "Yeah. I think we've got to go back to him," Haldeman said, without enthusiasm for Friday.

"Try again," the president said reflectively. Then he sat in silence. Haldeman had made his point. Nixon's doubts about Friday were again nagging him. Finally, he asked, "They have any other names?"

"No. No new ones."

"It's just so hard to find a God damn southerner. If we could just get out of the South," Nixon said, bridling with frustration at his own restriction.

• • • •

Haldeman returned to the Oval Office in the early afternoon, carrying a memorandum to the president from Leonard Garment, who like Mitchell, was a former Nixon law partner. Garment had come to Washington after the campaign, and while Nixon did not rely on him as he did Mitchell, he respected Garment's mind and judgment. When they practiced together, it had been Garment who had prepared Nixon to argue before the Supreme Court, for Garment had headed up the litigation operation of their law firm. At the White House, Garment was known as the "house liberal" though he was not as liberal as Nixon often pictured him.[11]

"Well, Len's got his thoughts on one piece of paper, on the Court,"[12] Haldeman informed the president. "He has two nominations."

Nixon, because Garment was Jewish, guessed that one of the two names was Edward Levi. But this was wrong. Haldeman said that Garment "makes his case that your objective should be not only the philosophical view but the ability to persuade others on the lower courts, the bar, others." Garment had recommended "two men, that by adding them to Burger and Blackmun, you have a foursome that's strong enough to effect fundamental changes and to begin to do so soon enough to make a difference in 1972—Howard Baker and Caspar Weinberger." Haldeman got no reaction from the president, so he read the next paragraph. "He says, 'Whether or not Friday and Lillie have these qualities is largely guesswork. In the case of Baker and Weinberger, you have personal knowledge of their intelligence, level of energy, ability to organize and present information and ideas, and argue a case.'"

"Why doesn't he want a woman?"

To answer, Haldeman jumped to the fourth paragraph: "He says, 'A persuasive case has not been made for the appointment of Judge Lillie. The appointment of a woman is not that much of a political plus. Many men and women view this as simply catering to the feminist lobby, and in the case of Lillie there is a growing feeling that she's not qualified.' That's in his circle," Haldeman added.

"Mum hum." Nixon was intrigued. But he quickly said, "The problem

[with] Weinberger though, it just won't fly. I've thought of that [at some length]." Nixon's voice trailed off as he thought further.

"Howard [Baker wouldn't] be bad," Haldeman suggested.

"Howard would be fine. I've got to talk to Mitchell about [him]."

"He's kind of interesting," Haldeman said, encouraging the idea. Adding, "He's not an effective senator."

Nixon agreed. "It's just that he's never going to be the leader in the Senate."

"No."

Nixon said that Garment did not understand the politics and polls regarding the Jewish vote.

Haldeman offered his assessment. "The Jew thing is just, ugh, it is impossible. No gains to be made there. They're not going to vote for you on that anyway. The Israeli types will vote for you if you do something for Israel and against you if you don't."

"Forget it," Nixon said, waving it away. "I don't see this problem on Lillie. Why do you think [Garment thinks she's not qualified?] She's as qualified as anybody he'll know."

• • • •

At 2:00 p.m. I joined Bill Rehnquist, Dick Moore, Bud Krogh, David Young, and John Mitchell for a meeting in Ehrlichman's office. It was an opportunity for Rehnquist and Mitchell to delve into what Young and I had learned about Friday and Lillie on our visits. I led with a bit of song and dance about our visits, entertained all questions, and I am sure—notwithstanding my efforts to the contrary—thoroughly embarrassed both Rehnquist and Mitchell with the sloppy work they had done on Herschel Friday, while more than corroborating their choice of Mildred Lillie.

Earlier I had encountered a newsman who had covered the Justice Department before the White House. He had heard, off the record, that I was vetting the Court candidates. No comment. Was I visiting with all six? I suggested he see Ziegler, who was in charge of releasing White House information. But his next question numbed me for a moment, then gave me a good laugh. As the meeting was breaking up, I repeated the story for several of the group.

"So he asked me if Bill Rehnquist was under consideration," I explained, after setting up the story. That got everyone's attention, as I hoped. "So I said, why would you ask that? He answered, 'Well, that potential first occurred to me last month when I was over at Justice and ran into Bill.' He said he flat out asked Bill if Nixon might appoint him to the Court. He told me Bill answered by saying it would never happen. 'I'm not from the South, I'm not a woman, and I'm not mediocre.'"

My small audience burst out in laughter, except Rehnquist, who had overheard my story and turned beet red. When the laugher stilled, he nodded his head up and down with a boyish grin. "Yeah, I said that, but it was off the record."

• • • •

Following the meeting in Ehrlichman's office, Ehrlichman and Mitchell went to the president's EOB office.[13]

"Well, we're on the Supreme Court," the president announced, not that anyone had any doubt. Speaking to Mitchell, he asked, "What is your present evaluation?"

For a change, Mitchell had some encouraging news. "First, I'm happy to report we've gotten over our Chief Justice problem." Mitchell's manner expressed his pleasure with how he had handled it. "He's going to stay in bed until he recuperates from this current illness and then go about his business and not add to our problems. We had an extensive conversation that really resolved the earlier kick. He's feeling a little better and has the drugs out of his system.

"With respect to our candidates, I have been talking to Ed Walsh today after they had their task forces in the field in Little Rock and in L.A. With respect to Judge Lillie, the essence of it is [they've looked at] her relations on the court, her inability to get along with other judges, et cetera, her rate of reversal and so forth. It's Ed's assessment—bear in mind that they have not had their committee meetings to kind of assess what's going to come out, they are going to start meeting tomorrow afternoon to go over it, wind it up with the California people on Wednesday—his assessment is that Judge Lillie will not be found qualified."

"I'm not surprised," the president said, but there was disappointment in his voice. He did not seem to listen to Mitchell's statement that the ABA knew of no woman more qualified than Lillie. "What about Sylvia Bacon?"

"No question that she's not going [to qualify]."

"She a district court judge, no?"

"No, she's a Superior Court judge here [in the District of Columbia],"
Mitchell said, dismissing her. Mitchell was still interested in Judge Lillie,
and reported that she was also receiving positive support from professional colleagues. "The three-member panel of the ABA that interviewed
Lillie said that she's got a great personality, good character and all that,
but yet they've come up with this. This is Ed's judgment, and I guess all
the rest of them [agree]." Mitchell had informed Walsh that the president
would want to know if her reversal rate was a problem.

"Reversal rate?" Nixon said, nonplussed. "Who, who, who, who are the
judges that had the greatest?"

"The dissenters, for Christ sakes," Mitchell finished his thought.

"Holmes and Brandeis dissented more than they ever [concurred], so
they were, they were then reversed. Bullshit, reversal rate. God damn
them."

Mitchell wrapped up his report on Lillie by saying that her husband
"needs further checking out." Mr. Falcone did not keep good records,
which was part of the problem. Mitchell then turned to the ABA's evaluation of Friday. According to Walsh, Friday would pass the bar; not that
they would find him qualified, rather, they would "not oppose" his nomination. Mitchell said he had asked Walsh how they came up with this position, and had been told, "on the basis that he was not nationally known."
Understandably, Mitchell thought this dubious at best.

The president, however, wanted to know if Walsh thought that there
was any woman who was qualified for the Supreme Court. Mitchell said
they had talked about Sara Hughes, who had been on the Federal District
Court bench in Texas for many years and was seventy years old. But
Mitchell did not really have a satisfactory answer. Nixon said he did not
blame Ed Walsh for the problem. Then the president, in an unusual action, told Ehrlichman, "I want to talk to John [Mitchell], but I want to talk
to him alone. I'll tell you later what was talked about. I want to be able to
say that only John and I have talked about it, right, that you don't know a
thing about it." With this, Ehrlichman left the meeting.

Nixon now spoke in a hushed, confidential tone. The president was
ready to get down to it. He and Mitchell would decide this question together as they had so many political questions. "I think it's well that we

discuss this privately and decide what we're going to do," he began. "Let me put it this way, I think that with regard to the woman"—he paused, lost in thought for a moment. "I had thought that appointing a well-qualified woman [was important politically]. I mean, let me put it this way. I think we've got the perfectly strong group of people [as candidates]. Our first consideration must be what kind of a person is going to be on the Court. The second, we've got to do it, if we can, in a way that is not going to hurt the presidency. Now this is the question we've got to address ourselves to. The woman thing was simply being, in terms of the person, this woman [has] to be hard-line as hell. And second, will the presidency be taken on? But if the bar comes out with a not qualified, then the [question is whether to go without bar approval]."

Thinking aloud and weighing the problems and potentials, Nixon concluded that if the bar gave a non-qualified to Judge Lillie, he would have to find another nominee, someone like William French Smith, whom the bar could not possibly reject.

It was decided. "I need them qualified!" Lillie was probably not going to make it.

The president was forced to raise other names for consideration. "Suppose you were to take [Lewis] Powell, he's sixty-six?"

"No, sixty-four."

"A good man."

Mitchell agreed. They talked about Powell's background. As the conversation progressed, the president acknowledged that he could not go with Senator Byrd. "We can't go with Byrd, you know that. He'd get the burn. But, hey, how about Baker?"

"Howard is a fine individual."

Nixon had liked Garment's proposal; it had confirmed an earlier thought of his own. Baker was in his forties, which meant he could serve on the Court for many years. "He's a very persuasive political guy and you know that Court is political as hell. He's a good leader. He'd be a God damn persuasive judge." Garment's seed was sprouting.

"You know, my only limitation for Howard Baker [is that we could lose a Senate seat]." Mitchell was not sure whom the governor of Tennessee would appoint to Baker's Senate seat if Baker were to go to the Court. Nor was the president. Still, he found appeal in the Baker idea.

It remained to be decided how far to play the Lillie card. They were going to have to deal with a "PR problem" if they did not appoint a woman, Mitchell noted.

"Think the women will be mad if we don't take a woman?" the president asked.

"Yes, sir, yes."

Mitchell told the president that if the bar found Lillie not qualified, then they would not be able to find a conservative woman anywhere who *was* qualified. He added that all the women in large law firms tended to be liberals.

Returning to the subject of new candidates, Nixon said that he wanted to put Howard Baker and William French Smith into play. Then the president returned to Lewis Powell. Mitchell surmised that the bar would not, and could not, oppose any of these men. Nixon raised yet another name, his law school friend Charles Rhyne, but Mitchell remained unimpressed with him. As Nixon looked at his alternatives, he was reminded of the Haynsworth-Carswell debacle, and the reality that the public did not recall those he had placed on the Court as readily as those who had been rejected. "Let me ask you, leaving out the Senate seat," the president posed, "wouldn't Baker be a man who would [knock] the hell out of them?"

"If we can get him up there under the proper circumstances, yes."

Clearly, having to figure the bar's reaction was frustrating both men. When Nixon realized he was starting to drive his attorney general a bit crazy with potential combinations, he backed off, and finally told Mitchell, "That's fine. I'm following you." Nonetheless, Nixon instructed him to get Walsh's reaction to Powell as a potential. He liked Powell as a backup, so he pressed Mitchell to pursue it. "Would you do that?"

"I will do it and, and, hopefully it will work."

"All right, do that. I'm going to go with Powell. Sixty-four years of age and by God, for him, he'll stay on till he's seventy-five like everybody else and that's not bad. Wouldn't you say?"

Somewhat reluctantly, Mitchell agreed.

It took awhile, but Nixon had moved the discussion to the point where he was ready to let Mitchell know it was time to abandon Herschel Friday. "I think they're going to rip Friday up, John." Nixon was telling Mitchell to replace Friday with Powell. It was for this reason that Nixon had excused Ehrlichman. When Ehrlichman had sent me to vet Friday, he had undercut Mitchell's selection—a selection that should never have been made. Without Ehrlichman present, it was easier for Mitchell to let go of his own choice.

Soon it was evident that Nixon also believed he needed an alternative for Lillie. At the moment, Nixon was leaning toward William French Smith. The president told Mitchell to get a reading from Walsh on Smith. He wanted to get all this accomplished that week. When Mitchell protested, "They can't start the second maneuver with Smith and Powell until they act—" Nixon, uninterested, had another thought. "Now, do you have openings on the Circuit Court of Appeals, or anything out there? Is there any place that we can put Mildred Lillie on another court?"

"No, [not really]." Mitchell explained his difficulties. To place Lillie on this court would require taking a selection away from someone else, a situation filled with political problems. Nixon dropped the idea.

Eventually Nixon reached a fundamental question about his replacement for Friday. "Do you think Powell will take this?"

"I'm going to talk to him today," Mitchell said. Mitchell was not sure whether Powell would take a seat on the Court or not.

Nixon, impatient to get matters resolved, asked Mitchell if he would talk with Powell right then. Mitchell had no objection, and the president requested that the White House operator get Lewis Powell for the attorney general. But Powell was traveling and unavailable.

• • • •

Mitchell left this meeting with no truly viable candidate to fill either of the vacancies on the Court. The president had rejected Friday, and Mitchell knew the bar would reject Lillie. They were going to play the Lillie card a bit longer, however; if the bar rejected her, the president would get political credit for having tried to appoint a woman nonetheless. But that was a game, and when it ended they would be left with no cards. Mitchell had to worry about the prospect of Lewis Powell, who had told him only a few years earlier he was not interested in a Supreme Court appointment. As for Howard Baker, Mitchell had no idea how he would react to an appointment. It is fair to say that the appointment process was in a complete shambles.

Over a month had passed since first learning of the openings on the Court. What should have been a political opportunity, easily capitalized on, had become a growing liability, difficult to resolve. The president had publicly committed to fill these seats but now would not meet his own deadline. With each passing day, the pressure was compounding to fill the vacant seats so the Court could get its work done for the new term, which had commenced on Monday, October 4, 1971.

PART THREE

10

POWELL AND BAKER

October 19, 1971

DEADLINES CERTAINLY CAN CONCENTRATE THE MIND. For over a month Richard Nixon had been fussing thoughtlessly with his Supreme Court selections, resulting in a political shellacking by the media. The fact that he had failed to meet the deadline that he had imposed the prior week annoyed him. Yet this missed cutoff proved to have a remarkable impact on his thinking. It forced the president to take full charge of the process, using Mitchell like a staffman.

On Tuesday, October 19, he had nobody vetted or ABA-approved, let alone ready to take either of the two open seats. By Thursday, the 21st, he would announce two nominations. He had toyed with names, aiming for one southerner and two solid conservatives. He had played with punishing the Senate, by suggesting Byrd. Despite his personal feelings, he had tried for a woman and now needed a graceful exit from Mildred Lillie. He had tossed names of people he knew nothing about at the ABA, and they had embarrassed him.

He was painfully aware of the media hammering. The president's Tuesday morning news summary featured more attacks on his list of six potential Supreme Court nominees. It reported that Harvard professor Lawrence Tribe said that "Judge Mildred Lillie was overruled unanimously in four key cases this year and he charged that it was 'with extraordinary frequency' that her decisions were 'insufficiently defensible' that they were overruled." *Time* magazine's page on "Nixon's Not So Supreme Court" asserted that the list of candidates "once again demonstrated RN's inability or unwillingness to nominate renowned jurists to the highest tribunal." Interestingly, but incorrectly, *Time* believed that John Connally was responsible for the Byrd ploy, which made it obvious that "RN was opting for mediocrity and playing politics at the same time." But what caused Nixon to add a bit of cryptic marginalia was the critical commentary by CBS's Eric Sevareid claiming the president was "selecting Court appointees that will be of electoral help [even] though his press advisors are appalled at the list of six." The president messaged Haldeman: "H—Can't we muzzle our staff on this?"

It was too much harmful news. It was time for the games to end.

• • • •

While the president felt he must wait for the bar's evaluation of Mildred Lillie, he planned to press forward on other fronts—hard. Although he and Mitchell had tacitly agreed to drop Friday, they needed to firm up Powell, or Baker, or Smith, or whomever, for Friday's seat. And the president needed an alternative for Lillie. Decisions had to be made, so the president summoned Mitchell to the Oval Office for further discussion.[1]

Nixon opened the conversation. "I've got a couple more ideas on our Court thing. You haven't talked to—"

"—I have talked to Lew Powell this morning, early this morning," Mitchell cut in, knowing exactly what was on his mind.

Anxiously, the president asked, "He'll do it?"

"He will do it, he'll do anything you ask him to."

"Good."

"He doesn't care to," Mitchell quickly added. "He's got a problem which he's checking out for us. His eyesight."

"Oh Christ."

"And it's an unusual disease that has a slow process of deterioration. It doesn't bother him now."

"He's fine?" the president asked hopefully.

"He is checking with his doctor, and will get back to me as soon as he can today. He's had this ever since he was in the Air Force Reserve, so it's a very slow process, something that floats in the eyes that impairs his continued reading. He said that he now, of course, works with the books and the briefs and everything else. It's just a question of whether or not the doctor's judgment will be if he steps that up and accentuates the reading process as to whether it's going to impair his ability to perform. He is the highest type of individual, you know, that would take these things into consideration."

"I know." The president added that "most guys would never tell."

"No, they wouldn't. They'd go for the honor and let the chips fall where they may. But he puts it on the basis that anything that you would ask him to do he would do."

Nixon wanted assurance that Powell would report back soon. The best Mitchell could give him was, "He said he'd be back to me as soon as he could today."

"And then you'll call?" Nixon asked, sharing the pressure he felt with Mitchell to get these matters resolved.

Mitchell gave his assurance, and said, "Then I will get in touch with Walsh and provide the scenario."

"You will emphasize to him that now we're going to go for Powell and we want him approved tomorrow."

"Well, and we also want that woman approved."

"Well, that's the other thing. We think it would be very bad, in the event that they don't approve the woman. I'm just saying this, sort of tongue in cheek, it looks to me like it's a stacked jury, no women on the jury. Just point that out. Don't tell him I'm saying it, just say, look, you aren't going to look very good." The president wanted to know if the bar had any trouble with Lillie on anything other than her reversals.

Mitchell believed that was the only thing that had arisen—but that they would reject her for it anyway. "I think, here again they'll see it on the fact that it's an intermediate court, that her opinions are not distinguished and, you know, the usual crap that you can make a case out of."

"That's too bad."

For the second seat, they were again at square one. Again searching for names. Over the course of a long conversation, in which they ran countless permutations and combinations, they considered and rejected nominating a number of sitting judges. Getting the most attention was federal appellate judge William H. Mulligan of New York, the former dean of Fordham Law School, who had been recently appointed to a federal appeals court. Nixon liked Mulligan because he was a Catholic. Mitchell, himself a Fordham Law graduate, was worried that Mulligan would be considered a mediocre selection. Nixon moved on, but he was not about to abandon this judge.[2]

Mitchell told the president, "I'm pointing out the paucity of people that are available for the appointment to this Court that will receive acclaim."

"Look, I'm not concerned about acclaim. Let me put it this way. I am willing to settle for half a loaf of acclaim." The president then repeated that "they didn't say Burger was too damn distinguished, did they?"

Mitchell had been doing some digging. "No, we looked at the editorials yesterday—"

"Blackmun? Was he distinguished?"

"No, quite the contrary. He wasn't distinguished at all. But you could justify them on the basis of their sitting on the circuit court for a period of years."

"That's right. So that takes care of it. There are just not any acclaimed people, John. Except on the left."

"On the left or, or the—"

"Or old."

"Or the older ones. Now they talk about people like Wright,* for Christ sakes, he's really a left-winger. He's on his third marriage and you wouldn't know what would happen to this guy. He could be another Douglas before you turn around."

"Yeah, I see. I didn't know that background. And as far as you're talking about [Edward] Levi from Chicago or [Phillip B.] Kurland from the law school in Chicago, those people, I just"—Mitchell stopped, sighed, and continued—"they're not going to follow your philosophy."

"I wouldn't trust them," Nixon added. "I'm just thinking you've got to move fast. If they turn Lillie down, I want to put the names up right away."

*Charles Alan Wright would later join the president's defense team when he was threatened with impeachment.

The president wanted Mitchell to submit William French Smith along with Lillie's name, and have them both considered by the ABA.

After some banter, the president mentioned William Mulligan yet again. But Nixon wanted Mitchell's reactions to Garment's other suggestion. "Len Garment recommends Weinberger. Why not?" Then he answered with another question about Weinberger's conservatism, or lack of it. "Couldn't [we] be sure?"

Mitchell said, "I couldn't be sure about Cap. I wouldn't have the faintest idea. Cap's a very able, brilliant individual. Of course he's half Jewish or at least his name is Jewish, and he has a public life which they seem to hang some criteria on. He's from California."

They were going in a circle, and it was up to the president to break it. "The Baker thing's intriguing. I just don't know what they'd do." Maybe the bar would even find him "well qualified," Nixon hoped. Mitchell was sure of it. After a brief rehash of how they had handled Burger without the ABA, Nixon got back to business. He wanted to place the names of Powell and Baker with the bar, if these men were willing. But he remained interested in Mulligan, and continued to nudge Mitchell to include him as well. "What I'm getting at is, let's suppose that they come up with Baker and say not qualified." Then the president would have to submit another name. "We'll be screwing around here until the end of the year. I was thinking that Mulligan wouldn't take them long."

"No," Mitchell agreed. But there was another way to handle the ABA. "On the case of Howard Baker, you might say the hell with them, and go ahead and send his name up. Assuming he's had a reasonable law practice."

"Well, why don't you take that up with [Baker]? See what kind of a law practice he had and how reasonable it was. Whether he made some money and so forth. In other words, go with Baker like we did on Burger. Then let the bar do what they did and do their [own thing]. Baker can get confirmed just like that. They'll back [him], I'm sure. Because first of all, [Senator Hugh] Scott would work his ass off for him to get him the hell out of the Senate."

"So would Griffin."

Nixon agreed. "And Griffin would work his tail off to get him out of the Senate. In other words, Baker is actually [in] with the liberals, you know, and even though he's sort of running against Scott, he'd get all the senators. So you've got it made." Nixon was warming to Baker. "I think he'd make a damn good judge."

"Do you think he's that conservative?"

"Oh Christ, yes. Yeah, I think he is. I think he would go with Burger on a thing like this. I mean, he isn't the greatest stand-up guy, but I think he's young, and so forth. He's not going to be like a Douglas or a Black."

"I don't believe so."

"Howard is basically a Dirksen type of fellow.* He'd come out more often than Potter Stewart on our side."

"Oh, I'm sure of that." But Mitchell admitted he did not know all of Baker's "foibles."

"No, I think Baker would be good. I'll tell you that if they turn the woman down, [then] we just throw up our hands and send Baker up. Check his law background," the president instructed.

"Baker and Powell. They'd have a hell of a job complaining about either one of them," Mitchell said.

"They'd never complain about Powell. You mean the Senate? Or the bar?"

"I'm talking about the Senate," said Mitchell. "Now what the bar will do to Baker I don't know."

"Now, they wouldn't say not qualified," the president added with disbelief.

"I don't believe they would, either."

"He's a senator," the president said, giving it a ring of importance, though he admitted that senators were more important in Washington than elsewhere.

The president instructed Mitchell to forget about who might be appointed, or elected, to fill Baker's Senate seat if they appointed him to the Court. "Don't be worried about the Senate seat. This is more important. Just be categorical about that. Appointing Baker to that Court isn't going to hurt us one damn bit. I mean, my point is that the Court can help us more than any [individual] as a senator—to fight the busing issue."

---

*Senator Everett Dirksen of Illinois had been the much-admired Republican minority leader of the Senate, a moderate who worked well with all sides. Presumably Nixon knew that Howard Baker was Everett Dirksen's son-in-law.

By now, Nixon had fully embraced the concept of Powell and Baker. "Two southerners. It's good."

"If they're looked upon as southerners."

"Yeah. They're both southerners to me. Border states, what the hell. Would you say it might [have an impact]?"

"It might have a bigger political impact than any other combination that you could put together," Mitchell said.

"Because what?"

"Because of the Senate and Baker," which was Mitchell's shorthand way of saying he would be easily approved, "and because of Lew Powell, an outstanding president of the ABA, et cetera. It would take care of the South and the border states—"

As the conversation continued, the president digressed to talk about leaks, saying that Haldeman was a "God damn good man." Mitchell agreed he was one of the "finest people" he'd ever met. The president told Mitchell that he was "pissed" at the continuing leaks and off-the-record comments by his staff. "We've got enough trouble with the press without having one of our jackasses in here [popping off]," Nixon said. But he needed more information about Baker. "On the Baker thing, maybe we can find out right now how long he practiced law?"

Mitchell wanted to go directly to the source. "I was thinking of getting him down and sitting down with him to go over it when I get back [to the office]."

"All right. Do that. Why don't you do it right away?" Nixon wanted Mitchell to hit Baker "cold turkey." But he had another idea. He picked up the telephone, and told the operator to get him Haldeman. Instantly he had him on the line, and told Haldeman to get him a book with information on Howard Baker. The *Congressional Directory,* or *Who's Who.* He wanted to know how long Baker had practiced law. And he needed it "right away."

Waiting for Haldeman, they discussed sending both Powell and Baker to the Senate without waiting for bar clearance. Nixon, of course, loved this idea. "Now you're talking, now you're talking," he enthused.

"See, this is not really a clearance process."

"No."

"This is an advisory operation."

"That's right. Why not send him up? Now we know that Powell will be cleared by the bar, and just send Baker and Powell up, and send them up if Lillie gets turned down." Nixon did not want Mitchell to have to continue going around and around "with all those kikes on that, you know, who the hell's on the ABA. It's a bunch of, I mean there're some Jews, and also there are these—"

"A few of them."

"Were you active in the ABA? I was not."

"I was in a [section dealing with bonds]."

"I wouldn't go to the God damn ABA, even if they could give me"—he changed his thought—"the ABA, just like all professional organizations, is an incestuous group."

Haldeman entered and reported on Baker. "He's forty-five, he'll be forty-six in November. Born in November '25."

The president asked, "Where did he go to law school?"

"University of Tennessee Law College. He went to Tulane and the University of the South and then to University of Tennessee Law College, L.L.D. 1949."

"Yeah. Go ahead."

"And was in the Navy '43 to '46, discharged in '46. It doesn't say when he practiced. He was running for the Senate in '66, so there was twenty years from the time he got out of the Navy until the time he went [to the Senate]."

"That's not bad. What did he do in between? You got anything else?"

"It doesn't say."

When the president asked Mitchell for his take, he said, "Howard was in a firm in Knoxville. I know because we used to work with them."

"Thanks, Bob," the president said, and Haldeman departed.

Mitchell resumed. "Getting back to this scenario, it really depends on how hard you want to play the turndowns. If we've got turndowns we could say the hell with it, they wouldn't approve this woman." Mitchell advised the president how he could have a win-win. "You'd use it for both purposes. In other words, you get off the hook with the woman, and also the reason why you're not submitting the names to them again because you just don't believe in their judgment."

The president could not have liked the idea better. Mitchell left to call

Baker and drop a bolt from the blue: He was under consideration for a seat on the Court.

• • • •

Anxious to get results, and learn how Mitchell was progressing with Baker and Powell, the president telephoned his attorney general shortly before 1:00 p.m.[3] There is one person whose telephone calls are always put through in Washington, regardless of what is going on. Mitchell took the call, and before the president could get a word in, Mitchell filled him in.

"Hi, Mr. President."

"Yeah, hi."

"I have Howard with me now."

"Oh, I see, fine. I wanted to tell you one thing. Are you somewhere where you can talk?" Obviously he was not. But Nixon passed on news that Haldeman had given him, that a California businessman both Mitchell and Nixon respected, Asa Call, was opposed to Mildred Lillie, and that in Los Angeles opposition to her was building. They speculated briefly that the opposition was because she was a woman. "Well, we'll see. The bar may take us off the hook on the damn thing," Nixon noted.

Mitchell laughed. Given the circumstances of the conversation, Mitchell responded with nothing. Nixon clearly understood why.

"You haven't heard from Powell yet?" the president asked.

"No, but [I] expect to shortly." This was correct, but incomplete, for he had talked to Powell at 11:11 a.m., immediately on his return from the Oval Office. With Howard Baker sitting across his desk, he could only report that Powell had more information for him, and was calling back.

"How does this one [referring to Baker] look?" Nixon asked.

"The exploratory stage."

When Baker was gone, Mitchell called Nixon to report.[4] "I have a report in both areas," he told the president.

"Right."

"We sort of knocked Howard off his feet with surprise," Mitchell began. Baker's first worry was money. (One minute and 4 seconds of this conversation has been withdrawn for privacy reasons by the National Archives.) "As he points out, the $60,000 salary [of a justice at that time] gets down to thirty pretty quickly after that tax bite."

Nixon was sympathetic, but he pointed out the Court's insurance and retirement benefits, and the like.

"Oh, I've given him all of those," Mitchell said, pointing out that Mr. Justice Douglas seemed to have made quite a bit of money through his writings.

"Right, make speeches."

"Yeah," Mitchell said, chuckling.

"Good, now, what about the other fellow?" Nixon asked, referring to Powell.

"He has talked to his doctor at great length. He is very much concerned about his eyesight. He says that he has had to ration his reading. To put it succinctly, he thinks that it would be a fraud on the people. He doesn't know whether he'd be there three years, or two years, or four years, or what it would be. He's a very conscientious individual and I tried to point out to him that the fact that if he got there that might be the most salutary thing for the people of this country. Of course I think if you called him up and asked him, he would do it if he was blind."

"Um hum."

"The question, I think, is to what might come out of the fact that knowingly you sent him to that Court with this type of an impediment, in view of the recent Harlan situation."

"Yeah."

"He, of course, does not have the same problem that Harlan has, but he still has [a problem]."

"He may be overly conscientious about how much he has to read and all that sort of thing, too."

"It is quite possible, but he still says he has to ration his reading. And while the doctor says it's possible that his eyes would last for ten years, it's also a possibility that with excessive use they would fail in a shorter period of time."

"Um hum, um hum, um hum."

"So that's the situation."

"Well, let's pursue the Baker one at least," Nixon said with a nervous laugh. "Let's get one there if we can. I don't know, Powell is just so good, that I—"

"Absolutely."

"I just think the fact he raised such a thing indicates that we ought to press him."

"Well, he is that type. He's the finest individual I think I've met in the bar."

" Damn it. Two years of him is worth more than twenty of a lot [of others]."

"I would believe this would be the case, and particularly at this time."

"This time it would give us a terribly prestigious appointment, and this and that. I frankly think you ought to press it on him, John. Will you do that? And I'll call him if necessary. I'll be glad to. But I really feel that the point is that I think that right now, the Court needs him. The point is we need him for whatever length of time it works out. And also this is something that he just really ought to undertake."

"I wonder if you'd like to talk to him and get your own assessment of this eyesight business?"

"Well, would I have him come in or do it on the phone?"

"Do it on the phone, I would think. Because you'd want to do it as early as possible."

"Where is he, in Richmond?"

"No, he's in New York, and the White House operator's been getting him for us. I think a full understanding on his part, which I've tried to convey to him, of the timeliness of his acceptance, coming from you, might, you know, be a weight in the judgment factor."

"All right, fine, I'll give him a call."

"All right, sir. And I expect to hear back from Howard before five."

"The Baker thing could be a good one. Now if we don't get Howard, and the Lillie thing strikes out, I suppose that you can—" The president left his comment dangling.

Mitchell knew where he wanted to go. "Well, it may be that we can bite the bullet and go with Mulligan."

"Now that's the thing that I'm thinking. I just think the Mulligan thing is, you know, we thought of him originally, and God damn it, so what if he's mediocre. He's not mediocre in my opinion. He's the former dean of a law school."

"Absolutely."

"And that's a hell of thing, John."

"It is with all the other deans that they have been trying to push on us, with all their liberal philosophy."

"Everybody else says a dean's a big thing, right?"

"That's correct."

"So he was the dean of Fordham, a good Catholic law school, and they say that isn't such a good thing, huh?"

Mitchell laughed.

• • • •

At 2:53 p.m., the president placed his first call to Lewis Powell, but the White House operator failed to find him. The president could only tell Mitchell that Powell "had checked out of the hotel and left no number to call, so I presume that he is on his way back to Richmond."

"Um hum."

"So, I've tried. I just called him just now. I was tied up for awhile when you told me earlier. Now what do you think we should do? Leave a call for him?"

"I would because I think we'll have time to do that—" Mitchell did not finish before the president started talking again.

"But you had the feeling that it might still be an open question. You know, the way I look at it is that if I just say, look, you're a conscientious man and all the rest, but right now, your country needs you and I'd like for you to take this, and as soon as you feel at any time you can't do it, why you come to me and, and then we'll work it out."

"I think that would be the way," Mitchell counseled.

"I'd say that two years of Powell is worth twenty of somebody else, and that's the damn truth."

"In this particular circumstance, as I keep pointing out to him, that's absolutely correct," Mitchell said.

Nixon, after reaffirming that Baker was his top choice for the second seat, added, "Could I ask you to do one other thing?"

"Yes sir."

"Have you ever tried the Mulligan name out on a, say, a fellow like Ehrlichman, to see what he thinks? I mean, I just don't know. Are we too concerned about this mediocre business with him? I'm just thinking on this and I'm going to put it to Powell. But if he doesn't go, then I just lean to Mulligan right now."

"Well, I'll talk to John about it and let him think about it."

"Say after all he's a dean of a law school."

"And I'll tell you what I might also do," Mitchell added, "because John keeps turning to him for the PR, let me talk to Dick Moore and have him go and sit down with Ehrlichman."

"Good, all right, that's the way to do it. And tell him in the highest of confidence."

"Yeah."

"In the Lillie thing, tell him we've got a problem there but we think, but I lean strongly to [Mulligan] for reasons that have to do with Fordham, I like the dean thing. I like the fact it isn't the number one law school. God damn it, I didn't go to a number one law school, John. Ah, where'd you go? You go to Harvard?" Nixon was being facetious, knowing his attorney general had gone to Fordham.

"Not recently."

"No."

"As a matter of fact, I was touted off going to Harvard."

"Well, the whole point is that this number one law school bullshit is getting me down a little, isn't it you?"

"It has for about thirty years. They just don't produce the product."

"Well sure, look, you've seen a lot of Harvard men around, they're soft in the head," the president said. "And they don't work as hard. But, now, this Fordham man may be all right. I've seen some pretty good Fordham graduates, haven't you?"

"Yes, I have. As a matter of fact, they're spread all over the Northeast and doing a hell of a lot better than the people from Harvard."

"And let me tell you, if you take on the dean of Fordham, they're taking on then the Notre Dame dean, and a hell of a lot of others. Santa Clara, Loyola."

"About, ah, about eighty percent of the schools."

"Right, but I mean they're taking on all the Catholic deans," the president insisted.

"Yep, very much so."

"Well, would you run that by Dick Moore? And then, and I don't want them to bring it to me because I don't like this business of my being lobbied by the staff and things."

"Yep."

"But just say you are just checking yourself, see. Will you do that?"

"Yes sir, I will."

"That's better, and say that this—put it on Burger, say that he's raised his name. Would you do that?"

"I will do it directly."

. . . .

Following a two-hour meeting with Ehrlichman, Weinberger, George Shultz, and Alexander Haig in his EOB office on the 1973 fiscal year budget, the president again tried to reach Lewis Powell. Again, no luck. The president called Mitchell to report.[6]

"I still haven't heard from Powell," he told Mitchell. "I've left a call just a few minutes ago but—"

"I wonder if he's in transit?"

"Well, he's been in transit for quite awhile."

Mitchell had his own problems. "I haven't heard back from Howard Baker yet either, although he said he'd call me back before five. I guess he's searching his soul."

"Sure."

"Another thought's occurred to me, Mr. President," he said. Indeed, that thought had just walked out of his office a few minutes earlier. "If we can't get Baker and Powell, if that doesn't pan out, you might consider this Bill Rehnquist over here that everybody is so high on."

"Well, let me ask you what are his qualifications?"

"Well, first of all—"

"He's an assistant attorney general," the president interrupted. Clearly the president had not forgotten the fact that he had already dismissed Rehnquist for his lack of stature.

"Yeah, in charge of the Office of Legal Counsel. In fact, Walsh has stated on a number of occasions why in the hell don't you put up somebody like Rehnquist?"

"Yeah."

"So I think that would clear."

"Right."

"He is, as I say, an arch conservative."

"Oh I understand that, but I mean—"

"He was a great student, and a pretty tough guy."

"How about the qualifications thing, that's the thing?"

"I would be inclined to believe that there would be no difficulty with it."

"How long has he practiced law?"

"Oh, Bill's been practicing, I guess, at least fifteen, maybe more."

"Where is he from?"

"He's from Arizona. Of course, he may be tapped with the Kleindienst-Goldwater business, but he's pretty eminent," Mitchell said. The reference to Kleindienst and Goldwater appears to relate to Rehnquist's involvement in the 1964 Goldwater presidential campaign, when Kleindienst helped in getting Goldwater the Republican nomination. For Nixon, that could not have been a negative.

"Did he go to law school there?"

"No, I think he went over, went to law school over at Stanford, with Ehrlichman, if I'm not mistaken."

"Yeah. Was he, um hum?"

"Just a thought I had. Everybody's so high on his ability and talent," Mitchell explained.

"He's a hell of an able guy," the president agreed. "Now, what's his age?"

"Oh, Bill's, must be in his late forties, early fifties."

"But he's younger than that, I think."

"Pardon?"

"How long did he, how long did he practice law then?"

"Must, must be fifteen, eighteen years at least."

"Then he came to the government with us?"

"Yes."

"Then he's practiced longer than that, cause he wouldn't be that old. See, 24 plus 14 is only 34, I mean, 38. He may be only forty." The president figured Rehnquist graduated from law school at twenty-four.

Mitchell knew that was not correct. "He's past that. I gather he's been practicing longer and has really had a lawyer's lawyer practice, you know. Handling their appeals and advising."

"Has he done appeal work?"

"Oh, yes, yeah. Sure, he's done quite a bit of appellate work in all of the courts. Has been great before our congressional committees. Just a question of whether or not he'd fall under the category of distinction or not."

• • • •

Finally, at 7:49 p.m., the White House operator told the president she had located Lewis Powell, and put him on the line.[7]

"Hello," the president said. His voice was deep and melodious. While these calls were not his forte, he seemed to be enjoying this one. "You just got back from New York?"

"That is right, Mr. President."

"Right. I know John Mitchell has talked to you."

"Yes, he has."

Nixon got right to the point. "And what I wanted to emphasize with you is that the importance of the factor that he, of course, covered in his conversation, that, in terms of the Court, and in terms of the kind of appointment we make, we think that nominating you would be very important. Now, of course, I understand the problem that you have mentioned with him which, which only somebody who has the conscience that you have with regard to the Court, and yourself, would do. But I just wanted to emphasize what I felt, that our concern here is not, you know, the question of the number of years that are involved but, at the present time, the need for a top-notch appointment to the Court, and I just wanted to talk to you a bit about it to see how you felt about it under those circumstances."

"Well, you're certainly wonderful to call me, Mr. President. I feel very small indeed to put you to this trouble." The National Archives has withdrawn the next 1 minute and 45 seconds of conversation based on privacy, but there is little doubt that Powell explained his medical problem to the president. Powell concluded: "It's simply that I thought it was far wiser to put someone on the Court who could be sure of staying there an appropriate period of time, and have the sort of influence that, you as a lawyer know, the great judges have had who have been able to stay there for many years. So that was the, the situation as I saw it and stated it to the Attorney General."

"Yeah. Well, let me ask you this. Let us suppose that I determined, and uh, I want to talk to John about this further, but that I determine that in view of the present situation on the Court, uh—you know Warren Burger is extremely anxious to have a top-flight appointment at this time, and what happens in the next five years is terribly important without going beyond that even; you know, who can look that much further—but I determine that your appointment at this time is what the Court needs. Would you undertake it if I were to ask you to do it?"

"I think the answer is affirmative, Mr. President. I am a fairly patriotic guy and—"

"Oh, I know that. I know what you've done through the years."

"Right, well, I would like, if I may, to reserve judgment until tomorrow morning. I'd certainly like to talk to"—Powell restated to be more explicit—"I have three senior partners in my law firm and I would, of course, try to keep this completely confidential, but in fairness to them, matter of fact, I've just walked in the door and I haven't even had an opportunity to confer with my wife."

"Sure, that's important."

"But I would say this, and I'm sure you'll understand the spirit in which I say it. I would be confident you could do far better than to put me on the Court." Again, twenty-two seconds of conversation are withdrawn, likely in reference to Powell's eyesight. Powell then offered a different caution. "One other thing I mentioned to the Attorney General that I'm sure you are quite conscious of, I've been active in my state, and particularly in education, and there will be plenty of black leaders who will think that I was not aggressive enough in aiding integration in Virginia."

The president was not disturbed in the least. "That doesn't affect matters, no, that doesn't bother me a bit."

"And I've written extensively and, well, I don't think I've taken an extremist position on, on any issue."

"Right."

"I'm sure that the Attorney General's Office is familiar with what I've written," Powell added, overestimating the thoroughness of the selection process.

"No, that's something that should be of no concern whatever. The point we're really very much worried about at the present time is that, if we can have a really top-flight appointment, it will tend to pull the teeth of some of those who, you know, regardless of who we appoint who has any kind of a philosophy that isn't on the left, they'd tear them to pieces, you see, and that we don't want to have happen. It seems to me in your case, because of your preeminence at the bar, your high, you know, acceptance among your colleagues and across the country, and so forth, the ABA, and so this would be something that nobody could—well, let's put it quite bluntly, nobody could claim that you were a mediocrity." The president chuckled as he made this last comment.

"Well, I've observed the political scene long enough to be quite confident that some of the elements who opposed Clement Haynsworth—"

"Right."

"And I thought he was a great appointment—"

"He was."

"—Would oppose any southerner, and they probably would oppose me, but that is not a consideration that I attempt to evaluate, and—"

"Right. Well, let us do that."

"I leave that to the Attorney General and his people."

"Right."

"I have stated my concern. It's a genuine one but, if I may, I would respond to your question this way. Let me talk to my wife—"

"Yes."

"And my two co-senior partners. I am one of the three seniors in the law firm." Powell then made another reference to his health.

"I know. I understand that," Nixon responded. "But very few people can look at themselves as objectively. Let me say this, that John [Mitchell] and I have talked this over—only the two of us—and we're not going to let you be bandied around unless we're ready to go on it, you know—"

"Right."

"But we feel that this could have a rather dramatic effect, despite the age factor and the rest, can have a dramatic effect in indicating an appointment of a top-flight man, and basically from the South but totally qualified, could have a very good effect at this time. As you know, the problem we have is finding others in this area who, frankly, meet the qualifications. That's our problem, I mean, they're either—"

"Oh, it's—"

"Many of them are much too old or much too liberal or, frankly, not old enough. And that's what you really get down to."

"Yes, and you have fairly determined opponents who are not going to be content with anyone whom you name—"

"I know that."

"Unless you name someone totally divergent from your philosophy."

"That's right, which I'll never do. I mean, believe me, if we have to go through every lawyer in the book, we're just not going do that. I'm sure you can understand how strongly I feel on that."

"I admire that very much."

"I think the Court needs it, that's the point, and I know Burger feels this way, see if Burger and Blackmun and Stewart—"

"Well, they are superb appointments."

"Well, we have good men there, and with you on it, let me say that I think too you've got to have this in mind as you talk this over. That time moves a lot faster than it used to. I mean opinions, decisions will be made in the next five years that are enormously important, you know, on many of these issues. The whole course of our system for many years to come may be determined in this period and I just want you to know that the Attorney General and I feel that, if you can see your way clear to do this, that we'll take the responsibility on the political side and all the rest. That's our job. But in terms of [the eyesight problem, the president was not concerned]." Nixon then added, "When talking to Burger, my goodness, when you see the workloads of our present justices—and I don't need to name them, you can guess who they are—it's just unbelievable what the poor man goes through. And you could carry half a load and do more than some of them do with a full load."

"Well, I doubt that, but—"

Nixon laughed. Powell joined him in the laughter, and the president continued, "Well, I think so. Will you give consideration, having in mind the fact that we've determined that we would like to have you, and if you can do it, fine, and if you could give John [Mitchell] a call and give him your decision in the morning, I would appreciate it."

"I will call him in midmorning."

"Fine."

"It may not be possible for me to, to—"

"No hurry, no, no. But may I say that I just want you to know that we strongly feel that we've considered all these things, considered them very carefully, that you are what the Court needs at this point, in view of all the hullabaloo that's been raised about mediocre people and the rest. I mean, I get that constantly, the point that they can never take you on, on that point and I feel strongly about that myself."

"Well—"

"Although, as we all know, whether a man is mediocre or not isn't determined until after he's been on that Court awhile."

"That's right. History proves that."

"As a matter of fact, I was looking over some of the editorials on Burger when we named him and several said, well, he's mediocre. Well, who knows that he was mediocre until he was on it for awhile? And he's proved to be a great Chief Justice, in my opinion."

"Well, I wish you could have seen him in England. You'd have been very proud of him." Burger had been the titular head of a contingent of American lawyers visiting London for a special meeting of the American Bar Association.

"Is that right? Yeah?"

"Yeah, he was. He was great there and all Americans were proud of him and there were twelve thousand of us who were there, including the wives, and the English really respected him."

"Well, just let me say that this is the way we feel. We would like for you to weigh that very heavily into your decision and your talk with your wife and with your partners, and if you would give John a call at your convenience tomorrow sometime before noon or around noon, that would be fine."

"I'll call him before noon."

"Fine. All right."

"Mr. President, let me say, however this turns out, that I am ever so grateful—that is a poor word but I can't think of a better one—for your taking the trouble personally to call me."

"Well, that shows you how much we want you," the president said with a soft laugh.

"Thank you very much."

"All right, thank you."

When the president hung up, he sat and thought for a few minutes. If Nixon had wanted Powell before the call, he wanted him even more now. Powell's dignity, patriotism, humility, and conscientiousness could not but have impressed the president. Yet he had not been able to close the deal. At 8:19 p.m. he called Mitchell to report.[8]

"I talked to Powell."

"Good."

"And, well, as you know, he is a great fellow, and he said that he would talk to his partners in the morning and so forth and, and would call you before noon. Now I think it's sort of a—"

"[He's not going to turn you down, is he?]"

"Well, there's a chance, there's a chance. I said, well, I just wanted him to know that we feel very strongly. For the good of the Court and so forth and the country, and he ought to weigh and all that sort of thing. But he said, well, I just think you can get somebody better, you know, who can serve longer, et cetera, et cetera. So that's the way it is. Okay? So lean on him hard, whatever he says tomorrow."

Possibly emboldened with a bit of alcohol (there was a slur in his voice and a different attitude), Mitchell spoke bluntly. "You must not have leaned on him very hard, because I started off with him on that basis, and I got the rapport that he would do whatever you wanted him to."

Defensively, Nixon responded, "Oh I leaned on him very hard. I said we've decided it and we felt he should take this under consideration, that he weigh this as he made his decision."

"And he's still talking to his partners and this one and that one and the rest?"

"Yeah."

"Well, he's probably being conscientious."

"In the morning, when he gets to you, just say, well, after you've talked to your partners, we want you to do it. How about it? Okay?"

"Yes sir, I will do that. Now, there are two other factors involved. Things are not going well with the bar, as you might expect. But I have been talking to Walsh and he's going to keep that session open until we program him the way that we want it to go."

"Right."

"The second thing—"

"They're going to turn Lillie down, aren't they?"

"Well, I would believe so," Mitchell speculated.

"Fine. How about Howard?"

"I can't find him. You know, he promised to call me back by five o'clock and I can't even find him. However, he's been conferring with George Romney* and the Lord, or what he's doing I don't know. But I'll stay after him so that we'll have an answer on it all and try and put the pieces together before late tomorrow afternoon when the bar gets through up there [in New York]."

"Good."

· · · ·

Baker was first told that he was a candidate at 11:35 on that Tuesday morning. Now it was mid-evening, and Baker was AWOL. Apparently he was frantically considering his finances, or searching his soul. Or both.

---

*Romney was the former president of Ford Motor Company, who became governor of Michigan, and opposed Nixon in the 1968 presidential primaries. He was in the Nixon cabinet as secretary of Housing and Urban Development. He was not held in high esteem by either Mitchell or Nixon.

11

WHILE HOWARD BAKER

DITHERED

October 20

RICHARD NIXON was homing in on Powell and Baker, but he wasn't finished considering other options. The first item of business on Wednesday, October 20, was one more check for a woman. The president called in his personnel staffman, Fred Malek, to undertake a quick review of every female attorney he had appointed in the executive branch. Were any qualified to sit on the Supreme Court? Malek, not a lawyer, could offer none off the top of his head. But he promised to review the situation. The president did not want to find he had overlooked an obvious choice—one of his own selections within his administration.

Mitchell still had heard nothing from Howard Baker, no doubt to his surprise and annoyance, and he was going to be out of the office most of the day to give a speech at noon in Philadelphia. He called the president.[1] "I wanted to give you an interim report because I have to leave to go out and talk to those AP [Associated Press] editors in Philadelphia," Mitchell began, explaining that he had to leave at 9:30 a.m. He continued, "[Chief Justice] Warren [Burger] talked to Powell last night and he said he had a good conversation with him." Mitchell said he was expecting a call from Powell any time.

"You get the feeling with regard to Howard that he'd like to do it?"

"Yes, yep."

The president, aware of Baker's financial problems, said, "Well, God, we can arrange something. Well, I don't know, loans are hard to raise, but hell, that shouldn't be any problem. Anybody that's going to have a job that pays sixty thousand for the rest of his life, even these days, John, [that] ain't bad, huh?"

"Well, particularly when you have all your pensions and everything else, you know that your future is taken care of."

"Sure. He'll still get his senatorial pension. It won't be a hell of a lot but it'd be ten thousand dollars a year."

"Well, probably add it to his [military] service and so forth, you know that all adds up. So hopefully that will, those—"

"Can I ask you one other thing?"

"Yes sir."

"I wonder if we shouldn't, just as a backup thing, did you tell them not to look into Sylvia Bacon, or how'd we leave that? Are they not checking her?"

"Well, that almost fell by its own weight. Because of her age, limited experience and so forth," Mitchell responded.

"You mean that you just think they would vote her not qualified?"

"Well, yes, this is the—"

"Inevitable. I'm just trying to think of the answers that we have when people say, well, why didn't you check the woman adequately? Okay?"

"I think we can posture that all right. And Walsh is going to keep that group up there [referring to his evaluation committee, which was working in New York City], after he advises us of their conclusion. So that we know how to structure them in connection with how you want to move on this," Mitchell said. These vague statements were understood by both to mean Mitchell was going to lay the blame on the ABA. "Are you going to be available this afternoon?" Mitchell asked.

"Yes sir, all day."

"All right, sir, it'll probably be late this afternoon because they're going to continue up there this morning on [Herschel] Friday, and then get into Lillie. So I gather that will be late in the afternoon."

"Are we pretty sure that they're going to do what we want on the Lillie thing? When I say what we want, I mean if they're going to give her a bum rap? I don't want, you know, no opinion. [If they reject her] they ought to say not qualified. Is that what they're going to do?" This, of course, would take Nixon off the hook.

"This is Walsh's opinion as to how it is going to come out. From the preliminary information."

"He is aware of the fact that we're going to have to put it on them?"

"I told him that in no uncertain terms last night and he anticipates it," Mitchell said.

"Right. The bar has just big, broad shoulders and they're going to be—"

"They're going to have to [take the blame]."

"They're a stacked jury, they're going to take, you know, the wrath of the women." Nixon was satisfied, and moved on. "Another point occurred to me. Do we have any place that you could push a woman up to the circuit court at the same time we do this on the Supreme Court? Is there anything open there? Let's suppose we [create the opening], suppose we went the way of the New York one, you know what I mean, Mulligan. [Then] toss a woman in there. You see what I'm getting at, John? I think the idea that all this hullabaloo about women having been raised has got to indicate that we sure have [women] under consideration. That it isn't just a not never."

"I quite agree." However, Mitchell did not think he had a woman ready, nor an opening for an appellate court, particularly in New York. If there was such an opening in the District of Columbia, Nixon wanted to move Sylvia Bacon up. After discussing other courts where they might place Bacon, the president said, "Okay, you're leaving to go to Philadelphia and you'll be gone—"

"I'll be back here by three-thirty, I believe."

"Well, I'll be here all day." But before Mitchell left, the president wanted his read on Baker. "And, let's see, is it your analysis at the moment, you think Baker is considering it?"

"Ah yes, I would [say so] very strongly. And it would seem to me that with the problems he's talking about, there must be some way to work them out."

Nixon wanted Mitchell to move on Baker. "I'm not under any circumstances going to submit it to the bar. I mean, he's just going to go. Okay?"

"Yes sir, and Powell?"

"And the same with Powell, right?"

"Very good, sir."

"We just can't be bothered with [the bar]. Okay, John."

• • • •

The president spent his morning on other business in the Oval Office, and went to his EOB office at 12:30 p.m., where he had a light lunch, and then pulled out a yellow legal pad, loosened his necktie, and sat in the easy chair beside his desk. He had decided, come hell or high water, he was going to announce his nominations to the Supreme Court in an address to the nation the next evening—October 21. Even before he was certain who the nominees would be, he began collecting his thoughts about what he was going to say. Anticipating that his prose would need polishing, he called Haldeman to say that he wanted a fast writer to work on his text for tomorrow night, and would use Bill Safire. He told Haldeman that "he wouldn't tell Safire tonight who the nominees would be." In fact, he could not. He still didn't have any.

As the afternoon progressed, the president took periodic breaks. At 2:23 p.m. he telephoned Chuck Colson to talk politics, but when the Court came up in passing, the president did not give Colson a hint of what he was up to, nor his thinking.[2] By late afternoon, he was restless to find out what Mitchell had learned on Powell and Baker. He called the attorney general at 3:43 p.m., but the operator reported Mitchell was en route from Andrews Air Force Base. When Mitchell arrived back in his office at 4:10 p.m., he immediately returned the president's call.[3]

"What are the latest reports?" the president asked.

"I've just gotten in. Howard Baker has not called . . . ," Mitchell said. (The National Archives has withdrawn six seconds from the end of this sentence for privacy reasons.)

"Oh, still delaying, huh?"

"Yes, sir," Mitchell said, but tried to look at it favorably. "I gather he's probably looking for something hopeful, at least I trust that's the case."

"Did Burger did talk to [Powell]?"

"Burger did talk to him."

"Burger must have felt very damn good that we're considering him, or how did he think? Did he think it was a good idea?"

"Yes."

"Even though he's so old?"

Mitchell—then fifty-nine years of age—chuckled. "Even though he's so old."

"What did he say? What was his reaction? I'm curious."

"Burger's reaction?"

"Yeah, what'd he say about the age factor? Well, he's good for eight, ten years, huh?"

"Well, that's just what he has been saying, what he repeated last night, and of course, he also felt that it would give his main interest—the Court—a big shot in the arm. Of course, everybody's looking out after their own interest and when he reported back after having talked to Lew Powell, it sounded awfully good. Burger thought that Powell would go ahead and do it [notwithstanding his medical problem]." Mitchell told Nixon he was not surprised that Burger felt good about Powell, given "those fossils" who were his brethren.

"Yeah, those farts," Nixon added for good measure. But the president was concerned about Howard Baker, saying, "He just can't screw around forever."

"I don't understand this because when I talked to him late last night, he was just going to meet with his banker that was flying in and he was supposed to have an answer for us this morning."

"I wonder if you shouldn't call him."

"I think I better. I'll give him a call. At least you'll know what's [going on]."

"Now the other thing is this, in my view, John, that if both of them strike out, I really come down hard on, I'd go for Smith in California."

"Smith?"

"And there's no question he's going to get a well qualified in my view. I just can't see, God damn it, if he doesn't, nobody else will, you know? Elite school like either Cal or Harvard, I don't know which, and a big law firm and chairman of the Board of Regents of the University of California. Now by God, that's pretty hard to knock, isn't it?"

"It certainly should be," Mitchell agreed.

"So that's that. Now the other one is, I think I'd go for Mulligan. I mean, in terms of votes, it's worth the cost. So, what the hell, he's dean of a law school and he's on a court at least. I just don't know, I think if you appoint one outstanding one and one mediocre, that's not too bad, is it?"

"I would think that they'd have to give you some good marks and some good credit, but they're not going to do it if they can help it."

"You're just afraid of Mulligan, are you?"

"I'm not afraid of Mulligan as a person. As a judge and his philosophy, I have some concern about them getting on you as not [nominating] the distinguished gentleman that should be, et cetera. But I think they'd probably do that anyway. They'll probably do it with Smith."

• • • •

While waiting, Nixon needed someone with whom he could talk things over. Haldeman, not being a lawyer, could not give him the reactions he needed. He thought of his old friend just down the hall. At 4:20 p.m. he called Dick Moore, and asked him to come to his EOB office. If fate was to attend any of the president's conversations, this proved to be the one.[4]

The president explained the situation when Moore arrived. "I've taken this judge thing out of the hands of our staff, for reasons you're well aware of," Nixon said, referring to leaks, as Moore seated himself near the president's easy chair and ottoman, where he was working. "They're all leaking too much. Getting these poor bastards [beat up] before we get the results from the God damn ABA. The ABA's probably going to come down negative on Lillie. So she'll be turned down."

"Not qualified?"

"Yep. Now, if that happens, all we're going to do is we're going to say that [the ABA rejected her]. And Mitchell's going to crack the ABA, none of the women [could] meet their qualifications." The president then explained his concern with being attacked for "appointing mediocrity," noting, "of course, anybody that's of our philosophy would be a mediocrity." The president said this criticism did not trouble him. Yet, "I don't want to give them too big a target. As a result, we are now running by, on the southern side, the Powell [nomination]. He's sixty-four years old. But he is [a] preeminent lawyer."

"I don't know him."

"Oh." This surprised the president, for it showed Moore was a bit out of touch with the legal community. The president gave him Powell's background: "past president of the American Bar, a great scholar, writes for everything, and so forth and so on. He's everybody's first choice. He's from the South. And he's a hell of a guy, you know. We're only buying ten years from him."

"I'd like to see you have more position than that."

"I know, but we buy that in order to get something else, [a young man like] Howard Baker. Baker's practiced law, a very good practice, for seventeen years, [although he has never] argued cases in the Supreme Court. And he's six years in the Senate, forty-five years of age, you know, [and] of the two of them, [Baker] is probably the weakest." The president said they hoped to know today on Baker. (Twenty-four seconds of material are withdrawn here by the National Archives, apparently related to Baker's financial situation.) Nixon concluded by saying, "This God damn Douglas makes money."

"Writing for *Playboy* or [*Evergreen* or something]," Moore added. Gerald Ford had attacked Douglas for writing in the *Evergreen Review,* a publication conservatives considered pornographic.

Neither man believed Baker would turn down the nomination. As Nixon told Moore, "If he takes it, though, you've then got a guy who's there thirty years. And who, also, if a Republican is around, is a potential candidate for Chief Justice. Because he's a much stronger personality than Potter Stewart, plus he's Republican." When Moore agreed, the president continued: "Howard would understand that. God damn it, [Potter Stewart's] just a weak man. I think a fine judge, but he's never going to be Chief Justice."

Still, Baker might not take the offer. The president wanted to take Moore through his thinking on potential alternatives. At some length Nixon explained Judge William Mulligan's attraction, then William French Smith's, as alternatives to go with Powell. Moore, realizing he could be getting himself between Mitchell and the president, said little about either man. But Moore also sensed the president's frustration, and the uncertainty of the situation. Here was an opportunity to change Nixon's mind. Moore was aware of the president's earlier reaction to and rejection of his—and my—candidate, but he decided to try again. "You, I gather, have some, you're aware of Bill Rehnquist, and his [background]."

"Yeah, I know him. But—"

"You didn't—"

Nixon said matter-of-factly, "But they're just going to say he's not qualified. I mean, they're just going to say, what the hell, he's a young fellow—" In a nice way the president was saying, We've already looked at Rehnquist, but I'm not interested.

Moore continued. "He's the most conservative, so—"

"I know he's conservative. I know all that. He'd be a fine member of the Court, but how the hell could you just put a guy who's an assistant attorney general on the Court?"

Rather than agree, Moore next mentioned something no one had told the president. "Mr. President, he was second in his class at Stanford, he served as a law clerk to Robert Jackson." It clicked.

"Oh, did he? Law clerk to Jackson."

"To Robert H. Jackson, who you know is the cream of the crop," Moore stressed, laying it on thick. Moore added that Stanford was one of the great law schools, that Rehnquist had had a fine law practice, and "now he's got three years as the President's lawyer's lawyer—interpreting the statutes and the Constitution, at the Department of Justice."

Nixon emitted an appreciative, and contemplative, humming noise, not quite a purr.

Moore nudged further, giving Nixon a historic moment to think. "You could sell him, qualification like that. You take a Supreme Court law clerk and the fact he's a justice, it's only happened once before. It would be an impressive thing."

"You think the bar would give him a well qualified?"

"I think they'd give him, I'd like to [believe] it."

But the president realized that was no longer the issue. "I'm not going to ask the bar, though. What's John [Mitchell] think of him? For clerking for the Supreme Court, given his [real qualification]. What's he think?"

"He thinks highly. John thought he would be great. So did John Dean, who brought him up in a discussion that I was privy to when we were talking about Poff's withdrawing."

"He's from Arizona?" the president asked, not sure of Rehnquist's home base.

"Yes, he is. He was born in Wisconsin."

"Did he have any kind of law practice out there?"

"At one point he was a partner of [a firm]. The man that was the lawyer that Barry Goldwater used [during the 1964 campaign. I've got his résumé]," Moore said excitedly. "I could, I could get it, and send it right in."

"You know, you look at him now, there's an Order of the Coif* man, second in his class while at Stanford," the president said appreciatively. "Stanford's an elite law school. Right?"

"Right. It's the western of the elite, sort of an answer to Harvard."

After denigrating Harvard, the president observed, "You get to the top of your class in any law school, you're pretty [damn qualified], that's what."

Moore tried to add a bit more icing. "In terms of Rehnquist, it's sort of recognizing that there's a great law school on the West Coast, that can produce—"

"Where'd Bill Smith go to law school? Probably Harvard?"

"Bill Smith went to Harvard undergraduate, then he went to Harvard Law School."

There was one fast way to deal with this Rehnquist idea. Nixon picked up the telephone and asked the White House operator to get him on the line. While waiting, Moore continued selling, mentioning again that for the past three years it had been Rehnquist who, as legal counsel at the Justice Department, was the government's constitutional lawyer. Once again the president reached for the telephone, this time requesting the attorney general. Moore said that Rehnquist was forty-six or forty-seven years of age.

"Be a hell of a judge," Nixon finally told Moore.

"Yes. I can't tell you what [complimentary statements] I've heard from people at the department that think seriously about this, his qualifications, his ability." Moore mentioned how effective Rehnquist was when testifying before Congress. "They can't fool him. I mean, he did the work of Jackson. He knows the Court, he knows the tricks."

"He's clerked for Jackson, who is one of the best judges on the Court. Should have been chief judge," Nixon said. "He's certainly more qualified than White was. The Whizzer was, of course, deputy attorney general. The Whizzer wasn't all that smart. He's good, but he's not great."

---

*Order of the Coif is an honorary legal fraternity made up of law students with high standing in their law school class.

"But Rehnquist has got [brains] and he's also got ways to express himself," Moore noted, referring to Rehnquist's writing skills.

The telephone rang. The operator had the attorney general on the line.[5] Mitchell led with good news. "I was on the phone with Lew Powell when you called and he is available. We started to talk about some things he wanted to check with me but I'm sure they're of no serious consequence."

"But he's going to go then?"

"Yes sir." The attorney general turned next to Howard Baker. "I have not been able to get a hold of our little senator friend. I don't know whether—"

"Let me ask you this. I just got Dick in here, Dick Moore, a minute ago." Often the president would pretend that persons were not present when he engaged in telephone conversations with others. He would wink, usually very awkwardly, at the guest to signal that it was a charade.

"Yeah," Mitchell said.

"And I may reevaluate. [Moore] comes down very hard on your man Rehnquist. He just thinks that, you know, second in his class at Stanford, was clerk to Robert Jackson, and then from your account apparently conservative." To Nixon, when you made a good argument, you "came down hard." Nonetheless, while he was complimenting Moore, the president was careful to make Mitchell think he was acting on his recommendation. He did not want to offend his trusted friend (and soon to be campaign manager) since Mitchell really wanted to return to New York and get back to making money practicing law.

"Absolutely."

"And would make a brilliant justice. Would you agree?"

"Yes sir."

"What would the country say about him? He sure is qualified, isn't he?"

"I would believe so. I don't think there's any question about it. It's an opinion expressed by Ed Walsh when we were talking about this. From his point of view, he certainly would. What is the political mileage out of it?"

The president did not really have an answer, so he shifted gears. "We've got Powell and now—Powell has said yes?"

"Yes sir."

"That's great," Nixon exclaimed.

"[Powell] has started to talk about some things he wanted to talk to me about but I can imagine that they are nothing of consequence."

"Now, on Powell, I want Powell. I want to go forward and announce that before it starts leaking."

"Well, there isn't anybody gonna leak it that, that I know of—"

"Well, I don't want you to tell Walsh," the president said.

Mitchell laughed. "I will not, of course. And what we have to do is to program this Walsh committee business so we can use it, use them—"

Nixon's mind was still relishing Powell. "Well, how about announcing Powell this afternoon?"

"I wouldn't do that until we've first—"

"—Heard from Walsh?" Nixon said, finishing Mitchell's thought.

"Yeah, we want to program that committee so we can blame the woman on that."

"I see. But I mean, Powell is not getting a woman's seat. Well, I get your point. All right. You'll hear from the Walsh committee when? This afternoon?"

"Yes sir. Ed Walsh has got a call in to me now."

"Yeah, all right, call me back when you get it. But remember, let's figure on the Rehnquist thing. The political mileage basically is the same kind of mileage if we were to go with Smith. The idea being that we are appointing a highly qualified man. That's really what it gets down to."

Mitchell agreed.

"And also he doesn't quite have the smack of the corporate lawyer as much as Smith."

"No, he's more of a general practitioner."

"Incidentally, what is Rehnquist? I suppose he's a damn Protestant?"

"I'm sure of that. He's just WASPish as WASPish can be."

"Yeah, well, that's too damn bad. Tell him to change his religion." Richard Nixon was having fun again. He had Powell, and he had just fallen in love with Justice Robert H. Jackson's onetime law clerk. Plus he was enjoying his waltz with Howard Baker. He felt he couldn't lose at this point.

Mitchell laughed. "All right, I'll get him baptized this afternoon."

"Well, baptized and castrated, no, they don't do that, I mean they circumci—, no, that's the Jews. Well anyway, however he is, get him changed," the happy president said.

"All right, let me pursue this further with Lew Powell, and I'll see if I can run down Baker and then I'll talk to Walsh and get back to you."

When the president hung up, he turned to Dick Moore. "We've got Powell."

"Good." Moore could tell how pleased the president was to bring this nomination to a finality.

The president told Moore he was to tell no one. When Moore assured him he was not a leaker, Nixon agreed, "I know you're not." The president said, "Everybody's so interested on the staff and they're afraid we're going to make a big boo-boo. We're not going to make boo-boos. I know exactly what I did on all these others; we just have to do it this way."

Moore wanted to pursue his Rehnquist recommendation. "And I won't press the point, but [on] the Rehnquist nomination," Moore said, and then told the president he was "a big tall" fellow, whose easy demeanor "hides the conservative underneath." Moore said the point he wanted to make is the Senate "can't complain about a man's philosophy," so they "put so much emphasis on qualification." But with Rehnquist, "being a law clerk is almost conclusive that he is qualified for that Court."

"You're right, you're right." Nixon told Moore. "So the Mulligan thing isn't worth it. We can do other things." It would be either Baker or Rehnquist. "No big concern about Baker because he was very high in his class too . . . He's really good, he's smart as hell. Garment came up with him. He's Garment's candidate."

Moore suggested that "Mulligan needs a little more time on that court, on the Second Circuit," and that he might be ready for either the Douglas or Brennan seat, whichever became vacant first.

Nixon said, "We may get Baker. Powell and Baker would be a good strong team, even though they'd say two southerners." This did not trouble the president, however, since "It isn't the Deep South. It's not Thurmond's South. It's Middle South—Virginia and Tennessee. And incidentally, it isn't bad on another point. Looming over all this is the issue of busing. Both of these men are against busing, and that will help with [that issue]. Everybody will know that Howard Baker is against busing."

Moore wasn't finished with his sales job, however. He turned the conversation back to Rehnquist. "Really, any one of these goes well, coupled with Powell." He knew Nixon had to take this one step at a time. "But if Howard Baker does say no, I would say that—"

"Rehnquist is—"

"Rehnquist, I would say Rehnquist first."

"Why?" Nixon asked.

Moore explained that he knew William Smith was a good conservative, but on balance, Bill Rehnquist had "a bit higher level of qualifications." The two men continued talking about the relative qualifications of candidates, and the lack of viable women for the Supreme Court. Finally, the president asked Moore to check on where William French Smith had ranked in his class vis-à-vis Rehnquist.

• • • •

Late in the afternoon, I had a call from Dick Moore.[6] He was excited. Dick was not a person to hide his emotions. At the time I did not know what he had done, and only recall it all these many years later because of its curious nature, and clear import.

"It's been a very long time since I've done any legal research," Moore told me. "But I've got to do some research. I can't really tell you what it's about; you understand, I hope?" he asked, slightly embarrassed.

"No problem. How can I help?"

"First, do we have a law library? Where you guys do legal research?"

"We don't have a library but I have the annotated Federal Code in my office—"

"Not that kind of research. I'm looking for background on lawyers. Do you have a Martindale-Hubble? Or what is the name of that publication that lists law journal articles?"

It was apparent what Moore was looking for by that question. I told him there was a Martindale in the EOB library, upstairs, and gave him the telephone extension to call. "Now, let's say you're looking for scholarly writings by a person. You may find some listed in Martindale, but more likely you're going to have to go through the *Index to Legal Periodicals*."

"That's the index I was trying to remember. Do we have that?"

"No."

"Where do you suggest I find it?"

"Two places. We use two law libraries. The Justice Department and the Library of Congress." I then gave him the names and telephone numbers of librarians of both, and suggested that the reference librarian could help him find what he wanted.

Much relieved, Moore apparently felt he should share a tidbit with me. "While I can't tell you what I'm doing, since I've been sworn to secrecy, I can tell you that I passed along your recommendation for the Court at the highest level today. I presume he was on the law journal?"

"Editor, and number one in his class."

"Oh, number one. I didn't know. I thought he was second. Well, that only makes it better. Thanks for the help and the numbers."

There was little doubt in my mind what Moore had done. But I did not yet know that Nixon had reacted so favorably. Indeed, since returning from Little Rock and Los Angeles and filing my reports, I had heard nothing other than a call from Barbara Franklin, who was still looking for female lawyers. I was, as they say in Washington, out of the loop.

• • • •

The president called his attorney general again at 5:33 p.m. for an update.[7] He had spent the day in his EOB office, making notes on his legal pad about how to announce his Supreme Court nominees. He had one name, but not yet the other. Mitchell reported that based on his conversation with Powell, he had been doing some background checking. He hadn't found any problems. He explained that Powell "made a speech one time in which he condemned Martin Luther King for his activism—"

"Oh the hell with it. I'm for that."

"And he has backed wiretapping and so forth, so—"

"Everything's just great." This was all music for the president, who added, "And he's a hell of a scholar. Where did he go to law school? Not that that bothers me particularly."

"I hear so damn many of these things, I don't [know], I forget."

"Anyway, just get me a damn strong statement with regard to how superbly qualified he is and so forth."

"That I will."

"Have that prepared, because my feeling is to do them in tandem, and announce it, say, in a five-minute national TV around seven-thirty. I think it's the best way to do it, since we got Powell. How about Baker? Have you heard from him?"

"Baker surprised me. He is on an airplane coming back from Knoxville."

"That's nice."

"And has left no word about why he went or anything about it. He'll be in here at—"

"Maybe we leave him off the list."

Mitchell chose to pass over the president's comment, but it had to tell him that Nixon was having serious second thoughts about Baker. "Well, they say he'll be in here at quarter to six. His plane's due in at five forty-five so we should have the answer—"

"Well, you know, I still think that the Rehnquist thing is a damn good possibility, if he doesn't go. I know it doesn't do much politically, but when you think of the guy's record, it's a hell of a record."

"There's no question it's perfect for that."

"I mean, who's going to say that a law clerk to Bob Jackson is unqualified?"

"I've talked to Judge Walsh—"

"Yeah, how's he coming out?"

"They have turned down both of them."

"Good," the president quipped.

"Which was to be expected," Mitchell added sourly.

"Turned down Friday?"

"Yep."

"Well, I'll be damned."

"It was a six to six vote [by the committee on Friday]," Mitchell reported.

"And how about Lillie, what was it there?"

"Eleven to one."

"What'd they just say? Not qualified?"

"Yep."

"Great."

"And you know what they said?" Mitchell asked. "That she was probably as good as any woman that could be considered by the Court. This statement was made up there [by the committee]."

"Are they going to put that out?"

"No, no. They're not going to put anything out."

"Well, we'll put it out," Nixon declared. "Get that out."

"We'll get it out at the time and place when we want to," Mitchell reassured him.

"We've got to do it before we make the damn announcement." Nixon was very pleased by this postscript from the bar.

"That's what Walsh told me the statements [of the committee] were."

"That's nice, that's nice. And the stacked jury thing is going to really kill them."

"One other part of this scenario I would like to deliver to Walsh, at the appropriate time, [is] a letter disassociating ourselves from [the ABA]." Mitchell also thought it appropriate that he issue a press statement.

"Yes, I want you to prepare one. You prepare it. You put it out, the press statement. Good. Now you have to wait for the fellow, do you?"

"For Baker?"

"Yeah."

"Yes," Mitchell said.

They talked about timing. The president gave Mitchell his thinking. "I want to go tomorrow night, John. If Baker doesn't say no, or says yes tonight, then my view is to"—but before finishing the thought, the president stopped. He wasn't sure, any more, exactly what he wanted Baker to say. "I really lean very strongly to the Rehnquist one. Some way or another, I think that's such a surprise. You don't have the problem of Smith's law clients, and all that sort of stuff you know if you feel comfortable with him."

"I feel very comfortable with him."

"All right, well, that's the way I'll do it. It's either Baker or Rehnquist. All right with you?"

"All right, sir."

"So prepare something on—, God damn it, Baker shouldn't diddle us along like this, I mean that's—"

"He didn't even have the courtesy of calling up and saying he was going down there for this, that and the next reason."

"When does he get back here?"

"He's supposed to have arrived at five forty-five this evening, so we may still hear from him before too long."

"You've got a call in to him, have you?"

"Yes sir."

"I want it laid right on the line, we're not going to wait. Because I want to go. You see once this bar [vote] leaks out, you realize that that will cause [an uproar], and I'm just not going to be beaten over the head with it all weekend, see?"

"I agree."

"I'm going to make the announcement tomorrow night at seven-thirty p.m."

"All right. I think that would be great. And we'll program it towards that time."

"So I'm going to make the decision now to go at seven-thirty. I'll tell Haldeman quietly to get the [television broadcasting] time. Fair enough?"

"Very good, sir."

Within less than an hour, the president called Mitchell back.[8] He wanted to explain the mechanics of the announcement. He would have Ron Ziegler let the press know early in the day of the timing, so interest would build up throughout the day, and on the evening news. Come what may, he was going to announce "tomorrow night. I'm not going to give that number two fellow [Baker] any more time. He either comes tonight or we go for the other fellow [Rehnquist]. Because I've got to get this stuff on the road. Fair enough?" Also, the president wanted Mitchell to prepare background information on his nominees. "You pick up the background dope the best you can. I mean, a strong sales talk on each. Particularly if they were top in their class or near the top, say so, things of that sort. You know the kind of thing that shows they're scholars and all that bullshit."

Less than another hour had passed before the president called Mitchell again.[9] "One thing that occurred to me that you are going to have to fend off, of course, is our friend Volpe." They had not named a Catholic or Italian as he had urged, so they would need an explanation. They couldn't use age as an excuse, because Powell was a sexagenarian. But Mitchell reassured Nixon that he would handle John Volpe. The president had been thinking about the ABA's vote. "Why do you think they pissed on Friday of all things?" he asked.

"Civil rights," Mitchell answered. This was a different reason than he had earlier given the president; apparently he had acquired more information.

"I'll be damned. Really?"

"Yeah. That's what Ed Walsh told me."

"Well, they'll do the same on Powell then, won't they?"

Mitchell chuckled. "Well, they're not going to, nobody's going to have a chance."

"You mean, I will have named him, huh?"

"You will have named him and, and it won't be this pressure, you know, from all over the country, from [various interest groups on the bar]."

"Civil rights. I'll be God damned."

"Mmm hmm. Walsh admitted to me that that was it."

"Well, the woman thing, that's got to get out some way. I mean, naturally the vote will get out, won't it? Everything else has leaked out of there. Now believe me, we're going to leak this out if they don't," Nixon stated.

Mitchell was fully prepared to play hardball on this. "You can rest assured we'll get it out one way or the other. And Walsh knows it's coming. He's been well programmed—"

"And the eleven to one?"

"Yes."

"And I think the eleven to one is brilliant, because it's a jury that way, see, it's a stacked jury. All men. Huh?"

"Absolutely."

"And she's the best qualified woman but she's not qualified for the Supreme Court. Jesus, that's great. That's great." The president turned to his announcement. "Now, in preparing my remarks, I'm going to use Safire, because he's our fastest writer on this sort of thing. So he may ask a question or two but you know it will be by my authority."

"Fine. He's the biggest leaker in the place. Can you turn him off?" Mitchell inquired.

"Well, I'm not going to tell him until the morning."

"Oh, I see."

"Oh hell, I'm not going to tell him tonight."

"I see."

"Oh Christ yeah, that's my point. He's a leaker," Nixon agreed. "That's why once we decide, I'll start him running and lock him up." The president explained that was what he had done in prior uses of Safire.

"Great."

"Oh Christ, I know he leaks. Oh, he doesn't have the slightest idea that he's going to even be asked to do this job."

"All right, good, sir. I hear Howard Baker has just landed at the airport and he's waiting to talk to me."

"Waiting to talk to you?"

"Mmm hmm."

"At the airport?"

"He just got into the airport. He's on the phone."

"Yeah, okay, well, call me back." [10]

• • • •

The president had dinner with his wife, and they were joined by his secretary Rose Mary Woods, who was working late. At 7:40 p.m., he excused himself from the dinner table to call Mitchell.[11] Amazingly, Mitchell still had not talked with Baker.

"I've got Howard Baker coming in here in a few minutes, he's a little late. But we'll get this wound up one way or the other. He wanted to see you, but I told him to meet with me," Mitchell reported.

"Oh. The thing is, if he decides, if he says yes or no, if he wants it, fine, then that's what happens." The president was assuring Mitchell that the offer was still Baker's to accept or reject.

"Very good, sir. Well, he wanted to talk about politics and I told him— I didn't think that it was necessarily to do with politics—you weren't discussing it anyway." The politics Baker apparently wanted to discuss were the consequences of his leaving the Senate for the Court.

Nixon had instructions regarding Baker. "Now don't press him. If he doesn't want it, please do not push him."

"Well, I'll put it right on the line. One thing I want to make sure that all this financial mumbo jumbo that's been going on, I want to make sure that's cleared up."

"[Does he] have trouble?"

"I have no idea other than the fact that this has been going on since last night," Mitchell said. The fact that he raised it signaled concern to Nixon.

"Find out."

• • • •

At 10:10 p.m., Mitchell tried to reach the president. He was not available and when the president tried to return the call, Mitchell was out. At 11:27

p.m., the operator reached Mitchell for the president and they spoke for twelve minutes. The conversation was not recorded, but the gist would become apparent in the morning. Howard Baker had asked for more time. I believe he told Mitchell that he had visited the chambers of Associate Justice Potter Stewart to learn more about the Court,[12] and had traveled to Tennessee to sort out personal matters. Still, he needed to consult with his family before making a final decision. Mitchell had given him until the morning to decide.

While Baker dithered, the opportunity of a lifetime was slipping little by little from his reach.

12

THE REHNQUIST CHOICE

October 21

RICHARD NIXON AROSE on the morning of October 21, 1971, enthused about announcing his Supreme Court nominations. It was a day he thoroughly enjoyed being president. As usual, he made short work of breakfast, and was so anxious to get to his office he did not even bother to look at the front pages of either *The Washington Post* or the *New York Times*. Rather, he headed directly to his EOB office, arriving there at 8:15 a.m.

Rose Mary Woods had transcribed his dictated draft of the announcement speech—which he had worked on until almost midnight—by the time he arrived in the office. To structure his speech in a way that would maximize suspense, and hold audience attention, he planned to speak in general terms at first, before naming his choices. In this instance it was particularly fitting because he had not even made his second choice. One of the last things he had jotted on his yellow pad the previous night was:

I have nominated 2 best ~~lawyers~~ Constitutional lawyers—
   (1) Lewis Powell is [a] Virginian
     —he is every lawyers 1st choice
     —President of Bar
   (2) Rhenquist [*sic*] brilliant ~~young~~ Constitutional lawyer in govt.
     —1st in class

But when dictating, he had not included Rehnquist. He had left a gaping blank in his draft after dictating: "The Supreme Court is the highest judicial body in this country. Its members should be among the very best lawyers in the nation. The two individuals I am nominating to the Court meet that standard to an exceptional degree."[1]

He had less than twelve hours to fill in the blank.

He summoned Pat Buchanan.[2] Without really explaining what he was doing, or why—although it could not have taken Buchanan more than a few nanoseconds to figure it out—the president told Buchanan to dig out some information for him. He wanted to confirm that Warren Burger was the sixteenth chief justice. (In fact, he was the fifteenth.) In addition, he wanted Buchanan to "check with Colson, there's a poll which was taken on the Court's standing in the country." The president wanted the results.

"Right," his young speechwriter said.

"All right, let's see." The president paused, looking at his notes on his yellow pad. "I'd like you to write one brief paragraph—not too hard but more of a philosophical theme on the need to have judges [able to get] outside themselves, that's the tradition of the great justices." Nixon recalled using a quote from the political commentator Walter Lippmann during the 1968 campaign, about the balance of power within our society turning against the forces for peace. Nixon instructed, "I want you to get the exact quote from Lippmann."

"Yes sir."

The president wanted Buchanan's draft as short as possible. He wanted language to the effect that he did not want justices "to distort the Constitution, to promulgate their personal, philosophical, political views." He added, "I want it to be clear that they have this philosophy, of course."

"Of course."

"Both Harlan and Black had [such] philosophies, you agree?" He continued, "Then say that in my opinion, there should be no surprises. I pledged to rectify this balance." He wanted examples of the rights of society versus the rights of criminals. After repeating his instructions, he asked, "What's the news media [talking] about? I haven't [had a] chance to read [the papers]."

Buchanan gave him a fast rundown from the news summary and morning newspapers. The Court was the big news of the day. Splashed across the front page of *The Washington Post* was a story about the ABA's rejection of both Herschel Friday and Mildred Lillie. The *New York Times* had a story that would keep them guessing all day. It wrongly reported that word had been given to Democratic senator McClellan of Arkansas that Herschel Friday's nomination would go to the Senate anyway, on Friday, October 22. The only other item that had caught Buchanan's attention, that he mentioned, was the extensive coverage given Willie Brandt's receipt of the Nobel Prize.

When Buchanan left, the president called Haldeman.[3] "I'm not going to use Safire today because I worked on it myself last night," he reported. Haldeman had arranged television time at 7:30 p.m. as requested, and they discussed the mechanics associated with the announcement. The president wanted several aides dispatched to Capitol Hill to spread word of the announcements, just prior to his going on the air. But the only people he had discussed his selections with were Dick Moore and John Mitchell. "That's all. Nobody else, nobody else, nobody else." He did not want Ehrlichman involved. "Don't have Garment and all these other people get into this." He noted, "As far as the woman question is concerned, they said she's the best qualified woman and there is no woman qualified for the Court."

Haldeman was surprised to hear all this.

The president wanted Mitchell and Moore to prepare the background material on his choices, which he still wasn't sharing with Haldeman. "So you get ahold of Moore and tell him what [is needed], and work it out so everything arrives at the time I put it out, see what I mean? Let the evening news bastards go running off on the wrong thing. Don't you think, don't you agree?"

Haldeman agreed.

"It's like China," the president asserted. He had held his planned China initiative secret until his own dramatic announcement. He continued, "It's best to let them appear to be just assholes, you know. They didn't know, and so then all of a sudden we surprise them, then it's a bombshell. If you start guiding them, somebody's going to be a rat [and reveal it]."

A few minutes later, the president called Haldeman again.[4] "Tell Moore that he's to take responsibility for his fact-checking—of 125 words on each man." Haldeman wanted to know what was going to be done about the ABA rejections. Again, the president gave Haldeman, a former advertising man who had orchestrated most of his public relations and media plays, nothing. "Somebody from the administration is going to hit this hard, hard, hard. Okay?" Nixon did not want even to discuss this peripheral ploy with anyone. "Don't run it by anybody. I don't want this leaked to anybody. Don't run it by any of Ehrlichman's people or Dean." The president assured his concerned chief of staff that he was acting carefully. Both Mitchell and Moore approved of what he was doing, so it didn't need any further staffing.

At 9:30 a.m., the attorney general called.[5] Mitchell was in good spirits as he greeted the president to give him the latest report.

"Good morning, Mr. President."

"Did you work it out?" the president asked.

Mitchell cleared his throat. "Baker wants to go, and I told him that you still had [your] options open and I would refer to you his availability."

"Well, he wants to go now, huh?" Nixon was not pleased with this news.

"Yes sir, mum hmm."

"Well, God damn it, sure you couldn't talk him out of it, huh?"

"Well, not on the basis in which we've been pushing him into it. But I went through the same routine, and I think you have an option if you want to go the other way."

Nixon sighed. There was a long pause. Thankfully, Mitchell had not boxed him in. Mitchell, reading the situation, broke the silence. "I don't think it's going to disturb him too much if you use your options in another direction."

"Mum hmm."

"If you feel stronger in that other direction."

Nixon now had to make a choice. The tape of this conversation runs for seventeen seconds with neither man saying a word as the president's mind spun, computed, and calculated. He sighed, several times. Finally, he asked Mitchell, "Have you got anything that will help me decide this?

Could you take five minutes off and then call me back? What was [Baker's] record in law school and so forth? Do you know anything about that?"

"No, but I presume we might be able to dig it out."

"I need to know. I want to know whether he was just a playboy or whether he buckled down and did things. Because I'm preparing my remarks now and this all revolves around that these are guys that are qualified, you see?"

"All righty, I'll try and dig that out as fast as we can."

But the president wasn't sure he wanted to leave the door open for Baker. He saw a nice way out. "Now do you think we are in a position of telling him no? We just feel that under the political considerations that you've raised [regarding who would replace him in the Senate], Howard, are such that you shouldn't go."

"Yes, put it on that basis." Mitchell agreed this could be a face-saving exit for all.

"Yeah, and I've thought about it, and I have thought overnight too, and I just think his political considerations, that the judgment is that way. If he wants to go at a later time, why the place will be open for him. Put it that way, see?"

"I think we ought to get back to him right quick on it, though."

"All right. Fine. Call me right back. I need to know what his law school record was."

"Do you still want to keep your options open or do you just want me to turn him off?"

"No. I want the option open until I see what kind of a record he had. If he had an outstanding record, so that I can say that he and Powell both had outstanding records, that's one thing. But if it's a jackass record, then I really think I'm going to not, I'm going to close the option and go the other way. I have a feeling I'm going to go the other way. That's just my gut reaction. What do you think?"

"I feel that way for the better of the Court and I think that the PR on it is just about a breakeven."

"On the one side, you've got two southerners, which is not good."

"Mum hmm."

"On the other side, you've got a man who's unknown. But with a hell of a record. The unknown thing with Rehnquist is going to really not wash good. If he was high in his class, was he first or second or something like that?"

"He was first in his class," Mitchell corrected his earlier misstatement—just in time.

"You think he was first?"

"He was first, yes sir."

"Yeah, mum hmm." The president thought about this fact for a second. As Dick Moore had told me after making the same error, being first only made Rehnquist more attractive. "Well, that's a hell of a club."

"Phi Beta Kappa, of course," Mitchell added.

"Phi Beta Kappa, first in his class, law clerk to one of the great judges of this century, and practiced law as a lawyer's lawyer and so forth. Damn it, I really think we ought to go that way."

"All right, well, I'll turn Baker off."

It was done. Nixon had made his choice. But he didn't want to create a problem with Baker, whose life he had turned upside down. "I think you ought to say, Howard, in the view of the fact that you've had some doubts, but also, frankly, the President really feels that the political things that you've raised are questions, and the place will be open for you later if you want it, because we [may later] need two southerners on that Court anyway. And that maybe you'll want to take another crack at the leadership and so forth. Okay, [scratch] him off."

"Yes sir."

Mitchell immediately called Baker. The conversation lasted less than three minutes, according to Mitchell's records, and then Mitchell called the president back to let him know how it had been resolved.[6] "Hello, Mr. President. I have talked to Howard and he understands it fully and in good grace—"

"He can see it." The president was relieved. He continued, "He wasn't too enthusiastic anyway."

"I think it was with some relief, actually, on his part, but very warm and very gracious."

"Good." With that resolved, the president told Mitchell that he was writing his speech, and he had not told anyone other than Moore what he would do. He wanted Mitchell to call several people just before he went on the air: Herschel Friday, Mildred Lillie, and Senate Judiciary Committee Chairman Jim Eastland. He would have Dick Moore call Bob Byrd.

"Are you going to ignore the bar?" Mitchell asked.

"I'm not even going to mention the bar."

"That's good."

"I'm not going to mention it either way. But on the other hand, through the day, Ziegler will get hit on it, and he's simply going to say, well, the bar does not have a veto power, we're interested in their advice, but the President will make his appointments on his own recognizance, so to speak. Don't you think that's all right?"

"Yes sir. That's the line."

"In the meantime, I understand the woman story has leaked. It's out, huh?"

"Both of them. It's on the front page of *The Washington Post*. It couldn't have been better for us."

"Right. Now, on that, the only thing that hasn't leaked on the woman story is that little squib from within the bar that it said that they knew of no woman that was qualified. Could we do that?"

"Yeah, we will get that out one way or the other."

"I want that out. Tell Moore that [he] has to get it out today. Give it to Safire. He'll leak anything."

Mitchell had one other item. "In order to get their support, I think I'll call Leon Jaworski, who's the president of the American Bar, and Ed Walsh, so that they—"

"Right. I would call Jaworski and Walsh, and say we just appreciate enormously what they have done, and what the President has done now, he's just said the hell, we just can't submit these people to them and have them beaten down for non-legal reasons. But that he has selected two men that he knows the bar [will find] well qualified, in both cases. And then tell him what it is. Fair enough?"

"Yes sir, will do."

"Now don't tell either, particularly don't tell Walsh—I don't know Jaworski—but don't tell him before six-thirty or so. The reason being is that they have staffs, and they may tell them, and the staff will leak. You know they've got these Jews that work—Walsh has—that work for him and they leak, the Jews leak, John, you know that."

Mitchell laughed. "I sure do. I will talk to him just before the event."

"I'm very pleased. Have you told Rehnquist yet?"

"Not yet, but I'm sure that he will be more than pleased."

"Pleased! Christ, he'll probably drop his teeth."

"I would expect so."

"Yeah, I don't want to see him. I don't think I should."

"No necessity for it."

"And I haven't seen Powell. I wouldn't know [Powell] if I saw him. I've met him but I don't know him."

"Well, he's a very distinguished-looking gentleman."

"Yeah. And I think really it's a good move. We're going to knock their God damn blocks off, fight it through. You say that Powell made a speech against Martin Luther King, that's the only thing you can find on his record that's bad, huh?"

"That's correct."

"What kind of a speech was it, too? Was it rabid or—"

"Oh no, no no no. It had to do with the argument that's prevailed here for the last four or five years [with regard to] civil disobedience situations."

"That's all right. That's a legitimate thing. I said many of the same things."

"Yes, and so—"

"Well, I think it's been a fine job, John, and you and Moore work out whatever you want, okay?"

"Very good, sir."

• • • •

Shortly after 10 a.m., Ron Ziegler and Bob Haldeman arrived in the president's EOB office to discuss Ziegler's morning briefing of the press.[7] Nixon knew much could still go wrong, as it often did. He instructed Ziegler that with regard to the American Bar Association's rejection of Friday and Lillie, he should say that it is the United States Senate, and not the American Bar Association, that has the right under the Constitution to give advice and consent. While the president welcomed advice from everyone, including the bar, only the Senate had the power to deny consent.

Also, he wanted Ziegler to get out that in rejecting Lillie, the bar had said that "they thought she was probably the best qualified woman in the country to be a judge, but that she wasn't qualified for the Supreme Court yet." The president said, "I tried to get it out through Safire, one of the leaks, but I want you to say it now. I think that's something you say."

Haldeman mentioned the *New York Times* story by Fred Graham that said McClellan had been told Friday would be nominated. Everyone laughed. They loved the error. The president instructed that "Moore has got to be in charge of the PR. This is his department and he's the only one that knows what's going to happen. I don't want anybody else in it."

Ziegler wanted to be clear what he could tell the press about when the president had made his decision. Could he say "yesterday evening"?

"No! No, no, no, no, no, no. That one I'm not going to tell you. Say I don't know. I don't think we want to get into that." What Nixon did not want out was the fact that he had chosen Rehnquist only a few hours before announcing it. It would make Rehnquist an afterthought, a last choice. He did not want Ziegler anywhere near this question.

Ziegler explained his concern. "I said at the one o'clock briefing yesterday that [the President] had not decided."

Nixon was not happy to hear this. But Haldeman felt that Ziegler could "still say you don't know when you decided." With this script settled, Ziegler left the EOB office.

Haldeman asked, "You want to take any stab at trying to sell the commentators ahead of time?" Nixon declined. "We need to get a positive reaction. That's what I'm getting at," Haldeman said. But the president wanted none of it. As far as he was concerned, the commentators were "the left-wing kikes, son-of-a-bitches for the most part." Nixon would give them information only after the fact. "Tell them to come in like they did after China. Don't tell the fuckers anything." He wanted everyone to keep their "mouth shut." A frustrated Haldeman sighed, got up, and left.

Not quite an hour had passed and the president had Haldeman back in his EOB office, to go over accumulated business before he headed to the Oval Office for a couple of scheduled interruptions—a meeting with the editor of the "Teenager" supplement of the *Cincinnati Enquirer* regarding volunteerism, and then a trip to the Green Room to receive diplomatic credentials of designated ambassadors of Malta, Senegal, Bolivia, Yugoslavia, and Argentina. But first, Nixon had more instructions regarding his speech.[8]

"After I do this tonight, it's very important that no calls come through," he told Haldeman.

"Okay."

"First, Burger. I'm not going to let him call me. He is not to call. All calls will go to Rose. Good. Did I come through?"

"Absolutely." Haldeman was not sure why Nixon was in such a testy mood, but the president was often like this before major announcements. The staff tended to steer clear before such events. In fact, after his television announcement had been delivered, he would accept a host of calls.

"Also, Volpe will be back. I'm not going to take [his call]. So I'm just not going to take any calls at all, period. Is that clear? That's all. Just say I'm out to dinner. Fair enough. Rose should take the calls, and listen, don't make calls around the country this time."

"Okay."

"There's no reason to. It's not that kind of thing where calls around the country to see what did you think of what he did and all that bullshit. We're not interested in that, see?"

"All right."

"It's too damn complicated to know what people understand," he growled. When Haldeman reminded him that these can generate some good statements, Nixon relented. "All right, fine. Call around the country only for the purpose of getting people to make statements. But don't have Herb Klein [Nixon's director of communication at the White House] call all these people and say, what did you think? all that sort of thing. Only have Herb call people that he wants a statement from." Then Nixon tipped his hand, telling Haldeman he was making "a hell of an appointment" relating to Virginia, so he might want to "cover Virginia very heavily."

A few minutes later, Ron Ziegler returned. He had more likely questions from the press he needed to discuss, and when doing so, the president stumbled onto an idea. The *New York Times* story, which reported he would be sending Herschel Friday's name to the Senate, was a wonderful opportunity to mislead the press in general, and CBS White House correspondent Dan Rather in particular. The president wanted Ziegler to make clear that the ABA's rejection of Friday did not mean they had veto power. Nixon believed that Ziegler's saying that would "make them think I'm going to appoint Friday and so forth."

Ziegler repeated, "And that will make them think, well, the President's going on television tonight to announce [Friday's nomination]."

"Suck 'em out," the president encouraged. More specifically, "Why don't you suck Rather in." Nixon continued, "Why don't you suck him [in] deeply and say, look, Dan, you're right, it's Friday. Better yet, Colson can say, where did you get that Friday report? This is one that had serious—"

"We want to know where you got that," Ziegler said, rehearsing the game.

Haldeman threw in the obvious answer. "Where they got it is McClellan's put it out."

"No shit," the president said. "Hey, it doesn't make it [right]. I just want [Rather] on that trail. I want to force him to be wrong. And find a way to get him to be wrong. Get him Safire, Safire leaks to everybody."

Ziegler quickly changed the subject. This was not the sort of game he played with the White House press corps. Caught once misleading them, and he was finished as press secretary. He was more concerned about having correct answers to respond to questions about the others on the list of six names that had been sent to the bar. Surely to Ziegler's relief, the president dropped the subject.

• • • •

At 10:30 a.m., John Mitchell called Bill Rehnquist.[9] If Howard Baker had been surprised by Mitchell's offer to consider him two days earlier, Rehnquist must have been stunned by the call. Dick Moore and Dick Kleindienst joined Mitchell for the historic moment.[10] The attorney general told an unsuspecting Rehnquist that within a few hours the president would address the nation and announce the nominations of Lewis Powell and William Rehnquist to the Supreme Court. Mitchell then told Rehnquist that he was dispatching Dick Moore to Rehnquist's office down the hall to give him more details and obtain information that the president needed for his speech.

Until this call, which I learned of shortly after the fact, the only people who had even heard Rehnquist's name mentioned in passing were myself, Bud Krogh, Dick Moore, Haldeman, Ehrlichman, Mitchell, and Nixon. Based on the report that Moore later gave me, I'm confident that Rehnquist had no warning prior to October 21 that he was even under consideration.

• • • •

When Moore arrived back in his office at the White House, he had a message that Haldeman wanted to see him as soon as possible. Haldeman passed on the president's instructions that he was to prepare 125-word background statements on each man that could be used by the president in his announcement, and then could be released by Ziegler's press office after the speech. Moore simply assumed Haldeman knew whom the president had selected. As Haldeman noted in his diary, Moore "spilled the beans to me." [11]

After Moore left his office, Haldeman called me. [12] He explained what was going on, and how he had learned by accident of the president's selections. He said he asked Moore if anyone was vetting these nominees.

"Who are the nominees?" I asked.

"The president isn't telling anyone, as I said. He's paranoid it will leak. I don't want him pissed at Moore for telling me. And if I talk to Mitchell, he'll wonder how I know. But I'm not sure anyone has done any checking on these people. I'm going to give you one name. I'm going to call someone else on the other." Haldeman was being a good chief of staff, quietly making sure the president did not screw up without advising the president of his actions. "Apparently he's going to name Bill Rehnquist," he finally told me.

"No shit." I was truly surprised. As soon as Haldeman said, "Moore told me you had recommended Rehnquist," I recalled Moore telling me he had passed on my recommendation.

"I don't want you talking to anyone about this, understand?" Haldeman said sternly. I assured him I would not do so. "I want you to assure me, as best you can, that you know of no problem with Rehnquist. Nothing that will embarrass the president."

"Bob, I'm sure that Bill Rehnquist would not accept if he had any problem. He knows this game as well as anyone. He was there with Haynsworth and Carswell."

"I know. That's what I'm concerned about. Those names, like Friday and Lillie, should never have come over here. Moore told me Rehnquist is damn near numb with shock. Nobody can vet themselves. I want you to think about this. The president's calling me, so I've got to go. He's giving lots of orders today. Call me back, within the hour. And say nothing, not even to your own staff, understand?"

"Yes sir."

• • • •

By 1:15 p.m. Moore had prepared his draft of the material on Rehnquist and Powell for the president, and went to meet with him in his EOB office.[13]

"I've got the material here. The remarks are longer than a hundred and twenty-five words, but I, in the interest of time, I thought I'd bring it in."

"Oh, that's all right."

Moore explained his drafts. "Gives you a little picture of these people." Then he hastened to correct his earlier error. "I thought [Rehnquist] was second [in his class], Mr. President, but one of his classmates* told me that, and then we spoke to him this morning and he acknowledged that he was first."

The president first read Moore's draft of Powell: "Everything that Lewis F. Powell, Jr. has undertaken, he has accomplished with distinction and honor, both as a lawyer and as a citizen. Excellence has marked his career since his days as a student at Washington and Lee where he was both Phi Beta Kappa and president of the Student Council and then the top of his class in law school. He also received a graduate degree from Harvard Law School."

Most of this information was new to Nixon, and he was fascinated to find out more about the man to whom he was about to give life tenure on the Supreme Court. "Mr. Powell is a loyal Virginian who has practiced law in the same firm in Richmond since 1931 except for four years of distinguished service in World II. In his distinguished legal career, he has received virtually every honor his profession can bestow. He has been president of the American College of Trial Lawyers, the American Bar Foundation and, most importantly, the American Bar Association. In that latter role, he provided leadership in the provision of legal services for the needy and the revision of the standards for the administration of criminal justice."

The president made a few minor editorial changes in the paragraph as he read, then proceeded to the end, which he struck, for it contained no substance. "Why don't you just say first rather than the top of his class?"

---

*Presumably this was Ehrlichman, who had told me the same thing. I had corrected Ehrlichman, for I knew better from conversations with Rehnquist.

"Yes, yes, of course. [But] I don't know if that—" Whether it was correct or not, by action of the president of the United States, Lewis Powell was now first in his class.

The president made a few other minor changes, and then picked up the draft material on Rehnquist, and read it: "The highest honor that can come to a graduate of an American law school is to be selected to serve as a law clerk to a Justice of the Supreme Court of the United States. Over the years, those who have achieved this honor would read like a 'Who's Who' of the leaders of the Bench and the Bar. There is a special satisfaction in nominating William H. Rehnquist because, on confirmation, he will return as an Associate Justice to the Court where he served as a law clerk almost twenty years ago."

The president looked at what he had just read. "I don't know whether the law clerk thing shouldn't be covered more by"—he paused, his eyes scanning ahead in the draft—"I think that's the interest of lawyers." Nixon struck the material, and proceeded reading: "William Rehnquist has always been outstanding in every intellectual endeavor he has undertaken. He was graduated from Stanford University with great distinction in 1948." Nixon stopped. He didn't like the "with great distinction." As he told Moore, "The way I would do that is he graduated from Stanford, he was Phi Beta Kappa, graduated in 1948, and then graduated first in his class at Stanford University." Nixon made these changes and continued reading. "He received one of the highest honors that can be bestowed upon an outstanding legal student, he was chosen as law clerk for Mr. Justice Robert H. Jackson, one of the outstanding members of the Court in the past half century."

Nixon had no major changes in the rest of the statement, which covered Rehnquist's private practice for sixteen years and his appointment as assistant attorney general, Office of Legal Counsel, serving as the president's lawyer's lawyer.

"Bob Haldeman said he would like background material," Moore said.

The president said that he was still holding this close. He did not want it going to Haldeman yet.

Moore was surprised. "We're keeping this pretty secret, sir," he assured the president.

The president asked Moore if he had anything else on Powell. He did, but not for the background statement. It was evident why he had not included it when he explained, "Well, only one thing you should know. Mr. Powell has never argued a case at the Supreme Court."

"I don't give a damn. Has Rehnquist?"

"Rehnquist has, yes. He's had one case there anyway."

The president was making further adjustments in Moore's material when the telephone rang. It was Haldeman, with the statistics for the speech that he had just requested, which the president jotted down. When he finished with Haldeman, he decided to give his speech a first run with Dick Moore as his audience. "Let me just give you a feel as to how this is going to run." Nixon cleared his throat and organized his papers.

" 'During a four-year term, the President of the United States makes over 3,000 major appointments to various government positions. By far the most important appointments he makes are those to the Supreme Court of the United States. Presidents come and go, but the Supreme Court—through its decisions—goes on forever. Because they will make decisions that will affect your lives, and the lives of your children for generations to come, I should like to share with you tonight my reasons for selecting the two individuals whose names I will send to the Senate tomorrow for confirmation as justices of the Supreme Court.' "

"I like the way it starts," Moore said.

" 'Over the past few months I have received thousands of letters from all over the country recommending scores of able men and women for appointment to the two vacancies on the Court. Because one of the vacancies is that left by the retirement and death of Mr. Justice Black, a former United States Senator, there has been great support for the appointment of a member of the Senate or House to the Court, so that the point of view of the Congress would be adequately represented. A great number of letters have recommended the appointment of a woman, since no woman has ever been named to the Supreme Court. A number of others have recommended the appointment of the representatives of religious, racial and nationality groups not presently represented on the Court. I believe the Supreme Court should, in the broadest sense, be representative of the entire nation. But with only nine seats to fill, obviously every group in this country cannot be represented by an appointment.' "

Moore gave an approving "Mum hum" as the president shuffled his papers before proceeding.

" 'These are the criteria, I believe, [that] should be applied in naming people to the Supreme Court. The Supreme Court is the highest judicial body in this country. Its members should, therefore, be among the very best lawyers in the nation. The two individuals I am nominating to the Court meet that standard to an exceptional degree. The second consideration is the judicial philosophy of those who are to serve on the Court. I emphasize the word judicial because whether an individual is a Democrat or a Republican cannot and should not be a decisive factor in determining whether he should be appointed to the Court. By judicial philosophy I do not mean agree with the president on every issue. It is the exception rather than rule that any two lawyers agree on any [close] legal questions. That is as it should be. It would be a total repudiation of our Constitutional system if the Justices on the Supreme Court were to be like puppets on a string, pulled at the preference of the president who appointed them. When I appointed Chief Justice Burger, I told him that the day he was confirmed by the Senate, he could expect that I would never talk to him about a case pending before the Court. He and all the other judges that I appoint will have no obligation whatever to clear it with the president.' "

As Nixon proceeded, he made markings on his draft. He was reacting to his own reading of the draft, and adjusting accordingly.

" 'In the case of both Chief Justice Burger and Mr. Justice Blackmun, and in the case of the two nominees that I shall send to the Senate tomorrow, their sole obligation is to the Constitution and to the American people." The president paused. "It should be 'to the Constitution of the American people, not to the president who appointed them.' " He marked his copy.

" 'As far as judicial philosophy is concerned, it is my belief that it is the duty of a judge to interpret the Constitution, and not to place himself above the Constitution or outside the Constitution. He should not twist or bend the Constitution in order to promote his personal political and social views. Judges who adhere to this philosophy find that they do not always agree in their interpretation of the Constitution. We have an excellent example of this in the two judges whose vacancies I now have the duty to fill, Mr. Justice Black and Mr. Justice Harlan. Mr. Justice Black was a liberal. Mr. Justice Harlan was a conservative. They disagreed on many occasions. As I learned not only from reading their opinions over the years and from appearing twice before them and arguing a case before the

Supreme Court, both were great judges with a brilliant ability to ask questions about the heart of the matter before them. And then they'd make a decision based on their interpretation of the Constitution.'"

After making more notes on his draft, the president continued.

"'In the debate over the confirmation of the individuals I have selected, it will be charged that they are conservatives. This is true, but only in the judicial, not the political, sense. During my campaign I pledged to nominate to the Supreme Court individuals who shared my judicial philosophy which is basically a conservative philosophy. There's one example which bears specific[ally] on that point. Many cases over the past few years have come before the Court involving the delicate balance between the rights of society and the rights of defendants accused of crimes against society. Honest and dedicated Constitutional lawyers have disagreed as to where and how to maintain that balance. Mr. Walter Lippmann wrote twenty-one years ago, "the balance of power within our society has turned dangerously against the peace forces, against governors, mayors, legislatures, against the police and the courts."'"

"Twenty-one years ago?" Moore asked. It was correct.

"'The two individuals I am nominating to the Court believe as I do,'" the president went on, "'that there's no decision to ignore this delicate balance between the rights of society and defendants accused of crime. The peace forces must not be denied the legal tools they need to protect innocent people from criminal forces. As great Constitutional lawyers, they are dedicated to the lawyer's, at the same time, to the lawyer's most precious principle, that the rights of innocent men must always receive the fullest protection of the law. It is with these criteria in mind that I have selected the two men whose names I will send to the Senate tomorrow.'"

Nixon cleared his throat. He told Moore this was where he would insert the material on Powell and Rehnquist. He would add: "I am asking that the Senate approve their nominations promptly, so that the Court can move forward on the backlog that is building up because of the two vacancies that have occurred in recent weeks."

Finally, "'Let me add a final word with regard to a subject that's very close to my heart and close to my legal background. Because of my years of studying the American system of government, I note with great distress a rising tendency, a growing tendency—'"

"'Rising tendency,'" Moore suggested.

" '—I note with great distress a rising tendency to criticize the Supreme Court as an institution. Let all Americans recognize that every individual has the right to disagree with the decision of the Court. After those decisions are handed down, however, it is our obligation to obey the law, whether we like it or not, and it is our duty as citizens to respect the institution of the Supreme Court of the United States. We have had many debates over the years on the role of the Supreme Court, and some of those debates have even ended up in our Congress. But let us never forget that respect for the Court, the final interpreter of what is the law of the land, is indispensable if America is to survive as a free society.

" 'Whether you agree or disagree with the views of members of that court, let us always hold in highest respect what's in my view the greatest judicial monitor of last resort in the entire world. Except for the contribution we have made to the cause of world peace, there is probably no more important legacy that the president can leave, in these times, than his appointments to the Supreme Court of the United States. I believe that Chief Justice Burger, Mr. Justice Black, by their conduct and their decisions, have earned the respect not only of those who supported them at the time they were nominated, but also those who either opposed them or who opposed their appointments. It's my firm conviction that the two men whose names I will send to the Senate tomorrow deserve the same respect that all Americans would be proud of, and they work diligently on behalf of their overriding responsibility, guardians of our Constitution and building respect for the law, order and justice of our land.' "

Moore liked it. They spent time tweaking it a bit, refining a few points, polishing the prose. The president then took Moore through his proposed introduction of Powell. " 'Mr. Lewis Powell is from Virginia, but like another great Virginian, Chief Justice Marshall, Lewis Powell is recognized by his colleagues at the various highest echelons as a man who represents not just Virginia, or a southerner. He is first and foremost a great American.' "

Moore complimented this as well, explaining how he could slide in the material he had drafted. He was pleased with the president's approach. "You're taking the high road. You're way ahead of them. You've got better men than any the [bar or media have] suggested. You've stuck to your principle of strict constructionist, appointing the kind of man you said you would to improve the Court, you know, who don't substitute their opinions for the law and it's really the soul of justice."

The president said he was going to state that Rehnquist was first in his class. That each of them was first. "They can't knock that [as mediocre]," Nixon noted.

"Now with that said, I didn't check the law school, but Rehnquist told me this morning that he was indeed first. As a matter of fact, he said that he kept track of his total. He had the highest marks in the history of the school, but he said that's, that's the kind of thing you can't document and he isn't [interested in doing so anyway]."

Nixon wanted to discuss the mechanics of getting information out. Moore told him he had visited with Ron Ziegler to arrange what they needed to do. "Now he doesn't know the names," Moore assured the president.

"That's right. He's not to be told."

"He told me he didn't want to know," Moore reported.

"No. And that nobody should know, except you."

Moore, of course, knew there must be one clear exception. "And Haldeman should know, he—"

"Haldeman, no sir. He doesn't [know, and understands I want it] kept quiet. I just think it better that he not know. You see, he'd have a hell of time not telling Ehrlichman, and Ehrlichman would have a hell of time not telling Dean, and Dean would have a hell of time not telling, you know, I just don't believe in telling anybody anything. I just don't [believe it's necessary]."

Moore did not tell the president he had let the beans spill with Haldeman. Rather he said, "There's only one way to keep a secret [is not tell anyone]." Suddenly, Moore was uncomfortable. "Do you, you don't, you don't need anything more from me on that?" He was pointing at the president's draft remarks.

"The only thing, I just wanted your [reactions]."

"Could I sit and read the [draft]? When I listen to you, I get pretty, I'm not the best critic when you get going, sometimes, I get enthused. Could I sit outside and read it, or in the corner?"

"Well, I'm not ready yet because I don't have [the Powell and Rehnquist material in it]."

"I loved it," Moore assured him.

"It's got to be something that relates to people. It can't be too legal."

Moore reread the speech. He wanted to make certain he had given the president his best counsel. When he finished, he suggested minor word changes in a few places, which the president appreciated. The president then sent Moore out to prepare the background material for release to the press following the speech, while he completed drafting it. By 6:00 p.m. Nixon had finished, and Rose Woods was typing a reading copy in large print, which he would review several times before delivery.

• • • •

Meanwhile, I'd been thinking, pacing around my large office, occasionally walking to the window overlooking the south grounds of the White House. In pushing Rehnquist for the Court, I had been screwing around. Unlike Dick Poff, whom I knew and had promoted because I had good reason to believe in him, I knew very little about Bill Rehnquist. With Rehnquist, I was playing a long shot merely for the adventure—a piece of history. It was unbelievable to me that by reminding everyone of Rehnquist, the idea had actually taken hold. My first thought was to confess to Haldeman what I had done. But surely, I figured, this had been run by Mitchell, so he was Mitchell's candidate as well.

I knew Haldeman's instincts in calling me and asking for a quick check were correct. It was doubtful anyone at the Justice Department would do any vetting of Rehnquist. To the contrary, they would all be thrilled that he was going to get the nod. It reflected glory on them. There was no doubt in my mind that Rehnquist was smart enough, but what about his judgment? Did I want Bill Rehnquist setting legal policy for the next three decades? His conservatism was extreme, unyielding. I had watched him prepare opposition to all matters progressive both while I worked at the Department of Justice and at the White House. All I could hope was that he would grow, not be inflexible, not be an ideologue. Hell, I was too young to be passing judgment on his wisdom or lack thereof. But he was not as balanced a person as Dick Poff, whom I'd also watched deal with important constitutional issues.[14]

Haldeman wanted to know if there was anything that might come up in a confirmation hearing that would embarrass the president—particularly since no one was really checking. There was not time to have my secretary go through my files, which might reveal something. But there was one classified file that was potentially a problem. I went to my telephone and buzzed my secretary.

"Jane, would you bring me that file that Bud Krogh sent to me about kidnapping American drug dealers abroad."

"We don't have it. Because it was classified, I sent it to the State Department, with your request for analysis."

"Do you recall if there was a memo in there where Rehnquist took a position for the Department of Justice?"

"I don't," she said.

"Thanks."

I could not call Bud Krogh, who would know. It might tip him as to why I wanted to know. But it stuck in my head that Rehnquist had thought it a dandy idea to snatch drug dealers from foreign streets and bring them home to stand trial. I had found the concept appalling. It was, in my mind, not unlike the time bomb sitting in my safe that would become known as the "Houston Plan"—a plan to conduct illegal surveillance (wiretapping, mail covers, military infiltration of campuses) that had been approved by the president, but which FBI director J. Edgar Hoover (no fading violet in such matters) refused to implement. I had no idea how many people were privy to the kidnapping scheme, but it was the kind of matter that, should it arise during a confirmation proceeding, could cause a nuclear detonation.

But the more I thought about this, the less I was concerned. Rehnquist could say—no doubt truthfully—that he was merely giving legal advice. He was not proposing, nor was he asked the sagacity of such a plan, only its legal implications. The kidnapping idea had been raised in Bud Krogh's office, and he was merely asked to give advice on its legality. He could do the same with all the draconian criminal laws that Don Santerelli was seeking for the District of Columbia. If any of these matters came up during his confirmation, he was merely acting as a lawyer. Only insiders would know that Rehnquist had never met a repressive law enforcement activity that he did not find legal.

Another concern came to mind, about something much more conspicuous. I called my secretary again.

"Jane, did we bring copies of my files over from the Department of Justice?"

"Only personal matters."

"How about my files on Justice Fortas and Justice Douglas?"

"Nope. Those all stayed there. Do you want me to borrow them? I think we can do that."

"No, there isn't time."

"Before you hang up: Haldeman's office called. He's waiting for your call. Right now," she said, feigning toughness.

I chuckled, and called Haldeman on his direct line. He picked it up, and told me that he received an absolutely clean bill of health for the nominee I had not been told about. "Now, how about Rehnquist, your candidate?"

"I gather he's my candidate if something goes wrong," I responded.

"You've got it. I understand this guy's really conservative."

"Bob, I'm not sure the U.S. Constitution is the operative parchment for Rehnquist," I said facetiously, quipping, "He may start with the Magna Carta." I told Haldeman I had no idea what a legitimate vetting of Rehnquist would uncover. I mentioned he might have some explaining to do about some of the legislation he had reported on. But I did not see that as a problem. I mentioned the kidnapping scheme that Krogh was working on, but explained I no longer had my files and did not know how involved Rehnquist had been.

Haldeman liked the idea of snatching drug dealers. "That's nothing that would embarrass the president. He'd support such a program."

I really had only one matter that I thought might cause a problem. I told Haldeman, "I think we should anticipate having to invoke either executive privilege or attorney-client privilege to keep them out of the problem areas, and Justice Department files. Once the liberals figure out what they have with Rehnquist, they're going to want to know much more."

"Give me a for instance?"

"Like Mitchell's activities in going after Fortas and Douglas."

"Is that a problem?"

"That's a problem. I don't know how deeply Rehnquist was involved. But I know he was often coming out of Mitchell's office when I was going in, and he was advising Mitchell all the way."

"So?"

"If the Senate Judiciary Committee's liberal bloc, you know, [Edward] Kennedy and Tunney, use the Rehnquist confirmation hearings to start digging into the role of the Justice Department in the Fortas matter, I picked up just enough while I was there to know it will be trouble. And Rehnquist will get dragged into it. It's a scandal waiting to happen."

"Well, you may be right. But I'm not concerned. I don't know much about that, but I do know that we don't have anything to worry about over here. We stayed away from all that. But I can't imagine Jim Eastland would let them get into that."

"If Mitchell cuts them off, refuses to provide information, it will be no problem."

"Do you have any doubt that he won't do that?"

"None."

• • • •

At 7:13 p.m., the president went to Alex Butterfield's office, adjacent to the Oval Office. The television and sound crews were working in the Oval Office. Under the watchful eyes of Secret Service agents they had spread a canvas tarpaulin over the deep blue oval rug that replicated the presidential seal. Lights had been set up, with a camera directly in front of the president's desk. Several hours earlier, Butterfield had turned the thermostat in the Oval Office to 60 degrees Fahrenheit, to get the room as cold as possible. Once the lights went on, it would heat up, but the air conditioning was too loud to run during the broadcast. Practice had proven that if the crew did not turn the lights on until the last minute, the room would stay comfortable for about fifteen minutes, thus preventing the president from sweating on camera.

Before coming to Butterfield's office, Nixon had changed to a fresh suit, white shirt, and necktie that Manolo Sanchez, his trusted servant, had brought over from the residence. Waiting for him in Butterfield's office was Mark Goode, his media consultant, who would make sure everything was set up properly. Every time the president gave a speech, he insisted on wearing a white shirt. Goode had tried in vain to get him to wear a blue one, which would soften his features on camera. "Blue shirts are not presidential," Nixon had insisted. Also waiting for him in Butterfield's office was Ray Voege, who had mastered the best makeup for the president.

At 7:28 p.m., the crew asked the president if he would take his seat at his desk for a sound check. He did, reading a few lines from his prepared remarks. At 7:38 p.m., the floor director counted down with his right hand from five to zero. The president delivered his remarks, which ran just over five minutes in length.[14]

The president's address to the nation was almost the same as he had given it earlier to Dick Moore. Of course, he had incorporated the names of his choices. Powell had long been rumored as a person the president wanted to place on the Supreme Court, so this was not as stunning a selection as his second. The Rehnquist choice surprised everyone.

For me, as I listened to the official announcement, I felt anxious, because the president was nominating a man I was sure would represent his conservative views, but he had not been vetted. Since then, my feelings have become more reflective. I must concede that seldom has any significant length of time passed that Rehnquist's presence at the top of the federal judiciary has not reminded me of the thoughtlessness of my somewhat irresponsible adventure as a young White House staffman playing for a piece of history.

13

AFTERWORD

NIXON'S LAST-DITCH DECISION to select William Rehnquist proved to be among the most significant of his presidency. Its impact is still being felt. His other choices—Warren Burger as chief justice, and Harry Blackmun and Lewis Powell as associate justices—were all men whose philosophies and rulings proved consistent with mainstream constitutional jurisprudence. The Rehnquist choice, however, has redefined the Supreme Court, making it a politically conservative bastion within our governmental system.[1] Rehnquist's many years of service, and his ability as a legal scholar, have brought about the rewriting of fundamental aspects of the nation's constitutional law.[2] With Rehnquist, Nixon found the conservative who would sit on the high bench for three decades, where he could work at undoing the legacy of the Warren Court. Nixon realized, perceptively, that in appointing a younger man as an associate justice he might also be appointing a future chief justice. In Nixon's words, he was appointing "a guy who's there 30 years. And who, also, if a Republican is around, is a potential candidate for chief justice." When

Burger retired as chief justice in 1986, there indeed was a Republican around, and President Ronald Reagan appointed the seasoned and tested William Rehnquist as chief justice.

It might have happened differently. The fact that Rehnquist was chosen at the last minute could have been disastrous for Nixon, because it made it impossible to vet Rehnquist adequately. The vetting process is designed to uncover anything that might disqualify a nominee if it should arise during Senate confirmation, and also to uncover lesser issues in order to prepare the nominee for how best to deal with them in public. Rehnquist had potential problems that were made worse by the lack of groundwork, and he had also left a paper trail explaining just how radical his views really were, which, if it had been discovered by Senate Democrats, could very well have killed his nomination.

The Suppressed Paper Trail

Since Rehnquist's initial nomination, I have wondered what would have happened if the Senate had had access to information about his activities at the Justice Department. There was an effort in 1971 to obtain such information, and then again in 1986, but in '71 Rehnquist invoked attorney-client privilege, which provoked Senator Birch Bayh to send a letter to President Nixon on November 4. Bayh sent a similar letter to Mitchell, who responded for both the president and himself on November 5, refusing to waive the privilege.[3] That ended the efforts in 1971 to learn about these activities.

In 1986, the Democrats on the Senate Judiciary Committee, with the tacit support of moderate Republican senators Charles Mathias and Arlen Specter, sought Nixon administration documents written by Rehnquist. When they requested all the documents relating to Rehnquist's work from 1969 to 1971, however, President Reagan invoked executive privilege.[4] After a series of news stories,[5] and given the reality that those requesting the documents had sufficient votes to issue a subpoena which could indefinitely delay Rehnquist's (and Antonin Scalia's) confirmations, an agreement was reached to provide a few specified documents. Senator Mathias, accompanied by staff, reviewed the documents. Not surprisingly, they found nothing.[6]

An index of the benign documents promptly surfaced in the *New York*

Times.[7] The senator was shown two dozen Rehnquist documents (which I doubt represented a week's worth of work for a post he held for some 112 weeks). They were all routine Justice Department business handled in a routine fashion.

What else might have surfaced? Aside from further information on his role in the effort to force Abe Fortas off the Court, which may yet come back to haunt Rehnquist, there are two possible smoking guns of which I am aware. One is highly specific, a short memo in which Rehnquist brushed aside the First Amendment. The other is far more general, if not devastating for a would-be justice: a nineteen-page memo outlining the Warren Court's expansion of civil liberties and protections of the rights of the accused, and clearly signaling Rehnquist's unsympathetic reaction.

Rehnquist's disregard of the First Amendment came on the heels of the publication of the Pentagon Papers by the *New York Times* on Sunday, June 13, 1971. By Monday morning, I had a request from the president via Ehrlichman: "the old man" wanted to know how he could put those bastards (as they were generally referred to) at the *New York Times* in jail. I was instructed to open my law books and find the right answer. I looked up the relevant criminal statutes, and studied the annotations. I was not encouraged the president could do anything to the *New York Times.* The infamous Sedition Act of 1798 had long expired,[8] and the First Amendment appeared a serious barrier.

But I knew what to do. I called Bill Rehnquist. Although I knew he was still recovering from his back surgery, he was in contact with his office.[9] I spoke to his deputy, Thomas K. Kauper,[10] and explained what was needed. By Wednesday morning, June 16, Kauper reported he was sending a memorandum which Rehnquist had approved. Recently I found it in my White House files at the National Archives.[11]

The memo set forth the "applicable federal criminal statutes for prosecuting government employees, private citizens, reporters and corporate newspaper entities who have taken part in the release and publication of the Defense Department study of the United States involvement in Vietnam." It pointed out that the only reason there was no precedent for prosecuting reporters or news organizations under the available laws was the result of "previous policy decisions not to bring cases against newsmen and news entities."[12] Rather than address these policy issues, or the First Amendment questions, the memo simply brushed them aside, treating them as non-issues.[13] If Senate Democrats had seen this memo either in 1971 or 1986, they would have grilled Rehnquist over it. He could have responded that he did not write it, and that it was merely a lawyer's answer to a specific question asked by his "client," but it would have given his opponents more ammunition and his supporters concern.

Rehnquist would have had a harder time ducking questions about the other potential smoking gun. Actually, it was more like a smoking cannon accidentally left on the testing range: a nineteen-page frontal assault on the Supreme Court's concern with protecting civil liberties of criminal suspects and defendants. Rehnquist was secretly building a weapon for Nixon's "peace forces." Rehnquist suggested a front group, a "commission" to handle the dirty work, and give the undertaking an air of legitimacy, by assigning eminent (and of necessity right-wing) legal thinkers the task of rewriting the Constitution in response to recent Supreme Court decisions in the field of criminal law. It was the first memorandum I ever received from him, while I was serving as associate deputy attorney general. When I departed for the White House, it was one of the few Justice Department documents I carried with me. He sent it at a time when we both had been in our posts at the Justice Department for less than ninety days, on April 1, 1969. Rehnquist considered it so sensitive that he classified it "administratively confidential," which kept it locked up for many years. It was, in fact, a brutal critique of how the Supreme Court had gone astray in the field of criminal law, and it clearly signaled Rehnquist's reactionary thinking on a wide range of controversial Supreme Court cases.[14] It could have launched the debate that was later visited on Judge Robert Bork's Supreme Court nomination, which showed what opponents can do with a nominee's writings.

Rehnquist reported that "changes in the constitutional rules governing criminal proceedings which have resulted from recent decisions of the Supreme Court . . . have hindered the enforcement of the criminal law, and have called forth adverse comment from informed, responsible sources." More specifically, he was concerned about decisions that had caused "(a) Sharp restriction of police interrogation of suspects during early stages of the proceeding . . . ; (b) Voluntary confessions and statements of a criminal defendant . . . [being] excluded as evidence at trial of a defendant; (c) Prosecutors [being] forbidden from commenting on the failure of the defendant to take the stand and deny or explain evidence against him; [and] (d) Multiplication of constitutional rules [resulting in] collateral attacks on conviction[s] through habeas corpus [appeals]." Following a pure Rehnquistian observation—"The Anglo-Saxon system of criminal justice is not designed to be the most efficient in the world"— he explained that the Supreme Court had "failed to hold true the balance between the right of society to convict the guilty and the obligation of society to safeguard the accused." Accordingly, he wanted the president to appoint a commission to review the relevant decisions (many outlined in his memo) to determine whether the "overriding public interest in law enforcement" required a constitutional amendment on behalf of law enforcement, whose powers had been cut back in favor of the rights of the accused. The proposal never got beyond my discussing it with John Mitchell, who thought it might create a problem if the Nixon administration could not control such a commission, which would not be easy.

This memo is a map of Rehnquist's thinking on the Supreme Court's role in criminal justice. Written at a time when Rehnquist had no inkling he would devote three decades of his life to the matters he had set forth, it is his candid assessment of a significant field of constitutional jurisprudence he believed needed to be radically changed. Reading it today, I realize that had anyone wanted to know what Rehnquist might do as a Supreme Court justice, he had explained it in 1969. Indeed, during his thirty years on the Court, many of the decisions he discusses have been revisited, narrowed, or overturned. Rehnquist's tough anti-crime position may have been politically winning—Nixon had used it successfully in his 1968 campaign—but for a Supreme Court nominee facing a Democratically controlled Senate, it could have been fatal. Here was a relatively young, right-wing nominee summarizing dozens of Warren Court decisions, including such sacred cows as *Gideon v. Wainwright* (guaranteeing a lawyer to all defendants) and the *Miranda* decision, and concluding that "there is indeed substantial doubt as to whether these decisions reach desirable results."

Another feature of this document that would have touched off a lively, if not deadly, debate is Rehnquist's disdain for those rulings that apply the Bill of Rights (the first ten amendments to the Constitution) to the states by incorporating these rights into the Fourteenth Amendment (which does apply to the states). Had the Senate known that as a justice he would seek to fundamentally redefine the Supreme Court's interpretation of the

Constitution, withdrawing the Bill of Rights (with freedom of speech and religion, prohibitions against unreasonable searches and seizures, the right to counsel, and the myriad other rights embodied in these first ten amendments) from state and local government, it would likely have produced a firestorm.

Would this memo have been enough to defeat Rehnquist? It is impossible to say. Rehnquist offered as little as possible of his thinking during his confirmation hearings, relying on the tradition that justices would be less than independent if they had to explain how they might rule on cases or controversies. However, when combined with the issues that did arise—and which Rehnquist mishandled—the possibility is tantalizing, for it would have pulverized his stonewalling.

Did Rehnquist Lie?

Rehnquist's lack of vetting left him ill-prepared to fend off attacks. Even during the hearings themselves, the White House was half-asleep. Unlike some controversial confirmation proceedings, for which the White House obtained daily transcripts and monitored them almost hour by hour, the Rehnquist-Powell proceedings were tracked largely from secondary sources: the daily newspapers and the president's news summary. The White House felt so confident that both nominees would be confirmed that the ad hoc group under Ehrlichman charged with that task was disbanded. Rehnquist's hearings were handled by the Justice Department: Mitchell, Kleindienst, and Wallace Johnson, who had taken my former post of handling congressional relations at the Justice Department. I had no direct involvement, other than occasional conversations and updates from the Justice Department (Kleindienst and Johnson), and a brief but informative conversation with John Mitchell when Rehnquist was being pummeled at the end.

The White House was therefore unprepared when, on the opening day of the hearings (November 3, 1971), Rehnquist was asked by Senator Birch Bayh of Indiana about press reports that he had challenged black voters at the polls in Phoenix, Arizona, in 1968. He responded that he had had "absolutely nothing to do with any sort of poll watching" in that year, whereas in earlier elections, "My responsibilities, as I recall them, were never those of a challenger," rather as a lawyer "who attempted to supply legal advice to persons who were challengers." [15]

After the confirmation hearings ended on November 10, charges that Rehnquist had challenged and harassed black and Hispanic voters continued to surface. Before the Senate Judiciary Committee voted to approve his nomination, Rehnquist was forced to submit a sworn affidavit in response to charges from six persons who had attested to Rehnquist's challenging voters. [16] On November 23, the committee approved the nomination by a vote of 12 to 4. [17] Senators Bayh (D-IN), Phillip Hart (D-MI), Edward Kennedy (D-MA), and John Tunney (D-CA) voted against the nomination and filed a separate report that outlined the voter-challenging charges, along with other problems they had with the nomination. [18] They believed that Rehnquist had improperly challenged voters based on claims made by a Mr. Tate and a Mr. Harris, who had witnessed the event: "Mr. Rehnquist made an improper attempt to administer personally a literacy test to a would-be voter. Mr. Harris says he approached Mr. Rehnquist, to whom he had been introduced, and 'argued with him about the harassment of voters.' A struggle ensued in which Mr. Tate came to Mr. Harris' aid." These affidavits were corroborated by affidavits from Rev. and Mrs. Snelson McGriff, who said it was either Rehnquist or "his twin brother" who was at this Bethune, Arizona, precinct in 1964. [19]

Rehnquist, in an affidavit and letter to Chairman Eastland, flatly denied the charges, which effectively ended the matter. [20] While questions of his improperly challenging voters echoed through the Senate floor debate in 1971, they did not threaten his confirmation. It came down to Rehnquist's word against the statements of a few unknown people who had submitted affidavits. Only fifteen years later, when he returned to the Senate in 1986 for consent to move to the center seat on the high court, did the question resurface with a vengeance. It became one of a few focal points of his confirmation to be chief justice. The issue was no longer Rehnquist's behavior as a poll watcher, but rather, whether he had been truthful with the Senate in 1971. [21]

Democrats believed that Rehnquist had lied, and they set out to prove it. To do so, they depended on a combination of live witnesses and affidavits—all eyewitness accounts of persons with personal knowledge that Rehnquist had challenged voters in a number of Arizona elections.

Rehnquist began by stating that he had "reread very carefully the statement I made to the committee in 1971" relating to these charges, and he had "absolutely no reason to doubt its correctness."[22] However, when his '71 statement was promptly read aloud, he began backing off, saying that he could not recollect his statement. Apparently realizing the contradiction, Rehnquist quickly added that if the words that had just been read were what he said in 1971, then *"I think they are correct"* (my italics).[23]

Senator Edward Kennedy next told Rehnquist that "Several witnesses have come forward and made statements about your activities as a leader in the Republican ballot security program in Phoenix in Arizona in the early 1960's," a fact surely known to Rehnquist because it had been reported on the front page of *The Washington Post.*[24] While the Republican chairman refused to permit many of these witnesses to testify, Kennedy read descriptions of the charges of several. Rehnquist denied knowing any of them, and he denied their charges.[25]

Collectively, these witnesses described "squads," or teams, that moved quickly from precinct to precinct to disqualify voters, confronting black and Hispanic voters standing in line at the polls by asking them questions about their qualifications, or holding up a small card with a passage from the U.S. Constitution and demanding that the voter read it aloud; also photographing people standing in line to vote. These descriptions were corroborated by a 1971 letter in the files of the Senate Judiciary Committee from Charles Hardy, an Arizona Republican who had become a federal judge, who was aware of the squads' activities and highly critical of them.[26] Hardy had not seen Rehnquist challenging any voters, however.

The most potent witness identifying Rehnquist with challenging voters was James Brosnahan, a former assistant U.S. attorney in Phoenix, who had been dispatched to investigate challenging activities in 1962. While Rehnquist remembered Brosnahan (who had earlier been a law clerk for a judge in Phoenix), he denied any knowledge that Brosnahan, accompanied by an FBI agent, had appeared in 1962 at a polling place where Rehnquist had been challenging voters.[27] He also repeatedly denied Brosnahan's charges, but in a guarded manner, saying that he did not "think" the charges were correct.[28]

Great effort was made by Senator Orrin Hatch of Utah to defend Rehnquist by discrediting Brosnahan. So damning was the testimony, Senator

Hatch all but refused to accept it. Brosnahan, an experienced trial lawyer, kept his cool as Senator Hatch lost his, becoming increasingly obstreperous and confrontational.[29] Finally, Brosnahan had taken enough of the assault, and he shot a rhetorical question at Hatch that ricocheted right off the Utah senator (clearly knocking him off balance), around the hearing room, and into *The Washington Post*, because it said it all: "Do you think I really would be here to testify about the qualifications of the chief justice after 27 years of trying lawsuits if I wasn't absolutely sure. If it was even close, I would be at Jack's restaurant in San Francisco for my Friday afternoon lunch."[30] The audience at the hearings erupted in applause. Bullying had backfired. James Brosnahan had publicly branded Rehnquist a liar, and he was corroborated by other witnesses.

All told, the Democrats produced fourteen people who swore they had witnessed Rehnquist challenging voters.[31] In rebuttal, the Republicans produced eight witnesses who claimed they had not seen or heard of Rehnquist challenging voters—but none of them could testify that they were actually with Rehnquist during any entire election day, nor did their testimony cover all the elections involved in the charges.[32] To read the testimony and affidavits, the conclusion is inescapable that Rehnquist's statement in 1971 flatly denying that he had challenged voters (in the elections from 1958–68) was false.

The evidence is clear and convincing that Rehnquist was not truthful about his activities in challenging voters, an activity that was legal and accepted at the time he did it. Had this underlying activity been discovered during the vetting process before his 1971 nomination, as it surely would have, it would not have disqualified him. Rather, it would have given him the opportunity to explain it, and he could have distanced himself from the unacceptable and sorry practice that once had not been uncommon. But to flatly deny ever engaging in challenging any voter—even for legitimate reasons—was foolish. I don't believe Rehnquist "harassed" black voters ever, for that is not his style or nature. Yet I have no doubt he challenged black voters at a time when it was perfectly legal in Arizona to do so. After reading and rereading his testimony, it appears to me he was saying to the Senate that he really was not sure himself. Yet his 1971 blanket denial forced him to remain consistent, and that blanket denial was a lie. The efforts to keep it in place were disingenuous at best, perjurious at worst.

. . . .

The second issue that the Senate faced concerned a single memo written in 1952, when Rehnquist was a clerk for Justice Jackson. It is a memo that has come to haunt Rehnquist, as much for his explanation of it as for its contents. Here, too, he suffered from a lack of vetting, since a different explanation would have allowed him to take responsibility for the nineteen-year-old document without derailing his nomination. But the reaction to this 1952 memo, and Rehnquist's dealing with it, suggests what might have occurred had the Senate found his 1969 diatribe on the Supreme Court's protection of civil liberties. The only difference being Rehnquist could not so easily have invented an explanation for his '69 document.

On December 5, 1971, amidst a lackluster debate in the full Senate, with Rehnquist appearing headed for easy confirmation, *Newsweek* magazine published a memorandum written by Rehnquist as a law clerk to Justice Robert Jackson.[33] Democrats jumped on it.

The next day, Senator Bayh, who was leading the opposition to Rehnquist as he had earlier against Haynsworth and Carswell, told the few senators in the chamber that "new and disturbing information concerning Mr. William Rehnquist's commitment to equal justice in this country was revealed today." He described the 1952 memorandum written by Rehnquist advising Justice Jackson to "reaffirm" the rule of "separate but equal of *Plessy v. Ferguson.*" The next day, Bayh continued to attack. "I am referring to the recent disclosure that the nominee urged, when he was a law clerk, Justice Jackson to vote against Brown against Board of Education. Not only did he urge him to vote against Brown against Board of Education, but some of the reasoning, and some of the rhetoric in that page and a half memo is almost impossible to believe."[34] There was only one Supreme Court decision worse than *Plessy* that a contemporary nominee might embrace, and that was the infamous *Dred Scott* case (which held that blacks were not citizens).[35] The signed memo to Jackson was entitled "A Random Thought on the Segregation Cases." The salient paragraphs of the page-and-a-half document stated:

> To those who would argue that "personal" rights are more sacrosanct than "property" rights, the short answer is that the Constitution makes no

such distinction. To the argument made by [plaintiff Brown's attorney] Thurgood, not John, Marshall that a majority may not deprive a minority of its constitutional right, the answer must be made that while this is sound in theory, in the long run it is the majority who will determine what the constitutional rights of the minority are. One hundred and fifty years of attempts on the part of this Court to protect minority rights of any kind— whether those of business, slaveholders, or Jehovah's Witnesses—have all met the same fate. One by one the cases establishing such rights have been sloughed off and crept silently to rest. If the present Court is unable to profit by this example, it must be prepared to see its work fade in time, too, as embodying only the sentiments of a transient majority of nine men.

I realize that it is an unpopular and unhumanitarian position, for which I have been excoriated by "liberal" colleagues but I think *Plessy v. Ferguson* was right and should be re-affirmed. If the Fourteenth Amendment did not enact Spencer's *Social Statics,* it just as surely did not enact Myrdal's *American Dilemma.*[36]

Reaction to Bayh's speech created a buzz in the Senate that was heard all the way down Pennsylvania Avenue, first at the Justice Department and then the White House. Suddenly, not only was there a real debate on Rehnquist's nomination, there was concern by his handlers. Other senators on both sides of the aisle were looking at the 1952 memo and addressing it on the Senate floor.[37] It was about this time that I literally ran into John Mitchell in the hall of the ground floor of the West Wing. He asked me to walk with him to his waiting limousine, parked on West Executive Drive. I asked if Rehnquist was in any trouble with the Jackson memorandum, and he told me, "Hell, he doesn't have the foggiest memory of ever writing it."[38] Mitchell assured me that Rehnquist would be confirmed with votes to spare.

Still, explanations were necessary, because no senator could politically agree to vote for a nominee who supported *Plessy* and rejected *Brown.* At the Department of Justice, Wally Johnson reported to Mitchell and Kleindienst, and soon action was taken.[39] Later that day, Senate Judiciary Committee chairman Jim Eastland arrived in the chamber, carrying a letter. He was given the floor by the president of the Senate.

"Mr. President, I have received a letter from the nominee about something which has been mentioned in the debate—the memorandum which he wrote to Mr. Justice Jackson," Eastland began, with a southern drawl that was not always easy to understand. Few men had done more in

their careers in the U.S. Senate to thwart the passage of civil rights legislation, and his annoyance with the opponents of Rehnquist was patent as
he spoke: "I did not think that he needed to write this letter, because the
memorandum was certainly what was the law at the time [referring to
Plessy v. Ferguson's separate but equal doctrine], which was in 1952. I
judge that he wrote this letter to be perfectly fair with the Senate. The letter is addressed to me," he added before reading it aloud to the Senate.
The pertinent portions are set forth below:

> Dear Mr. Chairman:
> A memorandum in the files of Justice Robert H. Jackson bearing my ini-
> tials has become the subject of discussion in the Senate debate on my con-
> firmation, and I therefore take the liberty of sending you my recollection
> of the facts in connection with it. As best I can reconstruct the circum-
> stances after some nineteen years, the memorandum was prepared by me
> at Justice Jackson's request; it was intended as a rough draft of a statement
> of *his* views. . . . He expressed concern that the conference should have the
> benefit of all of the arguments in support of the constitutionality of the
> "separate but equal" doctrine, as well as those against its constitutionality.
> . . . I am satisfied that the memorandum was not designed to be a state-
> ment of *my* views on these cases. . . . I am fortified in this conclusion be-
> cause the bald, simplistic conclusion that *"Plessy v. Ferguson* was right and
> should be re-affirmed" is not an accurate statement of my own views at the
> time.
> I believe that the memorandum was prepared by me as a statement of
> Justice Jackson's tentative views for his own use at conference.[40]

Rehnquist closed his letter to Eastland by noting that while he had used
Brown v. Board of Education "in the context of an answer to a question
concerning the binding effect of precedent," he had not been asked for his
views on the substantive issues underlying *Brown*. Accordingly, he
wanted to state for the record that he fully supported "the legal reasoning
and the rightness from the standpoint of fundamental fairness of the
Brown decision."[41] Rehnquist had trumped his opponents, by turning the
meaning of his memo upside down. Surprised by the contents of Rehnquist's letter, all Bayh could do was urge his colleagues to read it along
with the memorandum by Rehnquist to Justice Jackson to "judge the
veracity of it." He was more than suspicious.

Rehnquist's opponents were not alone in being surprised at his explanation. I was a strong supporter of Rehnquist, but I was amazed at his response. To be blunt, I thought he had lied. His explanation was so at odds with the style and contents of his memo to Jackson that it did not past the smell test. Given Mitchell's remark to me, I thought (and still believe) that Rehnquist overreacted to the heat he was getting, and felt he had to reconstruct history to get himself off the hook. To say I was disappointed is an understatement. If he did not remember writing the memo, which would not be surprising since it happened nineteen years earlier, he should have said so. If it did reflect his position in 1952—which I suspected to be the case for it was consistent with what I knew about him—why not admit it and say he had changed his views? Frankly, I thought his letter was inviting trouble. While it was not perjury to send a letter with a bogus explanation to Chairman Eastland, it was wrong, it was a false representation, and stupid.

By the next afternoon, December 9, Bayh and his staff had reanalyzed the 1952 memo to Jackson to determine if it could possibly represent Jackson's views based on his Supreme Court decisions and other writings. Bayh took his colleagues through the 1952 memo to show that Rehnquist's explanation did not fit with Jackson's views. Similarly, Senator Edward Brooke of Massachusetts, the Senate's only black and the first Republican to defect, expressed his serious doubts about Rehnquist's explanation.

The spreading disbelief in the Senate to Rehnquist's explanation was halted when corroboration for Rehnquist arrived from London. Donald Cronson, who had also been a law clerk for Justice Jackson and whose desk had been next to Rehnquist's, sent a telegram with his recollections, reporting that both he and Rehnquist had worked on the memo.[42] In addition, Cronson told the *New York Times* that both he and Rehnquist "personally thought at the time [1952] that the 1896 decision, *Plessy v. Ferguson,* was wrong."[43] Cronson added, "I think Justice Jackson asked us to prepare a second [memo] making the other argument [that *Plessy* should be reaffirmed]. My guess is that I physically prepared the first memorandum and he prepared the second, but we worked together on both. In what I have read about the second I can recognize some of my purple prose."[44] Cronson's so-called second memo was the one that had been initialed "whr."

Cronson's less than persuasive efforts were blunted when *The Washing-*

ton Post found Justice Jackson's longtime secretary, Mrs. Elsie Douglas. She had been with Jackson when both Rehnquist and Cronson clerked for him. Mrs. Douglas minced no words, and charged that Rehnquist had "smeared the reputation of a great justice" by attributing pro-segregation views to Jackson. And she "challenged Rehnquist's assertion that Jackson would have asked a law clerk to help prepare the remarks he would make when the nine Justices met to decide whether to overturn the separate-but-equal doctrine."[45] As others noted, the man who had made the opening and closing arguments at Nuremberg, and the justice who was known for his skills as an extemporaneous speaker, did not need Rehnquist to tell him what to say at a conference with his colleagues.

To resolve who was telling the truth, Bayh wanted to reopen the confirmation hearings. Accordingly, he asked the Senate to delay acting on the Rehnquist nomination until January 18, 1972, after the holidays. Rehnquist supporters, understandably, wanted to end this debate while they still had the votes to both cut it off, if necessary, and confirm. So Bayh's motion was easily defeated, and shortly after 5:00 p.m. on December 10, 1971—with Vice President Spiro Agnew presiding over the Senate— William H. Rehnquist was confirmed by a vote of 68 to 26.[46] He was the one-hundredth man to become a member of the Court since its founding, and ironically he would take the seat once occupied by Robert H. Jackson.

About an hour before this historic vote, Dick Moore called me. He was going over to the Department of Justice and wanted me to join him. The White House had known for days that Rehnquist was not in trouble, and would be confirmed; now it was time for a little celebration. Mitchell and Kleindienst were going to toast the new justice, and Moore thought I should participate. Without making an issue of my second thoughts, for I was pleased for Rehnquist, I begged off. I had earlier in November sent a memorandum to the president's appointment secretary, Dwight Chapin, suggesting the president mark the occasion when Rehnquist was confirmed.[47] In December, when I learned that Rehnquist would be invited to the Oval Office for a send-off to the Court by the president, I asked that my name not be included.

• • • •

Fifteen years later, during Rehnquist's 1986 confirmation hearings, the issue of his truthfulness about the *Brown* memo resurfaced. Senator

Howard M. Metzenbaum of Ohio, a Democrat, asked: "Does not the memorandum . . . have language that would indicate that you were indicating your views, not Justice Jackson's views?" Rehnquist agreed, "Yes, I suppose one could read it either way. The 'I's' in it certainly could have been mine rather, just looking at it as a text, rather than Justice Jackson's."

Metzenbaum explained to his witness that the committee had "other memos of yours" to Justice Jackson in which he had referred to "your ideas" when referring to Jackson, yet in this now infamous memorandum he claimed it was Jackson's thinking, but it still "talks about I, I, I." Why had he written it in the first person? Rehnquist avoided a direct response.

Senator Joseph R. Biden, Jr., of Delaware, the senior Democrat on this Republican-controlled committee, questioned Rehnquist about his position on *Plessy v. Ferguson* as a law clerk, to which Rehnquist said, "I saw factors on both sides, *I think*" (my italics). Biden, an aggressive and able questioner, pushed harder. Did Rehnquist "believe *Plessy* should have been struck down?" Rehnquist: "I had not come to rest on that, Senator." During his next round, Biden used a recent interview in *The Washington Post* which reported that Rehnquist's co-clerk Donald Cronson had said that Rehnquist had "strongly defended *Plessy* . . . at luncheon meetings with clerks." Biden asked if Cronson was correct. Rehnquist first said, "No, *I do not think* he is." But he quickly retreated. "Again, it is hard to remember back, but *I think* it probably seemed to me at the time that some of the others simply were not facing the arguments on the other side, and I thought they ought to be faced."[48] Biden pressed further: "Did you believe at the time you were a clerk for Mr. Jackson that *Plessy v. Ferguson* should not be overruled? Was that your view at that time?" Rehnquist: "Well, as I said to you yesterday, I thought there were good arguments to be made in support of it."

Next, Howard Metzenbaum laid out, and then asked Rehnquist to reconcile, all of his irreconcilable positions on the Jackson memo. They were:

(a) the use of the first person in the memo despite Rehnquist's claim that its views were Jackson's, not his;

(b) Cronson's statement, affirmed by Rehnquist, that he "did defend the view that *Plessy* was right" at lunches with other clerks;

(c) Rehnquist's statement in his 1971 letter to Eastland asserting that he knew the 1952 memo was Jackson's view "because the bold, simplistic conclusion that Plessy against Ferguson was right and should be re-affirmed is not an accurate statement of my own views at the time"; and

(d) Rehnquist's statement(s) to Senator Biden on overturning *Plessy*, that "I do not think I reached a conclusion. Law clerks do not have to vote."

Rehnquist's response shows how seriously he had gotten himself in trouble: "I would suspect that a logical interpretation [of his use of first person] is I perhaps imagined this was the way Justices spoke in conference." [49] Rehnquist continued trying to untangle his conflicting positions for Metzenbaum by adding, "Insofar as the statements [by Cronson, that Rehnquist was] arguing Plessy against Ferguson was right at the time . . . I do not doubt that is correct." yet if (b) is correct, it is in conflict with (a). [50] This was not explanation, but further contradiction.

It was when examining the historical record, and trying to give Rehnquist the benefit of my own long-held doubts, that I discovered additional evidence that tipped the scale for me. No senator examined this question more cogently, thoroughly, independently, and dispassionately than Senator Carl Levin of Michigan. Senator Levin, who was not a member of the Senate Judiciary Committee, undertook his own private investigation to ascertain the truth about the memo to Justice Jackson. Levin, a Harvard Law School graduate, exchanged several letters with Rehnquist, which he later sent to the Senate Judiciary Committee for inclusion in the record. [51]

Senator Levin's speech to the Senate, delivered on September 15, 1986, was careful in accurately citing the evidence and explaining why Levin had reached the conclusion he had reached. [52] Senator Levin stated: [53]

> I submit that the question is not what Justice Rehnquist believed 30 years ago and whether he still holds those beliefs today—it is how he represented to the Senate—in 1971 and in 1986—what he believed, what Justice Jackson believed, and for what this memo was intended.
>
> We now have had a better opportunity to examine the evidence relating to this memo than the Senate had in 1971. . . . [I]t is very difficult to conclude anything other than that the memo does not contain Justice Jackson's views, and must therefore have been either an expression of law clerk Rehnquist's views or an attempt on the part of law clerk Rehnquist to provide Jackson with the pro-Plessy point of view. In either case, the evidence casts serious doubt on Justice Rehnquist's account of the nature of his memorandum.

Levin next explained that he was adding his own observations based on the evidence developed by the Senate Judiciary Committee as well as "some questions I asked Justice Rehnquist in my two letters to him." The first letter asked Rehnquist "on what basis he stated that the views expressed in the memo were those of Justice Jackson." The senator had also asked if Rehnquist "could recall anything specific Justice Jackson had told him to indicate his views of the 'separate but equal' doctrine." Levin found "it difficult to believe [Jackson] would ever have expressed the view that 'Plessy versus Ferguson was right and should be reaffirmed.'" Rehnquist had responded that "he did not recall the specific content" of his discussions with Jackson, but he did remember that Justice Jackson was concerned "that the conference have the benefit of all of the arguments in support of the constitutionality of the 'separate but equal' doctrine, as well as those against its constitutionality." Levin continued:

> Frankly, I was not satisfied by this response. It still seemed to me, looking at the language of this memo, that it was a young law clerk talking in this memo, not a distinguished Supreme Court Justice. I centered on one sentence in particular: "I realize that it is an unpopular and unhumanitarian position, for which I have been excoriated by my 'liberal' colleagues, but I think Plessy versus Ferguson was right and should be reaffirmed." What "liberal colleagues" had Justice Jackson been excoriated by and when? Why would he have been excoriated by his colleagues for views he was about to express at an upcoming Court conference?
>
> In a followup letter, I asked Justice Rehnquist this precise question: "Did Justice Jackson tell you during these oral discussions that he had been excoriated by liberal colleagues for his views on Plessy? If he didn't tell you, then on what basis did you include this line in the memo?"
>
> Justice Rehnquist's answer was: "As I indicated in my answer to your question of July 23, 1986, I have no recollection today of the specific content of my oral discussions with Justice Jackson relating to the points that he tentatively intended to make at the Court's Conference on the Brown case. I do not recall Justice Jackson telling me in those discussions that he had been excoriated by liberal colleagues for his views on the Brown case. It is my strong sense, however, that Justice Jackson acknowledged during our discussion that he fully expected to be criticized sharply by some of his colleagues if he took the position that Plessy versus Ferguson should be reaffirmed."

This last sentence, Senator Levin informed the Senate, was the first time that Justice Rehnquist had publicly attempted to provide an explanation for the phrase "excoriated by my 'liberal' colleagues." While Senator Biden may have forced a crack in the Rehnquist stonewall, Senator Levin had just found a hole. Levin continued:

> And if we look at it in light of what the memo actually says, we realize that it is no explanation at all. Justice Rehnquist has a "strong sense" that Justice Jackson "fully expected to be criticized sharply" by his fellow Justices "if he took the position that Plessy . . . should be reaffirmed." But the memo clearly says "I have been excoriated." It doesn't say "I will be excoriated" or even "I might be excoriated if I take this position." It says "I have been excoriated," and the question remains, "by whom?"

Senator Levin next showed, based on notes of the other justices at the conference, that there was no colleague who would have "excoriated" Justice Jackson because, in fact, he never expressed such views, and his "fellow Justices . . . would hardly have spoken ill of him for expressing genuine convictions."[54]

To bolster his contention that the memo to Jackson did not reflect his views, Rehnquist had told the Senate in 1971: "The particular memorandum in question differs sharply from the normal sort of clerk's memorandum that was submitted to Justice Jackson during my tenure as a clerk." More specifically, Rehnquist had explained: "While he did expect his clerks to make recommendations based on their memoranda as to whether certiorari should be granted or denied, he very definitely did not either expect or welcome the incorporation by a clerk of his own philosophical view of how a case should be decided."[55]

Senator Levin had examined the papers of Justice Jackson which had been deposited at the Library of Congress. It was possible "to test the nominee's contention" that Jackson's clerks did not include their personal views, he explained. "In other words, the nominee was suggesting that the segregation memo could not have contained his own views because it was not normal practice to put his own views into memos since Jackson frowned on that sort of thing." With this fact in mind, Levin reviewed the "cert." memos Rehnquist had written for Justice Jackson, and found "numerous instances of personal opinions and informal observations being included with a review of the facts of the case." He cited three examples.[56]

Senator Levin concluded: "I am saddened to say I do not believe Justice Rehnquist's account of the Jackson memo." No supporter of Rehnquist has ever answered Senator Levin's remarks, during the Senate debate or since. Indeed, since 1986, many scholars who have examined the evidence have reached the same conclusion that Senator Levin reached on the Jackson memo.

For example, in 1988, Professor Bernard Schwartz was given access to Justice Jackson's draft concurring opinion in the *Brown* case, which was never issued. Schwartz writes that Jackson believed it so important that the Court have a single unanimous holding that he left his hospital bed to appear with his brethren the day *Brown* was announced. The draft reflected Jackson's considered views. Schwartz reports the draft showed that Jackson clearly believed that school segregation was unconstitutional. Schwartz concluded: "It is hard to believe that the man who wrote the sentences holding segregation invalid in his draft held the view only a few months earlier attributed to him by Chief Justice Rehnquist—'that Plessy v. Ferguson was right and should be re-affirmed.' So inconsistent, indeed, is this view with the Jackson draft that one may ask . . . what might have happened had Jackson's unequivocal draft statements on the invalidity of segregation been available when the Senate voted on the Rehnquist nomination . . . ?"[57]

In 1990, Joseph Rauh, a longtime Supreme Court observer and attorney for various civil rights groups who had opposed the Rehnquist nominations in both 1971 and 1986, reflected on the Court. Rauh, the last law clerk to Justice Benjamin Cardozo and the first law clerk for Justice Felix Frankfurter in the 1930s, reported that the issue at the Rehnquist confirmation in 1986 was not his prior positions "but whether he was telling the truth at his two confirmation hearings." Rauh concluded: "The evidence appears incontestable that he was not. . . . Rehnquist's betrayal of his sworn oath saddens me."[58]

In 1991, Professor Mark Tushnet (a former law clerk to Justice Thurgood Marshall) took another look at the high court's handling of *Brown v. Board of Education*. While Tushnet is very charitable in his analysis of Rehnquist's posture on the 1952 memo to Jackson—based on his reappraisal of Justice Jackson, whom Tushnet believes was ambivalent about race—he still does not buy Rehnquist's positions taken under oath. Tushnet says, "I believe that Jackson asked his clerks simply to put down on paper the ideas he and they may have been batting around in chambers. I have little doubt too that the memorandum, while expressing one aspect of Jackson's views, is put in ways that strongly suggest that it expresses all of Rehnquist's." [59]

In 1996, Professor Laura Ray examined the relationship between Justice Jackson and Rehnquist. When she turned to the 1952 memo, she noted there was "room for considerable skepticism concerning Rehnquist's claim that the memo reflected Jackson's views." And after parsing the evidence, including the writings of scholars who had preceded her, she concluded: "On balance, then, it is hard not to agree . . . that Rehnquist was expressing his own views in the *Brown* memo. With a seat on the Supreme Court almost in his grasp, Rehnquist may well have retreated from an uncomfortable position taken almost twenty years earlier in the only way that seemed open to him. That such a step might unfairly tarnish the reputation of Justice Jackson years after his death does not seem to have been a concern." [60]

After reviewing Rehnquist's Senate testimony, the conclusions of Rehnquist's doubters in the U.S. Senate, and the analysis and conclusions of academics who have examined Rehnquist's truthfulness in explaining his 1952 memo to Justice Jackson, I find that my reaction thirty years ago—that he was lying—has been established by clear and convincing evidence. As I sifted through the evidence and read the hearings and debates and commentary, I could not but think that had Rehnquist been properly checked and vetted in 1971, the 1952 memo would not have been sprung on him. Rather, he would have examined it, along with other memos he had written to Justice Jackson, in advance. He could have stated that it represented his views at the time, but that he had since changed his mind. But after he was nominated, it was impossible for him to reexamine what had truly happened, so he had to concoct something quickly, and rashly.

• • • •

It is now quite clear to me what happened: Rehnquist lied.

President Nixon: . . . I will give you one last bit of advice, because you're going to be independent, naturally. And that is don't let the fact that you're under heat change any of your views. . . . So just be as mean and rough as they said you were.

William Rehnquist: Thanks, Mr. President.

December 10, 1971
From their only private conversation

A Note on Sources

On October 16, 2000, the National Archives and Records Administration (NARA) released for public listening 420 hours of Nixon taped White House conversations, which cover the period of August 1971 through December 1971. These 4,140 conversations include the period—thirty-four days to be precise—when the decision was made by President Richard Nixon to fill two vacancies on the Supreme Court. All dialogue herein is based on verbatim transcripts, except for some of my own conversations reconstructed from notes, logs, records, and memory—indicated as such in the Notes. The White House recordings were transcribed by Sarah Shoenfeld, who holds a master's degree in history from Northeastern University, and Jennifer Gruda, a last-year law student at Georgetown Law Center. I reviewed them. I have only used those portions of the transcripts necessary to tell the story, and I edited them to eliminate unnecessary "ums," "uhs," "yeah," "right," "okay," and so on, as well as redundancies, and anything extraneous to the subject at hand. Occasionally, I have supplied implied words or necessary context within brackets, and in a few instances used brackets to note an inaudible word or two. Due to the imperfections of the tapes, some small errors may remain; nonetheless, readers can be confident that the words here were all spoken by the participants, notwithstanding my editing to make them easily readable.

In addition, I have drawn on materials from my own White House files, and the files of others at the White House, all from the National Archives—an estimated 3,000 pages in all. My relevant source material will be posted at www.hpol.org (Nixon tapes and transcripts) and www.oyez.org (documents), sites devoted to the Supreme Court that are maintained by Professor Jerry Goldman at Northwestern University. Other source material is set forth in the Notes and Bibliography.

Chronology

1971

September 17	Associate Justice Hugo Black notifies the White House that he is resigning for reasons of ill health
September 18	Press secretary Ron Ziegler announces that seven "men" are under consideration for the Court. Speculation centers on Congressman Richard Poff (R-VA)
September 23	Associate Justice John M. Harlan notifies the White House that he is resigning for reasons of ill health
	Nixon states publicly that he has asked U.S. Attorney General John Mitchell to "be sure that qualified women" are considered
September 27	The National Women's Political Council issues a list of ten women qualified to serve on the Court
October 2	Richard Poff withdraws from consideration for personal reasons
October 12	Nixon says he will announce his selections for both vacancies during the following week
October 13	John Mitchell sends six names of nominees to the American Bar Association for review:
	Senate majority whip Robert Byrd of West Virginia
	D.C. Superior Court Judge Sylvia Bacon
	Fifth Circuit Federal Court of Appeals Judge Charles Clark
	Herschel H. Friday, Little Rock, Arkansas, bond lawyer
	California Court of Appeals Judge Mildred Lillie
	Fifth Circuit Federal Court of Appeals Judge Paul H. Rooney
	Privately, Mitchell tells the ABA to focus on Lillie and Friday
October 18	John Mitchell asks Lewis F. Powell if he would accept a nomination

October 19   John Mitchell asks Howard Baker if he would accept a
              nomination

October 20   The ABA Committee on the Federal Judiciary finds Friday and
              Lillie not qualified to serve on the Court. Richard Moore,
              special counsel to the president, convinces Nixon to consider
              William Rehnquist.

October 21   Nixon tells Mitchell to rescind the offer to Baker. Nixon makes a
              televised address to announce the nominations of Lewis Powell
              and William Rehnquist

Notes

Abbreviations

NARA—National Archives and Records Administration, Washington, DC
WHF—White House Files (at NARA)
WHSF—White House Special Files
WSPF—Watergate Special Prosecution Force (at NARA)

Chapter 1

1. Letter of Earl Warren to President Lyndon Johnson, June 13, 1968. NARA, WHF.
2. Ibid.
3. Stephen E. Ambrose, *Nixon: The Triumph of a Politician, 1962–1972* (New York: Simon & Schuster, 1989), 159.
4. Press Conference No. 128 of the President of the United States, 11:38 a.m. EDT, June 26, 1968, in the President's Office at the White House. NARA, WHF.
5. Ibid.
6. John Ehrlichman, *Witness to Power: The Nixon Years* (New York: Simon & Schuster, 1982), 113. Ehrlichman told me he had spoken with Senator Griffin several times during the 1968 campaign both to encourage the Senate Republicans to defeat the Fortas nomination, and to get information from Senator Griffin for candidate Nixon on how their efforts were proceeding.
7. Laura Kalman, *Abe Fortas: A Biography* (New Haven: Yale University Press, 1990), 340.
8. Ibid., 342.
9. Ibid., 351.
10. This information was given to me by both John Mitchell and John Ehrlichman.
11. Kalman, *Abe Fortas*, 355.
12. The true nature of the Earl Warren Dinner is known to me because of a conversation shortly afterwards with Attorney General John Mitchell. When I mentioned the dinner, which had been written up as a social event by *The Washington Post,* and asked the attorney general if it had been a pleasant evening, I was unexpectedly told, "Hell, that was no party, it was a reconnaissance mission to figure out which of those

old farts is most likely to croak." Whatever conclusions were reached were not shared with me.

13. The guest list found in the Nixon White House Files at NARA includes the following: The President and Mrs. Nixon, the Vice President and Mrs. Agnew, the Chief Justice and Mrs. Warren, Mr. Justice Black and Mrs. Black, Mr. Justice Douglas and Mrs. Douglas, Mr. Justice Harlan and Mrs. Harlan, Mr. Justice Brennan and Mrs. Brennan, Mr. Justice Stewart and Mrs. Stewart, Mr. Justice White and Mrs. White, Mr. Justice Fortas and Mrs. Fortas, Mr. Justice Marshall and Mrs. Marshall, Mr. Justice Reed (retired) and Mrs. Reed, Mr. Justice Clark (retired) and Mrs. Clark, Mr. and Mrs. James Warren, Mr. and Mrs. John C. Daly, Hon. and Mrs. Earl Warren, Jr., Mr. and Mrs. Harry Van Knight, Jr., Dr. and Mrs. Stuart Brien, Mr. and Mrs. Robert Warren, Mr. and Mrs. Richard S. Dinner, Mr. Benjamin H. Swig, Mr. and Mrs. Robert McHugh, Miss Margaret A. Bryan, Secretary of the Treasury and Mrs. Kennedy, Attorney General and Mrs. Mitchell, Postmaster General and Mrs. Blount, Secretary of the Interior and Mrs. Hickel, Secretary of Agriculture and Mrs. Hardin, Secretary of Commerce and Mrs. Stans, Secretary of Labor and Mrs. Shultz, Secretary of HEW and Mrs. Finch, Secretary of HUD and Mrs. Romney, Secretary of Transportation and Mrs. Volpe, Hon. Thomas E. Dewey and Mrs. Dewey, Hon. Herbert Brownell and Mrs. Brownell, Hon. Warren Burger and Mrs. Burger, Hon. George MacKinnon and Mrs. MacKinnon, Hon. Edmund Brown and Mrs. Brown, Cardinal-designate Terrence E. Cooke, Hon. Walter E. Washington and Mrs. Washington, Mrs. Alice Roosevelt Longworth, Mrs. Henry Luce, Hon. Emil Mosbacher and Mrs. Mosbacher, Hon. Herbert C. Klein and Mrs. Klein, Mr. and Mrs. William T. Gossett, Mr. and Mrs. John H. Alexander, Mr. and Mrs. Randolph H. Guthrie, Mr. and Mrs. John Johnson, Mr. and Mrs. Norman Chandler, Mr. and Mrs. Jack Howard, Mrs. Katharine Graham, Mr. and Mrs. S. H. Kauffmann, Dr. and Mrs. Lee DuBridge, Mr. and Mrs. Charles Rhyne, Mr. and Mrs. Anthony D. Marshall, Mr. and Mrs. Art Linkletter, Mr. and Mrs. Bob Hope, Mr. and Mrs. Courtney Burton, General and Mrs. Mark Clark, Mr. and Mrs. Linwood Holton, Senator and Mrs. George Murphy, Senator and Mrs. Thomas Kuchel, and Hon. Ronald Reagan and Mrs. Reagan.

14. Ehrlichman, *Witness to Power*, 116.

15. I learned this fact while working at the Department of Justice.

16. Ibid., 19.

17. Bob Woodward and Scott Armstrong, *The Brethren: Inside the Supreme Court* (New York: Simon & Schuster, 1979), 18. Woodward and Armstrong correctly speculated that the Justice Department was leaking the information about Fortas when relying on the June 2, 1969, memorandum from FBI director J. Edgar Hoover to Attorney General Mitchell, in which Hoover states that a reliable source had informed the FBI that "in connection with the investigation involving former Supreme Court Associate Justice Abe Fortas, the Department [of Justice] furnished considerable information to William Lambert, writer for *Life* magazine, which not only enabled Lambert to expose the Fortas tie-in with the Wolfson Foundation but additionally kept Lambert advised" regarding its own investigation into the matter.

18. After an extensive search, on April 10, 2001 I was advised by Ms. Janis L. Wiggins, Archivist, Civilian Records, Textual Archives Services Division, that the Department of Justice records I sought were retained by the Department of Justice.

19. Robert Shogan, *A Question of Judgment: The Fortas Case and the Struggle for the Supreme Court* (Indianapolis: The Bobbs Merrill Company, 1972), 230.

20. Ibid.

21. Shogan, *A Question of Judgment,* 230–33.

22. Ibid., 231.

23. Shogan does not cite the provision of the federal criminal code, but based on the material he has provided it appears Rehnquist settled on Section 205 of Title 18 (Chapter 11), which read:

> Whoever, being an officer or employee of the United States in the . . . judicial branch of the Government . . . of the United States, including the District of Columbia, otherwise than in the proper discharge of his official duties—
>
> (1) acts as agent or attorney for prosecuting any claim against the United States, or receives any gratuity, or any share of or interest in any such claim in consideration of assistance in the prosecution of such claim, or
>
> (2) acts as agent or attorney for anyone before any department, agency, court, court-martial, officer, or any civil, military, or naval commission in connection with any proceeding, application, request for a ruling or other determination, contract, claim, controversy, charge, accusation, arrest, or other particular matter in which the United States is a party or has a direct and substantial interest—
>
> "Shall be fined not more than $10,000 or imprisoned for not more than two years, or both.

It should also be noted that this provision contained the following exception, which—if inferring the worst—would not have applied:

> "Nothing herein . . . prevents an officer . . . from acting, with or without compensation, as agent or attorney for . . . any person for whom . . . he is serving as . . . trustee, or other personal fiduciary except in those matters in which he has participated personally and substantially as a Government employee, through decision, approval, disapproval, recommendation, the rendering of advice, investigation, or otherwise, or which are the subject of his official responsibility, provided that the Government official responsible for appointment to his position approves.

24. Ibid., 232–33. Rehnquist was certainly correct (but again less than complete) in reporting that attorney general Lee issued an opinion to the House of Representatives that "A judge may be prosecuted in three modes for official misdemeanors or crimes: by information, or by an indictment before an ordinary court, or by impeachment before the Senate of the United States." But the 1796 opinion of attorney general Curtis Lee related to an Article I federal judge presiding in the Northwest Territory. Article I judges,

like the Northwest Territory judge addressed in Lee's opinion, are created by Congress (an example of a contemporary Article I judges is a Bankruptcy judge), while Article III judges emanate from the Constitution itself and have life tenure. Fortas was an Article III judge, as a member of the Supreme Court. In addition, Lee stated that impeachment, "being the most solemn, seems, in general cases, to be the best suit to the trial of so high and important an officer." Rehnquist's advice to Mitchell appears to be a concocted legal justification based on dubious precedent.

25. Ibid., 233.

26. Memorandum to the President, from Patrick J. Buchanan, May 6, 1969. NARA, WHSF.

27. "A Shadow Over the Supreme Court," *The Washington Post*, May 6, 1969, A-1.

28. "Some in G.O.P. Ask Fortas to Resign," *New York Times*, May 8, 1969, A-1.

29. Lambert claimed he had the story before he was given any assistance, and corroboration, by the Nixon administration; however, I recall hearing talk of Fortas's problems in conversations with Deputy Attorney General Richard Kleindienst long before *Life* published the story.

30. At the time, I was in charge of congressional relations for the Department of Justice. When the *Life* story on Fortas became news, I was asked by both Republicans and Democrats on Capitol Hill if the administration had been involved in this matter. I made inquiries with Deputy Attorney General Richard Kleindienst and was told, "Junior, there are some things it is better you do not know." Kleindienst proceeded to all but take credit for the leak himself.

31. Woodward and Armstrong, *The Brethren*, 19.

32. Bruce Allen Murphy, *Fortas: The Rise and Ruin of a Supreme Court Justice* (New York: William Morrow, 1988), 55.

33. Ibid., 571.

34. I was called to the attorney general's office on the morning of May 14, 1969. Will Wilson was with John Mitchell; they were discussing the Fortas case, and the weakness of building a criminal case against Fortas. Mitchell told me that if they could not convince Fortas to resign, the Justice Department might formally submit a report to the House of Representative calling for his impeachment. I was asked to prepare myself to talk with congressional leaders to determine if there might be bipartisan support for such an undertaking. Mitchell however was hopeful that "his talk with Chief Justice Earl Warren would do the trick." I was only to familiarize myself with the impeachment process. I left the meeting with the impression there was more interest in scaring the bejesus out of Fortas than successfully prosecuting him.

35. Murphy, *Fortas*, 551. ("When he first heard about Fortas's potential difficulties, Wilson later candidly confessed, he 'was excited about the prospect. I knew what kind of a potential coup we had. In all candor, we wanted Fortas off the Court.' " Murphy interviewed Wilson on November 2, 1982 in Austin, Texas.)

36. This celebration was reported to me by Deputy Attorney General Kleindienst, who told me that there would be no effort to impeach Abe Fortas, who had resigned.

Those present have been reconstructed from Mitchell's logs, May 14, 1969, NARA, Watergate Task Force Investigative Files, Box 122.

37. Murphy, *Fortas*, 375–76.

38. Richard Nixon, *RN: The Memoirs of Richard Nixon* (New York: Grosset & Dunlap, 1978), 419.

39. Curt Gentry writes: "When asked for background checks on three possible nominees for chief justice of the U.S. Supreme Court . . . the FBI Director found potentially derogatory material on all three—thus clearing the way for the man he personally favored, Warren Burger. 'Hoover picked Warren Burger,' [former assistant FBI director] William Sullivan would bluntly state. 'He made him chief justice.' One of the three Hoover had eliminated to clear the way for Burger was his former boss and longtime 'friend' William Rogers"—Curt Gentry, *J. Edgar Hoover: The Man and the Secrets* (New York: W. W. Norton & Company, 1991), 627.

40. Nixon set forth his specific criteria for a chief justice in his memoir: "a top-flight legal mind; he must be young enough to serve at least ten years; he should, if possible, have experience both as a practicing lawyer and as an appeals court judge; he must generally share my view that the Court should interpret the Constitution rather than amend it by judicial fiat; and he must have a special quality of leadership that would enable him to resolve differences among his colleagues so that, as often as possible, the Court would speak decisively on major cases with one voice or at least with a strong voice for the majority opinion"—Nixon, *RN*, 419.

41. Attorney General John Mitchell regularly gave syndicated columnist and *Newsday* reporter Nick Thimmesch interviews. In a September 28, 1971, column, Thimmesch reported on Mitchell's Supreme Court selection process, noting that "Mitchell relied on a basic working list [of nominees] compiled by the department's office of legal counsel." This was Rehnquist's office.

42. The author is personally familiar with this list. A search of White House Files failed to locate a copy of it, nor could it be found in available files from the Department of Justice.

43. Richard Kleindienst, *Justice: The Memoirs of an Attorney General* (Ottawa, IL: Jameson Books, 1985), 113.

44. Statement made by Mitchell in my presence.

45. Henry Abraham, *Justices, Presidents and Senators* (Lanham, MD: Rowman & Littlefield, 1999), 254–55.

46. Memorandum to Haldeman From Safire (cc: Keogh, Chapin), May 20, 1969, re: Presentation of Supreme Court Appointments. NARA, WHF. Safire advice on "The 'Jewish Seat' Problem" was: "Every President is tempted to say that he rejects the idea that any group or region 'owns' a seat on the Court. I think the President should not talk about this at all, because it only serves to focus attention on it and gains nothing. If the President is *not* going to appoint a Jew, nothing he says beforehand is going to placate that community. People like [former Supreme Court justice] Arthur Goldberg may say publicity that this should not be a consideration, but deep down Jews believe this. If the

President *is* going to appoint a Jew, he should not say beforehand that no ethnic consideration apply, because he was seem to by trying to lay the groundwork for not appointing one, and then seem to be changing his mind under pressure."

47. James F. Simon, *In His Own Image: The Supreme Court in Richard Nixon's America* (New York: David McKay, 1973), 104.

48. Nixon, *RN*, 419.

49. On May 22, 1969, President Nixon had a long, on-the-record conversation with newsmen regarding his selection of a chief justice. During that conversation, he stated: "Mr. Justice Frankfurter felt it was his responsibility to interpret the Constitution, and it was the right of Congress and the right of the State legislatures to write the laws and have great leeway to write those laws, and he should be very conservative in overthrowing a law passed by the elected representative of the people at the State or Federal level." *Public Papers of the Presidents, Richard Nixon, 1969* (Washington, DC: GPO, 1971), 392.

50. James F. Simon, *In His Own Image: The Supreme Court in Richard Nixon's America* (New York: David McKay Company, 1973), 6.

51. May 29, 1969, memorandum by William Rehnquist re: "Judicial Selection." NARA, WHSF.

52. Gentry, *J. Edgar Hoover*, 626.

53. John P. Frank, *Clement Haynsworth, the Senate, and the Supreme Court* (Richmond: University of Virginia Press, 1991), 26.

54. Ambrose, Nixon, 296.

55. "Senate Rejects Judge Parker, 41 to 39," *New York Times*, May 8, 1930, A-1.

56. H. R. Haldeman, *The Haldeman Diaries: Inside the Nixon White House* (New York: G. P. Putnam's Sons, 1994), 110.

57. I had discussions with Mitchell, Haldeman, Ehrlichman, and several other Nixon aides—as well as Senator Roman Hruska—about the consequences of forcing Fortas from the bench, and all recognized the bitterness in the Senate that Fortas's early retirement engendered for the Haynsworth nomination. Nick Thimmesch wrote in his September 28, 1971, *Newsday* column following an interview with John Mitchell that "Haynsworth was turned down by the Senate, a victim of the backlash from the Fortas episode."

58. Abraham, *Justices, Presidents and Senators*, 11.

59. Professor David Yalof, who had access to material that was not available to Henry Abraham, found that "this 'spite' interpretation seems misleading . . . when applied to Carswell's case in particular. . . . Justice Department officials may not have understood that Carswell's credentials were so far inferior to Haynsworth's . . . [and] claims that Carswell's credentials were 'inferior' or 'mediocre' came to Nixon's attention only later, after the nomination had already been placed before the U.S. Senate"—Yalof, *Pursuit of Justices: Presidential Politics and the Selection of Supreme Court Nominees* (Chicago: University of Chicago Press, 1999), 112.

60. *Atlanta Journal and Constitution*, August 1, 1992, Section F (Carswell Obituary), 6.

61. Gentry, *J. Edgar Hoover,* 626.

62. Ibid.

63. *Atlanta Journal and Constitution,* August 1, 1992, Section F (Carswell Obituary), 6.

64. *Irwinton [Georgia] Bulletin,* August 13, 1948, quoted in *Nomination of George Harrold Carswell,* Senate Judiciary Committee Hearings (Washington, DC: GPO, 1970), 22.

65. Frank, *Clement Haynsworth, the Senate, and the Supreme Court,* 102.

66. J. Myron Jacobstein and Roy M. Mersky, *The Rejected: Sketches of the 26 Men Nominated for the Supreme Court But Not Confirmed by the Senate* (Milpitas, CA: Toucan Valley Publications, 1993), 152.

67. *Facts on File, 1970,* 165.

68. Ibid.

69. Jacobstein and Mersky, *The Rejected,* 152. See also *New York Times,* April 27, 1999, B8 (Hruska Obituary).

70. Paul Simon, *Advice & Consent: Clarence Thomas, Robert Bork, and the Intriguing History of the Supreme Court's Nomination Battles* (Washington: National Press Books, 1992), 293.

71. Haldeman, *Diaries,* 147. Carswell did not remain on the Fifth Circuit Court of Appeals; he resigned and ran for the U.S. Senate, but lost badly in the primary race. Carswell would return to private practice a bitter man. In 1976, he pleaded no contest and was fined $100 on a battery charge for making homosexual advances to an undercover Tallahassee police officer in a men's room at a shopping mall—*The Washington Post,* August 1, 1992, B6 (Obituary).

72. Leonard Garment, *Crazy Rhythm: My Journey from Brooklyn, Jazz and Wall Street to Nixon's White House, Watergate, and Beyond . . .* (New York: Times Books, Random House, 1997), 213.

73. Haldeman, *Diaries,* 147.

74. Nixon's experience with Haynsworth and Carswell has many parallels with Cleveland's inability to get Supreme Court nominees William B. Hornblower and Wheeler H. Peckham confirmed by the Senate in 1893–94. See Jacobstein and Mersky, *The Rejected,* 101–10.

75. *Public Papers of the Presidents, Richard Nixon, 1970* (Washington, DC: GPO, 1972), 345.

76. Yalof, *Pursuit of Justices,* 113.

77. *Facts on File, 1970,* 326.

78. Woodward and Armstrong, *The Brethren,* 18.

79. Several years after Richard Nixon had resigned from office, Clark R. Mollenhoff, the Pulitzer Prize–winning Washington bureau chief of the *Des Moines Register* who served as a deputy counsel to the president (1969–70) in the early days of the Nixon administration, told me that he had knowledge of the tax audit of Justice Douglas, and intimated that it was not a random audit. At the time of the conversation it was not a

matter of interest to me, so I neither followed up nor pressed for information. Only the general gist of the conversation remained lodged in my memory.

80. Ehrlichman, *Witness to Power*, 113.

81. Gerald R. Ford, *A Time to Heal: The Autobiography of Gerald R. Ford* (New York: Harper & Row, 1979), 90–91.

82. Jack Caulfield, Memorandum to John Ehrlichman, June 4, 1969. NARA, WHSF.

83. Gentry, *J. Edgar Hoover*, 630.

84. James Cannon, *Time and Chance: Gerald Ford's Appointment with History* (New York: Harper Collins, 1994), 100–101.

85. Ibid.

86. I was assigned by Attorney General John Mitchell to keep abreast of the House Judiciary Committee's progress on impeaching Douglas, and when I reported no progress, Mitchell was less than pleased. I was told that Assistant Attorney General Will Wilson was providing assistance to Jerry Ford, but that I should not become involved, other than to observe.

87. Mitchell told me that Ford had taken on the assignment for the president, explaining that the initial plan was for Ford to keep a low profile; but Ford became concerned that if he did not do it himself, it would get bolloxed by others.

88. *Facts on File, 1970,* 261–62.

89. William O. Douglas, *The Court Years 1939–1975: The Autobiography of William O. Douglas* (New York: Random House, 1980), 372.

90. Nixon, *RN,* 420.

Chapter 2

1. First quoted by me in John W. Dean, *Blind Ambition: The White House Years* (New York: Simon & Schuster, 1976), 49.

2. Conversation based on Haldeman notes, NARA, WHSF, Box 44, Folder H, Notes, June–September 1971; see 9/17/71.

3. See Abraham, *Justices, Presidents, and Senators,* 159–65.

4. Interview with Alexander Butterfield (February 19, 2001), the White House staffman present at the meeting with the president and Ginger Rogers.

5. President Richard Nixon's Daily Diary, September 17, 1971. NARA. Through the following chapters the times and participants of presidential meetings, and telephone calls, have been taken from the president's Daily Diary, which is available for his entire time in office. It has not been cited in every instance.

6. NARA Nixon Tape No. 575-2.

7. NARA Nixon Tape No. 575-4.

8. NARA Nixon Tape No. 9-63.

9. See NARA Nixon Tape No. 575-5.

10. NARA Nixon Tape No. 575-7. The sound of Nixon opening and closing his desk drawer, and then his writing on his desk top, is clearly discernible on the recording.

11. For example, on May 22, 1970, Chief Justice Burger called John Ehrlichman to report that Justice Thurgood Marshall "is much sicker than anyone presently realizes." Burger suggested the president write to Marshall, which he did with a handwritten note: "Dear Mr. Justice Marshall, We have all been distressed to hear of your illness. I hope this note finds you on the road to recovery. Mrs. Nixon joins me in sending our very best wishes. Sincerely, Richard Nixon." NARA, WHF. In addition, the president's personal doctor was often able to get information on the health of justices when they were hospitalized, particularly at Bethesda Naval Hospital.

12. John Ehrlichman frequently recorded calls, but only a small number of such recordings have been located. None of Ehrlichman's recorded calls that have been located relate to the selection of Supreme Court justices. I did not record telephone calls. Based on my telephone logs, documents I found in the White House files, Nixon's recorded conversation and my memory, I has reconstructed such conversations as I recall them, including his conversation.

13. The commission, which was chaired by former California governor Edmund "Pat" Brown, included: U.S. Second Circuit Judge George C. Edwards, Jr., Senator Sam J. Ervin, Jr. (D-NC), U.S. Fifth Circuit Judge A. Leon Higginbotham, Jr., Senator Roman L. Hruska (R-NE), Congressman Robert W. Kastenmeire (D-WI), U.S. District Court Judge Thomas J. MacBride, Senator John L. McClellan (D-AR), Congressman Don Edward (D-CA), Donald S. Thomas, and Theodore Voorhees. The commission advisory committee was chaired by retired Supreme Court Justice Tom C. Clark, and included a who's who of legal scholars: Charles L. Decker, Brian P. Gettings, Patricia Roberts Harris, Fred B. Helms, Byron O. House, Howard R. Leary, Robert M. Morgenthau, Dean Louis H. Pollak, Cecil F. Poole, Milton G. Rector, Elliot L. Richardson, Gus Tyler, James Vorenberg, William F. Walsh, and Marvin E. Wolfgang.

14. Letters to Justices Black and Harlan, NARA, WHSF.

Chapter 3

1. The president called Mitchell from the family quarters to arrange the meeting. The call was not recorded. See President's Daily Diary, September 18, 1971.

2. The president's conversation with Haldeman, and then Mitchell, Ehrlichman, and Colson, is based on NARA Nixon Tapes No. 576-5 and 576-6.

3. See Winzola McLendon, *Martha: The Life of Martha Mitchell* (New York: Random House, 1979).

4. Pat Mehaffy was appointed to the United States Circuit Court for the Eighth Circuit in 1963 by President John F. Kennedy.

5. It is believed that this is a reference to United States Court of Appeals, 11th Circuit, Judge David W. Dyer. Nixon will repeated raise David Dyer's name, but Mitchell believes him to be too old. Judge Dyer retired from the federal bench in 1998, at 87 years of age, and passed away that same year. Of passing historical note, former Independent Counsel Kenneth W. Starr once served as a law clerk to Judge Dyer.

6. It has not been possible to identify William or Bill Pullman.

7. Norman P. Ramsey was appointed a judge to the United States District Court in Baltimore in 1980 by President Jimmy Carter.

8. Mitchell's log, Saturday, September 18, 1971. (He called Rehnquist at 4:25 p.m. It appears to have been a lengthy conversation, for he next spoke to Haldeman at 5:05 p.m., and left his office shortly thereafter.)

Chapter 4

1. *Wall Street Journal,* September 20, 1971, 1.

2. NARA Nixon Tape No. 576-8.

3. Ibid.

4. Julie Nixon Eisenhower, *Pat Nixon: The Untold Story* (New York: Simon & Schuster, 1986), 321. See also *Facts on File, 1971,* 751.

5. NARA Nixon Tape No. 576-11.

6. NARA Nixon Tape No. 9-93.

7. NARA Nixon Tape No. 577-3.

8. I recall Poff reading to me from several of his newsletters and speeches, but can no longer recall which specific documents, although I found them all in my White House files. A typical example, however, would be the following:

> A government of the people cannot function for the people unless it is a government by the people. There is no such thing as self-government if those subject to the law do not participate in the process by which those laws are made. Only a few are privileged to participate in the physical mechanics of the law-making process and these are those chosen as representatives by their fellows. For the latter, the opportunity for participation, and therefore the essence of the concept of self-government, is the right to cast a ballot to choose those who make the laws. If this opportunity is denied any qualified citizen, then he is not self-governed.

9. NARA Nixon Tape No. 577-17.

10. A few days later, the president would call Pat Buchanan. Although the conversation was not prompted by the memo Buchanan had sent, nor did it relate to the Supreme Court selection process, during the call the president would mention it:

> "Oh, on the Court. I saw your memo and you can be sure that we're on the right track," Nixon explained.
>
> "Okay, fine sir."
>
> "We can't tell anybody for obvious reasons . . . we've got to keep it awfully closely held." Then he turned to Poff. "It's, problem is that he did not practice much law, you know."
>
> "Right."
>
> "He just went right into Congress, so . . . we don't want to walk in there and have the damned people of the Senate turn him down for that reason. But there, we['re]

going to try to enlist Manny Celler and a few others. To say, well, that Judiciary Committee service for ten years is an equivalent."

"All right, sir, um hum."

"Right. But it seems to be moving all right. . . . I think actually that this is bound to have a very salutary effect on our southern friends, don't you think?"

"Sure."

"Substituting Poff for Black. God, it's, here you've got a strict constructionist conservative who signed the Southern Manifesto. And frankly, it's fine. Let some of those that are lib . . . the libs vote against him on that."

"That will really split the Democrats in the Senate, I would imagine. Right down the line on that point," Buchanan noted.

"Yeah. We just hope to Christ we get the votes."

"Yeah."

"Well, okay. Oh, so did Wilbur Mills, he signed it, you know," Nixon reported.

"He did?"

"Yep, Wilbur Mills signed the Southern Manifesto, so what the hell. We've got pretty good company."

"We ought to get a good list of the guys that did," the President suggested.

"Yes sir. Okay."

—NARA Nixon Tape No. 9-112.

11. NARA Nixon Tape No. 9-101.
12. NARA Nixon Tape No. 9-103.

Chapter 5

1. Interview with Alexander Butterfield, February 19, 2001.

2. NARA Nixon Tape No. 280-14.

3. Birch Bayh, Phillip A. Hart, Edward M. Kennedy, and John V. Tunney, "Individual Views of Messrs. Bayh, Hart, Kennedy, and Tunney," *Congressional Record – Senate*, December 3, 1971, 44635-44 (regarding Rehnquist's positions on wiretapping, preventive detention, "no-knock" statutes, and refusing to deter unlawful police actions by excluding evidence improperly obtained); see also, Sue Davis, *Justice Rehnquist and the Constitution* (Princeton: Princeton University Press, 1989), 11. (Davis notes that during Rehnquist confirmation hearing "when asked for his views regarding the Justice Department's policies in such areas as wiretapping, preventive detention, . . . he demurred, stating that he had acted as an advocate, presenting the position of the administration, but that if he had found any of them personally obnoxious, he would not have acted as he did.")

4. Although I have reconstructed this conversation from memory, I am aware of the precise day of the conversation because it appears in my White House telephone logs. I recall very clearly jesting with Rehnquist regarding Mary Lawton, an attorney who, I often found to have more liberal leanings than Rehnquist. Also encoded in my memory

are countless instances when we talked and his droll sense of humor, and quick wit, provided a delightfully amusing response. While Rehnquist and I certainly did not have daily or even weekly contact, and I often dealt with his deputy Thomas Kauper, I did have regular dealings with him over many years, which may be why I recall many of them although only a few appear in this book. He was (and is) a striking personality in his often professorial way—and memorable.

5. More specifically, the "veterans" were former FBI agent G. Gordon Liddy, who boasted then (and now) of his "black bag" jobs, or illegal entries, both authorized and unauthorized by his FBI superiors, and the former CIA operative E. Howard Hunt. For a detailed account of The Plumbers see Stanley I. Kutler, *The Wars of Watergate* (New York: Alfred A. Knopf, 1990).

6. Transcript of Conversation, July 24, 1971, 12:36–12:48 p.m. NARA, WSPF.

7. Krogh, Memorandum to John Ehrlichman, September 24, 1971. NARA, WHSF. Krogh noted:

> My experience has shown that the FBI investigations and a casual luncheon or conversation are not sufficient to extract the kind of information we need. I think something like a CIA de-briefing—taking two or three days—should be undertaken whenever a candidate reaches the top of the list. This interview should include a person associated with the nominee and one who is not. So, with respect to the possible selection of a legislator, a weekend would be spent questioning and probing into every facet of his professional life, personal life, trips, businesses, etc.
>
> John Dean and David Young would constitute a good team. They would report back to you anything which raised questions in their minds which might be checked out either by the FBI or by an independent check through Caulfield's resources. The results of these interviews, along with the FBI reports and other Justice Department reports, would be reviewed here, discussed and then recommendations prepared for the President. I think more emphasis should be placed upon *demeanor* evidence this time.

8. *Public Papers of the Presidents of the United States, Richard Nixon, 1971* (Washington, DC: GPO, 1972), 976.

9. The death penalty case pending before the Court that the chief justice did not want to rule on was *Furman v. Georgia*, 408 U.S. 238 (1972). Clearly he needed votes to reinstate the death penalty. When the Court later ruled, all the Nixon appointees would vote for the death penalty, but they still did not have a majority. Justices Douglas, Brennan, Stewart, White, and Marshall voted to uphold the ban on the death penalty; Chief Justice Burger, Justices Blackmun, Powell, and Rehnquist filed separate dissenting opinions to reinstate the death penalty.

10. This conversation has been reconstructed based on Ehrlichman's White House logs, my review of documents relating to the vetting of Poff, my White House log, my knowledge of the events and the personalities present at the meeting, and my memory.

11. NARA Nixon Tape No. 10-9.

12. This session was summarized in a lengthy memorandum that Young and I prepared right after the meeting, on Sunday, September 26, 1971, based on the notes we had made during the meeting with Poff. See Memorandum for Attorney General Mitchell [and] John D. Ehrlichman, from John Dean [and] David Young, subject: Meeting with Representative Richard Poff, Saturday, September 25, 1971, 2:30–6:00 p.m. Note: This memorandum has been withdrawn from my NARA files based on privacy. However, I had a copy in my personal files, and I have used it in a manner that does not invade the privacy of anyone.

13. Interview by Wayne Woodlief, Washington bureau, *Virginian-Pilot*, John W. Dean Files, NARA, WHF, Poff. (Note: Headline on the Xerox preservation copy not clear, but the body of the newspaper story is completely legible.)

14. Haldeman, *Diaries*, 358.

15. NARA Nixon Tape No. 579-3.

16. Byron "Whizzer" White had been deputy attorney general when nominated to the Supreme Court by President John Kennedy.

17. NARA Nixon Tape No. 579-7.

18. NARA Nixon Tape No. 597-10.

Chapter 6

1. Memorandum for the President, September 29, 1971, from John W. Dean, subject: "ABA Review of Poff's Judicial Qualifications." NARA, WHSF.

2. At the time, I was quite disappointed with this letter, and felt it poorly represented Poff. It failed to address Poff's scholarly work on the copyright law revision, his work on the vote for eighteen-year-olds, and presidential disability; the letter made no mention whatsoever of his work as vice chairman of the National Commission on Reform of Federal Criminal Laws. Because Poff was never one to talk about himself, I doubted if all the relevant information would be presented to the ABA Committee. In reviewing available files three decades later, it was obvious that the Justice Department did not do well by Poff in bringing his full background and experience to the attention of the ABA.

3. NARA Nixon Tape No. 580-13.

4. NARA Nixon Tape No. 581-4.

5. I have reconstructed this telephone conversation with Poff, the telephone conversation with Erhlichman, and the subsequent meeting with Poff at his office based on documents found in my files at NARA, including press accounts of my receipt of this call from Poff, handwritten notes that I recognize as being made by Poff, dictated notes that I telephoned to my secretary which I recognize as mine, and my indelible memory of the event.

6. John W. Dean Files, NARA, WHSF.

7. Haldeman, *Diaries*, 361.

8. Jack Anderson, "Poff Put Family Above Dream Career," *The Washington Post*, November 2, 1971, B11.

Chapter 7

1. "Poff's Withdrawal," *New York Times,* October 6, 1971, A-1.

2. I have reconstructed this conversation and the following conversation in my office with David Young, based on Ehrlichman's White House logs, Haldeman's contemporaneous handwritten notes found at NARA, David Young's White House files at NARA, documents found in my White House files at NARA relating to the search for women for the Court, and my memory.

3. I also talked to Haldeman in Florida, on October 2, 1971, who wanted to know the reason for Poff's withdrawal. Haldeman's contemporaneous notes read: "(Dean) Poff w/draw—irreversible. Told Kldst [Kleindienst] to call off ABA. drafted stmt—controversy on civil rights, would be divisive—not in best interest of country, court, family. real reason is combination—financial—nothing wrong but hard to document, he doesn't have the facts. human side—very troublesome, he's ok now—but needs gesture of support and understanding."—Haldeman Notes, NARA, WHSF. It was at this time that I suggested to Haldeman that the president call Poff, which the president did when he returned on October 5, 1971. See NARA Nixon Tape No. 10-49.

4. Listed alphabetically, Barbara Franklin had included: Sylvia Bacon, a judge of the District of Columbia Superior Court (Republican, thirty-nine); Constance E. Cook, a member of the New York State Assembly (Republican, fifty-two); Martha W. Griffiths, a member of Congress from Michigan (Democrat, fifty-nine); Margaret M. Heckler, a member of Congress from Massachusetts (Republican, forty); Shirley M. Hufstedler, a judge of the United States Court of Appeals for the Ninth Circuit (a liberal Democrat, forty-six); Cornelia G. Kennedy, a judge of the United States District Court for the Eastern District of Michigan (Republican, forty-eight); Jewel Lafontant, a black trial attorney in Chicago (Republican, forty-eight); Mildred L. Lillie, a justice of the Court of Appeals, Second Appellate District of California (a conservative Democrat, fifty-six); Soia Mentschikoff, a law professor at the University of Chicago Law School (a very liberal Democrat, fifty-six); Dorothy W. Nelson, dean of the University of Southern California Law School (a very liberal Democrat, fifty-three); Ellen Peters, a professor of law at Yale University Law School (possibly a conservative Democrat, forty-one); and Susie Marshall Sharp, an associate justice of the Supreme Court of North Carolina (a conservative Democrat, sixty-four).

5. I have reconstructed this conversation with Dick Moore based on my White House files, material in the Nixon tapes, and my memory of the event. Moore later reported to me that he had given both résumés to Ehrlichman, who simply forwarded the Rehnquist and Mentschikoff ones to John Mitchell's office, which was the standard procedures for all Court recommendations. See Memorandum for the Attorney General, October 5, 1971, from Tod R. Hullin, Administrative Assistant to John D. Ehrlichman, sending the two résumés "for your information/review." NARA, WHF.

6. NARA Nixon Tape No. 10-42.

7. NARA Nixon Tape No. 10-65.

8. John Ehrlichman, Memorandum for the President, October 7, 1971, NARA, WHSF. Ehrlichman requested a meeting on Friday, October 8, to discuss clearance procedures for Supreme Court nominees, which Ehrlichman and Mitchell had agreed upon. In addition, Ehrlichman added to the agenda a discussion of a proposed constitutional amendment regarding school busing to desegregate schools, and a problem with FBI director Hoover.

9. NARA Nixon Tape No. 587-3.

10. So surprised was the Washington establishment that it was a front-page, two columns-right story in the Sunday *Washington Post*. "Sen. Robert C. Byrd (D-W.Va.) is under consideration by President Nixon for an appointment to the Supreme Court. The conservative West Virginian, who ranks second in the Senate's Democratic leadership, has been actively interested in a nomination to the court, according to key Senate sources, since the retirement and death last month of Justice Hugo L. Black. The possibility of Byrd's nomination was said to have been discussed at the White House Friday morning. Byrd was subsequently called by a White House aide and urged to accompany Mr. Nixon on his trip to West Virginia's Mountain State Forest Festival later in the day. The two conferred privately aboard the President's plane." George Lardner, Jr., "Robert Byrd Considered For Court," *The Washington Post*, October 10, 1971, A-1. By Monday morning the *Post* made the subject the lead editorial. "It is deeply distressing to learn that Senator Robert C. Byrd of West Virginia is being considered by the White House for one of the nominations to the Supreme Court that the President must now make. We had hoped that the Nixon Administration, already burned twice by mistakes in its judgment about possible justices, was ready to stop playing around the fringes and to select persons of impeccable credentials. . . ." *The Washington Post*, October 11, 1971, A-18.

11. Presidential News Summary, October 11, 1971. NARA.

12. NARA Nixon Tape No. 11-26.

13. NARA Nixon Tape No. 11-33.

14. NARA Nixon Tape No. 11-35.

15. NARA Nixon Tape No. 11-40.

16. Haldeman, *Diaries*, 363.

17. NARA Nixon Tape No. 11-49.

18. NARA Nixon Tape No. 288-11.

19. *Public Papers of the Presidents, Richard Nixon, 1971*, 1034–35.

Chapter 8

1. NARA Nixon Tape No. 589-1.

2. NARA Nixon Tape No. 589-2.

3. I have reconstructed this conversation with Ehrlichman based on Erhlichman's White House logs, John Mitchell's logs, documents found in my White House files at

NARA relating to Herschel Friday, David Young's White House files at NARA relating to Supreme Court selections, and my memory.

4. For Mr. John W. Dean III, per conversation, William H. Rehnquist, October 12, 1971, with memorandum for the attorney general attached.

5. Memorandum for John Ehrlichman, October 6, 1971, from David Young, subject: Wilbur D. Mills. NARA, Dean files.

6. NARA Nixon Tape No. 590-2.

7. NARA Nixon Tape No. 590-3.

8. This conversation has been reconstructed based on a memorandum for Attorney General John N. Mitchell and John D. Ehrlichman, from John W. Dean [and] David R. Young, subject: Interview with Herschel H. Friday, October 13, 1971 (12:00–7:15 p.m.), and October 14, 1971 (9:45–11:30 a.m.). While this document is in my NARA files, they have not made it public. However, I have a copy in my own personal files.

9. "List for Supreme Court Narrows to Six Names," *The Washington Post,* October 14, 1971, A-1.

10. NARA Nixon Tape No. 11-86.

11. NARA Nixon Tape No. 592-6 (Note: This tape has been incorrectly labeled by NARA's finding aide as Tape No. 592-5).

12. NARA Nixon Tape No. 289-15.

Chapter 9

1. While Poff was still a viable candidate, I had discovered in the White House Central Files a letter from Senator Robert Griffin that had the membership—and their political leanings—attached. The ABA Committee had sufficient Republican votes, should they act along partisan lines, to support any Nixon nominee. There were twelve members, seven Republicans and five Democrats: Chairman—Lawrence E. Walsh, New York (Republican and former federal judge and deputy attorney general under Brownell); First Circuit—Sumner Babcock, Boston (Republican, moderate/conservative); Second Circuit—Cloyd La Porte, New York (Democrat, partner in Dewey Ballantine); Third Circuit—Robert L. Trescher, Philadelphia (Republican, moderate); Fourth Circuit—Norman P. Ramsey, Baltimore (Democrat, liberal); Fifth Circuit—John W. Ball, Jacksonville, FL (Democrat, conservative); Sixth Circuit—Harry G. Gault, Flint, MI (Republican, conservative); Seventh Circuit—Miles G. Seeley, Chicago (Republican); Eighth Circuit—Richard E. Kyle, St. Paul, MN (Republican, liberal/moderate); Ninth Circuit—John A. Sutro, San Francisco (Republican, partner in Pillsbury, Madison & Sutro); Tenth Circuit—Robert H. Harry, Denver (Democrat); and DC Circuit—Charles A. Horsky, Washington, DC (Democrat, liberal). NARA, WHF.

2. Ibid. (Senator Griffin's package also contained the letter from Judge O'Sullivan). Many books and essays have been written on the "rule of law." As good a summary as any would describe the rule of law as providing "that decisions should be made by the application of known principles or laws with the intervention of discretion in their ap-

plication"—*Black's Law Dictionary,* 6th edn. (St. Paul, MN: West Publishing Co., 1990). For Richard Nixon, a strict constructionist would adhere to the rule of law.

3. This conversation has been reconstructed based on a memorandum for Attorney General John N. Mitchell and John D. Ehrlichman, from John W. Dean [and] David R. Young, subject: Interview with Justice Mildred L. Lillie, October 14, 1971 (3:30–8:00 p.m.), and my memory of the conversation.

4. NARA Nixon Tape No. 593-6.

5. NARA Nixon Tape No. 593-7.

6. NARA Nixon Tape No. 593-11.

7. NARA Nixon Tape No. 593-12.

8. Mitchell's log indicates that he called me at 11:50 a.m., October 15, 1971. This conversation has been reconstructed based on my memory.

9. I have reconstructed this conversation with Moore based information in the President's Daily Diary, Haldeman's *Diaries,* David Young's White House files at NARA, and my memory.

10. NARA Nixon Tape No. 594-2

11. NARA Nixon Tape No. 595-4.

12. See Garment to Haldeman, October 18, 1971 ("A one-page on the Court that may (or may not) be useful. I'm too far away from the discussions to know. You would."), attached to Memorandum for the President, from Leonard Garment, subject: Supreme Court Appointments, October 18, 1971. NARA, WHF.

13. NARA Nixon Tape No. 291-11. (The audio quality of this conversation was exceptionally poor. But it was possible to construct the key points of the conversation.)

Chapter 10

1. NARA Nixon Tape No. 596-3.

2. Others included:

—New York Appellate Judge Charles Breitel, described by Mitchell as "a Jew from New York who's had a great record on the Court of Appeals." Mitchell believed that while he did not have great distinction, "because he's Jewish," the president could be successful with this conservative jurist. Nixon's reaction: "Sixty-two"—he paused—"Jewish." The idea of being boxed into appointing a Jew was not acceptable. "God damn them," he declared, and Mitchell moved on.

—Maine Federal District Court Judge Edward Thaxter Gignoux, who was suggested by Nixon but quickly dismissed by Mitchell. "Gignoux is not, in my opinion, Mr. President, reflective of your philosophy." Nixon's rejection was instant: "Forget it."

—Supreme Judicial Court of Massachusetts Justice Robert Braucher, described by Mitchell as a former Harvard law professor. "Everybody's ranting and raving about him, he's a conservative in criminal law, but what he'll do in the other fields, you just can't tell." Nixon's reaction: "Trouble is you say you don't know him. I don't know him."

—New York Appellate Judge Harold Tyler, who had been a district judge and was a Democrat. He had been recommended by Chief Justice Burger, but Nixon gave no reaction one way or the other.

—New York Appellate Judge Walter Mansfield, who had been recommended by Chief Justice Burger, and had recently been appointed to the Second Circuit Court of Appeals. But Mitchell thought Mansfield was "a weak character." This was going nowhere.

—Supreme Court, Massachusetts, Justice Paul Reardon, who Mitchell said was sixty]-five or sixty-six. Nixon did not so much as grunt when he was mentioned.

3. NARA Nixon Tape No. 11-131.
4. NARA Nixon Tape No. 11-133.
5. NARA Nixon Tape No. 11-138.
6. NARA Nixon Tape No. 11-143.
7. NARA Nixon Tape No. 11-153.
8. NARA Nixon Tape No. 11-155.

Chapter 11

1. NARA Nixon Tape No. 11-157.
2. NARA Nixon Tape No. 11-163.
3. NARA Nixon Tape No. 12-9.
4. NARA Nixon Tape No. 282-26.
5. NARA Nixon Tape No. 12-13.
6. I have reconstructed this conversation from my memory. It was so unusual for Moore to ask me for help in legal research that it could not be forgotten (and later we joked about his going to the Department of Justice law library, the first time he had been in a law library in decades, and trying to act inconspicuous when looking for law journal articles written by Rehnquist).
7. NARA Nixon Tape No. 12-15.
8. NARA Nixon Tape No. 12-17.
9. NARA Nixon Tape No. 12-25.
10. Shortly after 6 p.m. the president called Dick Moore. He told Moore that the ABA had voted against Mildred Lillie, and the bar found "of all the women in the country she was probably the best qualifed but, that they could think of, but that she was not qualified to be on the Court." Nixon said they would make sure that fact was leaked to the press. He continued. "I can't consult anybody on it, on the Rehnquist one, in case I don't get the Baker—Baker is the first choice and we'll know on him within an hour or two. But in case we don't get that, on Rehnquist, so far as Ehrlichman now, he is for it or not?" Moore assured the president Ehrlichman was for Rehnquist, and it was Moore's

impression that Rehnquist was his first choice. Moore also reported that he had checked on William French Smith, "who was not on the Harvard Law review, but he was Summa Cum Laude and Phi Beta Kappa at USC." Moore was still selling Rehnquist. He had made the point that Smith was not as highly qualifed as Rehnquist, just the case the president was having second thoughts. Nixon NARA Tape No. 12-19.

11. NARA Nixon Tape No. 12-26.

12. This I learned from a newspaper reporter, after the fact.

Chapter 12

1. The president's handnotes and dictation, and draft of the speech, are found in the president's speech files. NARA, WHSF.

2. NARA Nixon Tape No. 281-1.

3. NARA Nixon Tape No. 281-4. The calls to Haldeman from the EOB office were placed on an interoffice telephone. Only one side of these conversations was recorded by the room's listening device. But it is often apparent what Haldeman has said by Nixon's statements, or questions.

4. NARA Nixon Tape No. 281-6.

5. NARA Nixon Tape No. 12-28.

6. NARA Nixon Tape No. 12-30.

7. NARA Nixon Tape No. 281-70.

8. NARA Nixon Tape No. 281-26.

9. Mitchell, log, October 21, 1971.

10. See Kleindienst, *Justice*, 123.

11. Haldeman, *Diaries*, 376. Haldeman wrote: ". . . working with Dick Moore to get things organized over at Justice, and, of course, Moore assumed that I knew and spilled the beans to me. Turns out that they were set on Powell, the guy from Virginia who I expected, and thought they were set on Howard Baker as the second seat, but apparently, at some point toward the last minute last night or this morning, the P decided to go with Rehnquist instead of Baker, and they shifted over, even though Baker had been made the offer and they were waiting for his response at 9:00 this morning when he was supposed to have it in. He didn't call until about 9:30, at which time he said he would accept. By then the P had decided to go the other way."

12. I have reconstructed this conversation from my memory. Seldom did Haldeman call me on the interoffice telephone, and when he did it was always a matter of importance. Not only was the information he gave me memorable, but it made me feel like his confidante and a real insider privy to information no one else had. It was also one of those conversations where I discovered Haldeman's effectiveness as chief of staff; while the president was doing what he thought was his own thing, Haldeman was working behind the scenes to make sure the president did not make a mistake. I suspect this happened often, but history will never know it.

13. NARA Nixon Tape No. 281-34.

14. I have no doubt that I had many more thoughts than those set forth in my reconstruction of this moment. But I have only included those which these many years later remain fixed in my mind. Throughout my days at the White House, events took place that were of such a personal significance that they have remained relative clear in my memory; lesser moments have gone to those recesses where unimportant memories go. Learning of Rehnquist's selection was a momentous, and startling, moment for me. Not one easily forgotten.

15. Within minutes of the president completing his announcement, Attorney General John Mitchell announced from the Department of Justice that he was terminating the practice of submitting names of potential Supreme Court nominees to the ABA's Standing Committee on the Federal Judiciary. Mitchell's letter to ABA president Leon Jaworski, and the committee's chairman, Lawrence Walsh, said the arrangement was being ended because of "premature disclosures" of names sent for review. Mitchell noted that leaks "can be particularly unfair to a person whose name may have been referred to your committee but who may not be nominated to the court." Walsh later responded that he had warned the Justice Department that such leaks might occur, since this was inevitable when checking the backgrounds of those being reviewed.

Afterword

1. The Rehnquist Court has no true liberal justices, only moderates and conservatives. While there are two members of the Court who were appointed by a Democratic president (Ruth Bader Ginsburg and Stephen Breyer by President Clinton), all the others were appointed by Republican presidents (William Rehnquist by Presidents Nixon and Reagan, Sandra Day O'Connor, Antonin Scalia, and Anthony Kennedy by President Reagan, John Paul Stevens by President Ford, and David Souter and Clarence Thomas by President Bush. The two Democratic appointees (Ginsburg and Breyer) are considered centrist.

2. An analysis of the jurisprudence of the Rehnquist Court has been an ongoing effort. See, for example, Sue Davis, *Justice Rehnquist and the Constitution* (Princeton: Princeton University Press, 1989), and Stephen E. Gottlieb, *Morality Imposed: The Rehnquist Court and Liberty in America* (New York: New York University Press, 2000).

3. Letter from Senator Birch Bayh to the President, November 4, 1971, Dean file, WHSF, NARA.

4. *Nomination of William H. Rehnquist and Lewis F. Powell, Jr.,* Senate Judiciary Committee Hearings, November 3, 4, 8, 9, and 10, 1971 (Washington: GPO), 291, 377; (hereafter Rehnquist 1971 Nomination Hearings.) See also Al Kamen and Ruth Marcus, "Reagan Uses Executive Privilege to Keep Rehnquist Memos Secret; Senate Denied Access to Nixon-Era Papers," The Washington Post, August 1, 1986, A-1.

5. See, for example, Howard Kurtz and Ruth Marcus, "Democrats Seek to Subpoena

Papers," *The Washington Post,* August 2, 1971, A-1; George Lardner Jr. and Al Kamen, "Senator to Push for Rehnquist Memo; Democrats May Seek Subpoena for Nixon-Era Documents," August 5, 1986, A-4; and Michael Meyer with Lynda Wright, "Rehnquist's Rocky Road," *Newsweek,* August 11, 1986, 21.

6. Howard Kurtz and Al Kamen, "Rehnquist Bid Not in Danger Over Papers; Sen. Mathias Finds 'Nothing Dramatic,'" *The Washington Post,* August 7, 1986, A-1.

7. Special to the *New York Times,* "Index to Justice Dept. Documents Received by Panel in Rehnquist Hearing," *New York Times,* August 8, 1986, A-7.

8. The law was self-terminating, expiring March 3, 1801.

9. Rehnquist testified: " . . . I had a slipped disk operation in the latter part of May, and was either at home in bed or in the hospital until about the latter part of the second week of June. I am just trying to recall from memory. Then I started coming back into the office half days, and found that I was overdoing the first couple of days, so I stayed out again. And I think it was either on a Monday or Tuesday I was back in, perhaps for the third time, on a half-day basis." Rehnquist 1971 Nomination Hearings, 38. He never mentioned that shortly after his surgery he was staying in touch with his office.

10. I have corroborated my memory of these calls from my White House telephone logs, Dean files, NARA.

11. Memorandum for Honorable John W. Dean III, Counsel to the President, Re: Criminal Prosecutions for Disclosure of Classified Information Relating to Defense Department Vietnam Study, June 16, 1971, Thomas E. Kauper, Deputy Assistant Attorney General, Office of Legal Counsel, Dean files, WHSF, NARA.

12. Ibid., 4.

13. Ibid., 6.

14. Memorandum to John W. Dean, III, Associate Deputy Attorney General, From William H. Rehnquist, Assistant Attorney General, Office of Legal Counsel, Summary of Memorandum Re: Constitutional Decisions Relating to Criminal Law, April 1, 1969, with attached: Memorandum Re: "Commission to Evaluate Recent Constitutional Decisions in [the] Field of Criminal Law," WHSF, Dean: Box 44: Crime and the Rights of the Accused, NARA.

15. *Nomination of Justice William Hubbs Rehnquist,* Senate Judiciary Committee Hearings, July 29, 30, 31 and August 1, 1986 (Washington: GPO), 71; (hereafter Rehnquist 1986 Nomination Hearings.)

16. Ibid., 483

17. *Congressional Record—Daily Digest,* November 23, 1971, D 653.

18. See "Individual Views of Messrs. Bayh, Hart, Kennedy, and Tunney," *Congressional Record—Daily Digest,* December 3, 1971, 44635–644.

19. Ibid., 44640.

20. Rehnquist 1971 Nomination Hearings, 483

21. Rehnquist 1986 Nomination Hearings, 156.

22. Republicans wanted to get on the record the fact that Rehnquist's challenging voters in the 1950s and 1960s had recently been investigated for the Senate Judiciary

Committee by the FBI, which Republicans reported had turned up nothing. As stated by Chairman Strom Thurmond: "There is nothing new that I am aware [of] regarding this matter. I reviewed the FBI report and found absolutely no new information to support these charges. Justice Rehnquist, how do you respond to these allegations?" Rehnquist cautiously answered: "In the absence of any more careful description of the allegations, I think I would say, Mr. Chairman, that I have reread very carefully the statement I made to the committee in 1971 and have absolutely no reason to doubt its correctness today." Ibid., 130.

23. Ibid., 145.

24. See, for example, George Lardner Jr. and Al Kamen, "1971 Rehnquist Account Is Challenged by 3 Mem; 'Ballot Security' Role in '60s Called Active," *The Washington Post,* July 25, 1986, A-4; George Lardner Jr. and Al Kamen, "Another Phoenix Attorney Contradicts Rehnquist's 1971 Testimony," *The Washington Post,* July 27, 1986, A-5; and United Press International, "FBI Probes Rehnquist: Did He Harass Blacks?" *The Washington Post,* July 28, 1986, A-1.

25. In 1962 or 1964, Charles Pine, a Phoenix businessman, stated: "I saw [Rehnquist at the Bethune precinct] and I saw him approach at least one voter, if my memory is correct, two. He asked them, he said, 'Pardon me. Are you a qualified voter?' to this black gentleman. The man said, 'Yes.' And he said, 'Do you have any credentials to indicate that you are?' The man said, 'No.' And he said, 'Well, then perhaps there is a question of whether or not you are qualified.' And the man instead of standing in line, if he had advanced, by that time, he got to the voting table he would have found his name on the voting list, but he turned on his heels and left the voting precinct. I felt that the whole purpose of that was to discourage blacks from voting." Rehnquist 1986 Nomination Hearings, 145.

Mr. Pine testified to these facts in greater detail before the committee. Mr. Pine said he was a respected Phoenix businessman, and Democratic state chairman from 1972 to 1976. He described Rehnquist's team as "flying squads" that would arrive at a polling place, confront black voters to get them to leave, and then the squad would leave—ibid., 1048–53.

Mr. Quincy Hopper, a voter, stated "that he was at the Bethune school on election day 1964 and that [Rehnquist was] there at the school having voters read from the Constitution to test for literacy"—ibid., 145.

"Rev. Benjamin Brooks who is the pastor of the South Minster Presbyterian Church . . . stated that he is familiar with [William Rehnquist]. He saw [Rehnquist] at the Julian precinct where Pastor Brooks was an inspector on election day, the year that Paul Fannin and Phil Morrison were running for Arizona Governor [Rehnquist believed this was 1958], and Reverend Brooks stated that on that day [Rehnquist] challenged black, elderly working class voters for literacy by having them read the Constitution out loud"—ibid.

"Dr. Smith [a psychiatrist and psychology professor at the University of Arizona 1947–64] states that on election day in 1960 or 1962 as a poll watcher at Southwestern

Phoenix poll [Rehnquist] arrived with two or three other men. He says he recognized [Rehnquist] from political functions and was positive of his identification. Dr. Smith states that [Rehnquist] confronted a group of voters holding a card in [his] hand and said, 'You cannot read, can you? You do not belong here.' Dr. Smith says the voters were intimidated by [Rehnquist's] actions"—ibid., 146. When Dr. Sydney Smith appeared as a witness before the committee, he testified he was trained as psychoanalyst and clinical psychologist. He reported he went to the poll with John Grimes, the academic dean of Arizona State University. He stated that he saw Rehnquist confront black voters, and Grimes asked that he call the Democratic headquarters to report the incident while Grimes personally dealt with it. Dr. Smith did this, and when he returned Rehnquist and those with him were leaving. On cross examination it was revealed that he had told his wife and children of the incident at the time, and they discussed it again in 1971 when Rehnquist was first nominated. Dr. Smith said he had no idea what to do with his information but was surprised a man like Rehnquist was being placed on the Court. Dr. Smith testified that while he probably could not recall the route he had taken to the polling place, he could never forget the incident and Rehnquist's challenging words to voters, and he recognized Rehnquist because he was active in politics, as well as had seen his name and picture in the newspaper during the time period. In 1986 Dr. Smith's son, a registered Republican, told others of the incident, and Nina Totenberg of National Public Radio called Dr. Smith, and he repeated the story (between patients), which had resulted in his coming before the Judiciary Committee—ibid., 1054–65.

26. The letter stated: "In 1962, for the first time, the Republicans had challengers in all of the precincts . . . which had overwhelming Democratic registration. At that time, among the statutory grounds for challenging a person offering to vote, were that he had not resided within the precinct for thirty days preceding the election, and that he was unable to read the Constitution of the United States. In each precinct *every* black or Mexican voter was being challenged on this latter ground, and it was quite clear that this type of challenging was a deliberate effort to slow down the voting so as to cause people awaiting their turn to vote to grow tired of waiting, and leave without voting. In addition, there was a well organized campaign of outright harassment and intimidation to discourage persons from attempting to vote. In black and brown areas, handbills were distributed warning persons that if they were not properly qualified to vote, they would be prosecuted. There were squads of people taking photographs of voters standing in line to vote and asking for their names. There is no doubt, that these tactics of harassment, intimidation, and indiscriminate challenging were highly improper, and violative of the sprit of free elections"—ibid., 160.

27. Ibid., 146. "[Brosnahan stated] he received complaints of voter harassment at polling places. The complaints were that Republican challengers were challenging voters on the grounds that they could not read. He went to a precinct with an FBI agent. [Rehnquist was] sitting at a table where the voter challenger sits. A number of people complained to Mr. Brosnahan that [Rehnquist] had been challenging votes." Brosnahan later appeared before the committee and testified. He was a partner in a major San

Francisco law firm which regularly appeared before the U.S. Supreme Court, which concerned him given his negative testimony about Justice Rehnquist, who was en route to becoming chief justice. He testified that he knew Rehnquist as a practicing attorney in Phoenix, who had been a law clerk on the Supreme Court. He said at the polling place "the situation was tense," but when they showed their Department of Justice and FBI credentials, "it was clear to us by words and gestures that they were glad that we were there." The FBI interviewed those involved, and "the complaints had to do with [Rehnquist]. But given the time since the incident Brosnahan chose not to try to describe the complaints. Brosnahan stated he had read Rehnquist's 1971 testimony where "he describes his role in the early 1960's as trying to arbitrate disputes at polling places. This was not what Mr. Rehnquist was doing when I saw him on election day in 1962." Brosnahan had also read the letter Rehnquist sent the Senate in 1971 stating, "In none of these years did I personally engage in challenging the qualification of any voter." Brosnahan challenged this statement: "This does not comport with my recollection of the events I witnessed in 1962, when Mr. Rehnquist did serve as a challenger."

28. Ibid.,146–48.

29. Ironically, Brosnahan would later be selected by Independent Counsel Lawrence Walsh to prosecute former Secretary of Defense Caspar Weinberger for his role in the Iran-contra activities. Brosnahan's investigation, indictment, and prosecution was ended, however, when President Bush pardoned Weinberger as he was leaving office. Harriet Chiang, "A Great Case for an Adrenaline Junkie: S.F. lawyer takes on Weinberger," *San Francisco Chronicle,* October 28, 1992, D-3; and Martin Halstuk, "Weinberger Prosecutor Lashes Out; S.F. lawyer says Bush will pay 'terrible price' for his pardon," *San Francisco Chronicle,* December 26, 1996, A-2.

30. George Lardner Jr. and Al Kamen, "Rehnquist Hearings Leave Question of Veracity," *The Washington Post,* August 10, 1986, A-1.

31. Senator Metzenbaum similarly confronted Rehnquist with several additional witnesses who charged Rehnquist with challenging voters:

"Arthur Ross, now a deputy prosecutor in Honolulu . . . told the FBI that he saw [Rehnquist], and others, in 1962, with a card which had on it a constitutional phrase, asking prospective voters to read from it before entering the polls." Rehnquest 1986 Nomination Hearings, 157.

Snelson McGriff filed an affidavit stating he remembered a man who looked like Rehnquist challenging voters at Bethune precinct. "He would stop them in line and give them a card to read about the Constitution. I think there was a fight, and this man looked roughed up. He was taken to a police car. I have now seen pictures of this man in the newspaper, and if this isn't the man William Rehnquist, who is running for the Supreme court, then it was his twin brother"—ibid.

Jordan Harris filed an affidavit stating: "I was present as a deputized challenger for the Democratic Party in Bethune precinct, a predominantly black precinct. I met the party challenger for the Republican Party, Mr. William Rehnquist, because I noticed him harassing, unnecessarily, several people at the polls, who were attempting to vote.

He was attempting to make them recite portions of the Constitution and refused to let them vote until they were able to comply with his request. I know that this man was Mr. Rehnquist because the election board introduced me to him as challenger for the Republican Party"—ibid.

Robert Tate submitted an affidavit stating: "I was present at Bethune precinct. ...Mrs. Miller ... was encountered ... by William Rehnquist and requested to recite the Constitution. Mrs. Miller came to me crying, stating that Rehnquist wanted her to recite the Constitution. I looked around and there was William Rehnquist and Mr. Harris, struggling. I now remember him from pictures I have seen, lately, in the papers, and he was the same one involved in the above incident at Bethune precinct. He did not at the time, however, wear glasses"—ibid., 158.

"Mr. Melvin Murkin, an attorney in Phoenix, told the FBI that he recalled seeing [Rehnquist] give instructions to challengers in a polling place, and that voters in line began to leave as a result. He said he confronted [Rehnquist] and told [him] that people did not want to be embarrassed like that"—ibid.

Rehnquist denied each charge.

32. Republicans presented the following witnesses regarding Rehnquist activities in challenging voters:

James Bush, a Phoenix attorney, who testified he and Rehnquist organized and supervised a lawyers committee in 1960 and 1962 to address legal questions on election day. He testified that "neither Mr. Rehnquist nor myself spent much time away from headquarters" in those years. When asked if Rehnquist "could have been challenging voters when you were not present," Bush responded, "I cannot account for his action when I was not actually with him"—ibid., 1079–80.

Vincent Maggiore, a Phoenix attorney, testified that he was the Democratic county chairman in 1962 who called the U.S. Attorney's office. But "at no time did anybody come to me and state that Justice Rehnquist had committed any of these acts" that had prompted him to call the U.S. Attorney. He testified he knew Rehnquist at the time but knew of no wrongdoing—ibid., 1090–92.

Edward Cassidy, a retired policeman from Phoenix, testified he did not know Rehnquist. However, in 1962 he had spent the election day at the Bethune School, and was called into the school twice over disturbances that involved "a Mr. Wayne Bentson, the Republican challenger, [who] was less than tactful—guess that would be the way to describe him." By about 2 or 3 o'clock, Bentson had asked for protection, and the witness took him to his car, and that solved the problem. "At no time did I ever hear the Justice's name mentioned"—ibid., 1092. Cassidy informed Senator Hatch that the man he ushered out was 6 foot, or 6 foot one, and 200 pounds. "Pretty much the same size as Mr. Justice Rehnquist then?" Hatch asked, and Cassidy responded, "Fairly close I would guess, yes"—ibid., 1108. Cassidy left the precinct around 4 o'clock—ibid., 1110. Senator Hatch would later claim that others had mistaken Wayne Bentson for Rehnquist. But this was refuted by Brosnahan—ibid., 999.

William Turner, an international management consultant, testified in 1962 he organized a group of Republican poll watchers, or challengers, and also had done the same on more limited basis in 1958 and 1960. To the best of his knowledge Rehnquist was never a challenger—ibid., 1093–94.

Ralph Staggs, a semiretired homebuilder from Phoenix, had known Rehnquist since 1959, and while he had no knowledge of the elections in 1960, or 1964, he did have knowledge of the 1962 election, since he was the Republican county chairman for Maricopa County. He testified that "Rehnquist was not a member of the challengers committee [in 1962], and to the best of my knowledge, never was involved in any actual challenging in any of the precincts in Maricopa County, challenging any voters." Rather, he was chairman of the legal committee "to give advice to challengers." In 1962 Staggs sent Rehnquist to Bethune precinct "to clear up a problem that had been reported with improper voting there"—ibid., 1094–96. When asked by Senator Biden why he had filed an affidavit with the Senate Judiciary Committee in 1971, Staggs said he had called Rehnquist in 1971 and told him he would provide information to correct a news account he had read; but he later discovered it was wrong, and corrected it but the correct affidavit apparently never was received by the committee—ibid., 1100–01.

Fred Robertshaw, an attorney from Phoenix, testified he worked on the lawyers committee that Rehnquist and James Bush chaired. He testified that neither he nor others on the lawyers committee were challengers—ibid., 1096–97.

Gordon Marshall, retired corporate officer from Phoenix, testified that he "recruited and placed challengers." He testified that Rehnquist [whom he did not name but implied] was not "a man who intimidates, threatens, or harasses"—ibid., 1097.

George Randolph, an Arizona lawyer for 33 years, member of the U.S. Supreme Court bar for 29 years, and Senator Goldwater's legislative assistant and counsel to the Senate Labor Committee from 1957 to 1960, was involved in the Republican challenging program in 1960, 1962, and 1964. He gave legal advice to poll watchers and challengers in those years. He [stated incorrectly that he] had known Rehnquist since 1952, when he went to Phoenix. In 1962 and 1964 Rehnquist and Bush "conducted a school for challengers" where 25–30 people were told how to challenge. They were instructed "not to, under any circumstance, interfere with any voter"—ibid., 1097–99. Randolph told Senator Hatch that there was no voter-challenging program in 1954— ibid., 1105.

33. "Supreme Court: Memo from Rehnquist," *Newsweek*, December 13, 1971, 22.

34. *Congressional Record—Senate*, December 7, 1971, 45200.

35. *Scott v. Sandford*, 60 U.S. 393 (1856), known as the *Dred Scott* case, was a 7 to 2 ruling that African Americans had no right to sue in federal courts because they could not be considered citizens of the United States. Chief Justice Roger Taney, in denying Dred Scott his freedom from slavery, stated that blacks were "so far inferior that they had no rights which the white man was bound to respect." The Court further held that the Missouri Compromise's prohibition of slavery in territories north and west of Missouri was unconstitutional.

36. *Congressional Record—Senate*, December 6, 1971, 45420.

37. For example, Senator Tunney raised it—*Congressional Record—Senate,* December 7, 1971, at 45212—as did Senator Brooke at 45215.

38. I have reconstructed this comment. While I don't recall the exact words, I remember well the substance of Mitchell's remark. I recall this conversation because it was the first time Mitchell had ever mentioned to me that the president was considering a pardon for Jimmy Hoffa, the former Teamsters Union president, then in a federal prison. He was just telling me about Hoffa to keep me informed since the pardon would come through my office if he recommended it, and because of the media attention it would attract, it had to be handled on a confidential basis until it was announced. The Hoffa pardon meant nothing to me, but the Rehnquist confirmation did. I was able to date this conversation from Mitchell's log, December 7, 1971, NARA. (Mitchell had visited the White House barber, Milton Pitts, that evening.)

39. John Mitchell's log, December 8, 1971, NARA. (This log records Mitchell's calls with Wally Johnson at 11:15 a.m., as well as a call from Clark MacGregor, the White House congressional liaison man, at 11:25 a.m. At 1:20 p.m. Mitchell spoke with Kleindienst. Mitchell's activities very likely concerned Senate disquiet at the failure of Rehnquist to explain the Jackson memo.)

40. *Congressional Record—Senate,* December 8, 1971, 45440.

41. Ibid.

42. *Congressional Record—Senate,* December 10, 1971, 46115–116.

43. Ibid., 46116.

44. Anthony Lewis, "Ex-Colleague Says Rehnquist Opposed Segregation," *New York Times,* December 10, 1971, reproduced in the *Congressional Record—Senate,* December 10, 1971, 46112.

45. John P. MacKenzie, "Controversy Deepens Over Rehnquist Memo," *The Washington Post,* December 10, 1971, A-1.

46. *Congressional Record—Senate,* December 10, 1971, 46197.

47. John Dean, Memorandum for Dwight Chapin, Dick Moore, [and] Chuck Colson, November 3, 1971, WHF, NARA. ("Just a note to suggest that the PR experts might want to give some consideration and thought at this time to an appropriate ceremony, statement, etc. for the swearing in of the President's Supreme Court nominees. While I hate to count our chickens before they have hatched, I don't believe we are going to experience any serious problems and a little advance thinking on this might give the President some further pluses in filling these vacancies. If I can be of any assistance, please don't hesitate to call on me.")

48. Rehnquist 1986 Nomination Hearings, 276–77.

49. Ibid., 296.

50. Rehnquist also said, "I think there is also an interview with Mr. Cronson in 1971 indicating that I had told him that that was not a correct statement." In 1971, Cronson gave interviews to Anthony Lewis of the *New York Times,* December 10, 1971, and John P. MacKenzie of *The Washington Post,* "Controversy Deepens Over Rehnquist Memo." In neither interview does Cronson state that Rehnquist told him anything.

51. Rehnquist 1986 Nomination Hearings, 1158–62.

52. See *Congressional Record—Senate,* September 15, 1986, S 12537–46.

53. Ibid., 12541–43, for all the references to Senator Levin's speech that follow.

54. Richard Kluger, *Simple Justice: The History of* Brown v. Board of Education *and Black America's Struggle for Equality* (New York: Vintage Books, 1977), 606–07. In the portion of the book where Kluger reports on the inner workings of the Court's historic decision, he has reconstructed what occurred based on the papers of the justices, interviews with law clerks, and other writings. He reviewed Justice Jackson's role, noting that Jackson at one point "asked his two 1952 Term clerks [Rehnquist and Donald Cronson] for an advisory memorandum." After reporting on the contents of these documents Cronson's "A Few Expressed Prejudices on the Segregations Cases" initialed "DC" and Kluger reports that "If Rehnquist was telling the truth to the Senate and the words in his undated memo even remotely reflected Jackson's views, then the Justice must have undergone a considerable change of heart" by the time he presented his views to his colleagues in conference. While conferences are secret, the justices make notes of their colleagues' remarks, and Justice Burton's notes recorded Jackson's comments.

Kluger, however, does not believe Rehnquist was telling the truth. In a footnote of over 2,000 words, he states that there was "much evidence, both internal and external, that casts doubt on Rehnquist's account of the nature of his memorandum." Kluger first looked at the evidence of "the two living people who might have corroborated Rehnquist's explanation," Donald Cronson and Mrs. Elsie Douglas, Jackson's secretary. He found that both accounts conflicted with Rehnquist's explanation (as had several in the Senate). He then reexamined the Rehnquist 1952 memo, and point by point showed that there was nothing in the arguments remotely close to Jackson's thinking, while each of the positions promoted was highly indicative of Rehnquist's (past and present) thinking. Kluger concluded: "Taking the careers and judicial assertions of both men in their totality, one finds a preponderance of evidence to suggest that the memorandum in question—the one that threatened to deprive William Rehnquist of his place on the Supreme Court—was an accurate statement of his own views on segregation, not those of Robert Jackson, who, by contrast, was a staunch libertarian and humanist."

55. *Congressional Record—Senate,* December 8, 1971, 45440.

56. Senator Levin cited the following Rehnquist memoranda to Justice Jackson: in the Rosenberg case ("In my opinion, if they are going to have a death sentence for any crime, the acts of these ptrs [petitioners] in giving A-bomb secrets to Russia years before it would otherwise have had them are fitting candidates for that punishment. It is too bad that drawing and quartering has been abolished"); in a baseball antitrust case ("Before making any recommendation, I feel it is only fair to lay bare my strong personal animus in these cases. . . . I feel instinctively that baseball, like other sports, is sui generis, and not suitably regulated either by a bunch of lawyers in the Justice Department or by a bunch of shyster lawyers stirring up triple damage suits"); and a case involving Jehovah's Witnesses making speeches in a public park in violation of a local ordinance ("I personally don't see why a city can't set aside a park for ball games, picnics

or other group activities without having some outlandish groups like Jehovah's Witnesses commandeer the space and force their message on everyone"), *Congressional Record—Senate*, September 15, 1986, S 12543.

57. Bernard Schwartz, "Chief Justice Rehnquist, Justice Jackson, and the *Brown Case*," *Supreme Court Review* (University of Chicago Press, 1988), 267.

58. Joseph L. Rauh, Jr., "Historical Perspectives: An Unabashed Liberal Looks at a Half-Century of the Supreme Court," *North Carolina Law Review* 69 (November 1990), 242.

59. Mark Tushnet with Katya Lezin, "What Really Happened in *Brown v. Board of Education*," *Columbia Law Review* 91 (December 1991), 1911 n.190.

60. Laura K. Ray, "A Law Clerk and His Justice: What William Rehnquist Did Not Learn from Robert Jackson," *Indiana Law Review* 26 (1991), 554–59. Further note about Rehnquist truthfulness regarding the 1952 memo to Justice Jackson was reported in Brad Snyder, "How the Conservatives Canonized *Brown v. Board of Education*," *Rutgers Law Review* (Winter 2000), 459. Snyder notes the series of articles addressing this matter when Rehnquist presided at the Senate's impeachment trial of President Clinton. Jeffrey Rosen, "Rehnquist's Choice," *New Yorker*, Jan. 11, 1999, 28. In addition, Snyder cites a number of similar articles. *"See, e.g.,* Jim Dwyer, *Quite an Odd Couple to Sit in Judgment*, N.Y. DAILY NEWS, Jan. 7, 1999, at 6 (alleging that Rehnquist lied by denying that he had written a memo advocating segregation); Bob Herbert, *The Real Disgrace*, N.Y. TIMES, Jan. 10, 1999, § 4, at 21 (stating that "when his confirmation as Chief Justice was on the line, Rehnquist, in a cowardly move, [told] senators that the memo represented Jackson's—not [his] views"); Jason Vest, *Rehnquist's Glass House*, VILLAGE VOICE, Jan. 19, 1999, at 57 (arguing that "Rehnquist has little standing to preside over a perjury trial"). So did another former Jackson clerk, who described Rehnquist's explanation of the *Plessy* memo as "ludicrous." Murray Gartner, Letter to the Editor, *We're All Equal Under the Law: Whose Memo?*, N.Y. TIMES, Jan. 14, 1999, at A20."

61. *Congressional Record—Senate*, September 15, 1986, S 12546. Note: I have changed the word "qualifications" to "record" here.

Bibliography

Books

Abraham, Henry J. *Justices, Presidents, and Senators: A History of the U.S. Supreme Court Appointments from Washington to Clinton*. Lanham, MD: Rowman & Littlefield, 1999.

Ambrose, Stephen E. *Nixon: The Triumph of a Politician 1962–1972*. New York: Simon & Schuster, 1989.

Boles, Donald E. *Mr. Justice Rehnquist, Judicial Activist*. Ames: Iowa State University Press, 1987.

Cannon, James. *Time and Chance: Gerald Ford's Appointment with History*. New York: HarperCollins, 1994.

Davis, Sue. *Justice Rehnquist and the Constitution*. Princeton: Princeton University Press, 1989.

Dean, John W. *Blind Ambition: The White House Years*. New York: Simon & Schuster, 1976.

Douglas, William O. *The Court Years: The Autobiography of William O. Douglas*. New York: Random House, 1980.

Ehrlichman, John. *Witness to Power: The Nixon Years*. New York: Simon & Schuster, 1982.

Eisenhower, Julie Nixon. *Pat Nixon: The Untold Story*. New York: Simon & Schuster, 1986.

Foner, Eric. *The Story of American Freedom*. New York: W. W. Norton & Company, 1998.

Ford, Gerald R. *A Time To Heal: The Autobiography of Gerald R. Ford*. New York: Harper & Row and The Reader's Digest Association, 1979.

Frank, John P. *Clement Haynsworth, the Senate, and the Supreme Court*. Charlottesville: University Press of Virginia, 1991.

Garment, Leonard. *Crazy Rhythm: My Journey from Brooklyn, Jazz, and Wall Street to Nixon's White House, Watergate, and Beyond . . .* New York: Times Books, Random House, 1997.

Gentry, Curt. *J. Edgar Hoover: The Man and the Secrets*. New York: W. W. Norton & Company, 1991.

Gottlieb, Stephen E. *Morality Imposed: The Rehnquist Court and Liberty in America.* New York: New York University Press, 2000.

Haldeman, H. R. *The Haldeman Diaries: Inside the Nixon White House.* New York: G. P. Putnam's Sons, 1994.

Jacobstein, J. Myron, and Roy M. Mersky. *The Rejected: Sketches of the 26 Men Nominated for the Supreme Court But Not Confirmed by the Senate.* Milpitas, CA: Toucan Valley Publications, 1993.

Jeffries, John Calvin. *Justice Lewis F. Powell, Jr.* New York: Charles Scribner's Sons, 1994.

Kalman, Laura. *Abe Fortas: A Biography.* New Haven: Yale University Press, 1990.

Kleindienst, Richard. *Justice: The Memoirs of an Attorney General.* Ottawa IL: Jameson Books, 1985.

Lazarus, Edward. *Closed Chambers: The Rise, Fall, and Future of the Modern Supreme Court.* New York: Penguin Books, 1998, 1999.

McLendon, Winzola. *Martha: The Life of Martha Mitchell.* New York: Random House, 1979.

Murphy, Bruce Allen. *Fortas: The Rise and Ruin of a Supreme Court Justice.* New York: William Morrow, 1988.

Nixon, Richard. *RN: The Memoirs of Richard Nixon.* New York: Grosset & Dunlap, 1978.

Rehnquist, William H. *The Supreme Court: How It Was, How It Is.* New York: Morrow, 1987.

Savage, David G. *Turning Right: The Making of the Rehnquist Supreme Court.* New York: John Wiley, 1993.

Schwartz, Bernard. *A History of the Supreme Court.* New York: Oxford University Press, 1993.

Shogan, Robert. *A Question of Judgment: The Fortas Case and the Struggle for the Supreme Court.* Indianapolis: Bobbs-Merrill, 1972.

Simon, James F. *In His Own Image: The Supreme Court in Richard Nixon's America.* New York: David McKay, 1973.

———. *Independent Journey: The Life of William O. Douglas.* New York: Harper & Row, 1980.

Simon, Paul. *Advice and Consent: Clarence Thomas, Robert Bork, and the Intriguing History of the Supreme Court's Nomination Battles.* Washington: National Press Books, 1992.

Tucker, D. F. B. *The Rehnquist Court and Civil Rights.* Brookfield, MA: Dartmouth University Press, 1995.

United States Congress. *Congressional Record,* vol. 117, November 23, December 3, 6–10, 1971.

United States Congress. *Congressional Record,* vol. 132, August 15–September 15, September 16–22, 1986.

United States Congress, Senate Committee on the Judiciary, Nomination of George Harrold Carswell, Hearings. Washington, DC: U.S. Government Printing Office, 1970.

United States Congress. Senate Committee on the Judiciary, *Nomination of William H. Rehnquist; Report Together with Individual Views, to Accompany the Nomination of William H. Rehnquist.* Washington, DC: U.S. Government Printing Office, 1971.

United States Congress. Senate Committee on the Judiciary, *Clement F. Haynsworth, Jr. Hearings,* 91st Congress, 1st sess. Washington, DC: U.S. Government Printing Office, 1969.

United States Congress. Senate Committee on the Judiciary, *Nomination of Clement F. Haynsworth, Jr.; Report, Together with Individual Views, to Accompany the Nomination of Clement F. Haynsworth, Jr.* Washington, DC: U.S. Government Printing Office, 1969.

United States Congress. Senate Committee on the Judiciary, *Nomination of Justice William Hubbs Rehnquist: Hearings Before the Committee on the Judiciary, U.S. Senate, 99th Congress, 2nd sess., on the Nomination of Justice William Hubbs Rehnquist to Be Chief Justice of the United States,* July 29, 30, 31, and August 1, 1986. Washington, DC: U.S. Government Printing Office, 1987.

United States Congress. Senate Committee on the Judiciary. *Nominations of William H. Rehnquist and Lewis F. Powell, Jr.: Hearings, on nominations of William H. Rehnquist, of Arizona, and Lewis F. Powell, Jr., of Virginia, to Be Associate Justices of the Supreme Court of the United States.* 92nd Congress, 1st sess. Washington, DC: U.S. Government Printing Office, 1971.

Woodward, Bob, and Scott Armstrong. *The Brethren: Inside the Supreme Court.* New York: Simon & Schuster, 1979.

Yalof, David Alistair. *Pursuit of Justices: Presidential Politics and the Selection of Supreme Court Nominees.* Chicago: The University of Chicago Press, 1999.

Yarbrough, Tinsley E. *The Rehnquist Court and the Constitution.* Oxford & New York: Oxford University Press, 2000.

Articles

Chernack, Gregory S. "The Clash of Two Worlds: Robert H. Jackson, Institutional Pragmatism, and Brown," *Temple Law Review* 72 (1999): 51.

Culp, Jerome McCristal, Jr. "Understanding the Racial Discourse of Justice Rehnquist," *Rutgers Law Journal,* 25 (Spring 1974): 579.

Fiss, Owen, & Charles Krauthammer. "The Rehnquist Court: A Return to the Antebellum Constitution," *New Republic,* March 10, 1982, 18–20.

Greenhouse, Linda. "Senate Unit Wins Access to Memos Rehnquist Wrote," *New York Times,* August 6, 1986, A1.

Kamen, Al, & Ruth Marcus. "Reagan Uses Executive Privilege to Keep Rehnquist Memos Secret," *The Washington Post,* August 1, 1986, A1.

Kamen, Al, & Howard Kurtz. "Rehnquist Told in 1974 of Restriction in Deed, Reagan Permits Access to Some Documents," *The Washington Post,* August 6, 1986, A1.

Kleven, Thomas. The Constitutional Philosophy of Justice William H. Rehnquist," *Vermont Law Review* 8 (Spring 1983): 1.

Kurtz, Howard. "Reticence Frustrates Senators," *The Washington Post,* September 9, 1986, A4.

Lardner, George, & Al Kamen. "Rehnquist Hearings Leave Question of Veracity," *The Washington Post,* August 10, 1986, A1.

Muaro, Tony. "Theory Sees Rehnquist as 'White Supremacist,'" *Legal Times,* March 1, 1993, Courtside, 10.

Rehnquist, William H. "The Notion of a Living Constitution," *Texas Law Review* 54 (May 1976), 4.

———. "All Discord, Harmony Not Understood: The Performance of the Supreme Court of the United States," *Arizona Law Review* 22 (1980): 973.

———. "Dwight D. Opperman Lecture, Drake University School of Law, September 18, 1998: Remarks of the Chief Justice of the United States," *Drake Law Review* 47 (March 19, 1999), 2.

———. "Supreme Court: Memo From Rehnquist," *Newsweek,* December 13, 1971, 32–37.

———. "The American Constitutional Experience: Remarks of the Chief Justice," *Louisiana Law Review* 54 (May 1994): 1161.

———. "The Changing Role of the Supreme Court," *Florida State University Law Review* 14 (Spring 1986): 1.

Savage, David G. "Rehnquist Plan Sought Halt of Desegregation; Amendment Drafted for Nixon Administration Would Have Overturned Rulings, Ended Busing," *Los Angeles Times,* September 7, 1986, 1.

Schwartz, Bernard. "Chief Justice Rehnquist, Justice Jackson, and the *Brown* Case," *Supreme Court Review* 245 (1988): 245–67.

Shapiro, David L. "Mr. Justice Rehnquist: A Preliminary View," *Harvard Law Review* 90 (1976): 293, 294.

Taylor, Stuart, Jr. "President Asserts He Will Withhold Rehnquist Memos," *New York Times,* August 1 1986, 1.

Tushnet, Mark, & Katya Lezin. "What Really Happened in *Brown v. Board of Education,*" *Columbia Law Review* 91 (1991): 1867, 1880, 1911 n.190.

Young, Michael K. "In Rehnquist's Defense," *Texas Lawyer,* March 29, 1993, Commentary: Rebuttal (by law clerks to charge of Rehnquist being a white supremacist), 16.

Index